SHE

Hotel

2660 Woodley Rl/C.Ave NW

202-328-2000

WASHINGTON
DC

Christopher McIntosh

with contributions by
Nancy Rayburn and Bernard Burt

The
American
Express
Pocket
Guide

Mitchell Beazley

The Author

Christopher McIntosh, author of *The American Express Pocket Guide to Paris*, was formerly assistant editor of *Country Life* and deputy editor of *The Illustrated London News*. He has written travel articles for *Travel & Leisure* and other magazines, especially on France, Germany and Austria. His other books include *The Swan King*, a biography of Ludwig II of Bavaria.

Contributors

Bernard Burt (Where to eat, consultant on Hotels and Restaurants)
Nancy Rayburn (Nightlife and the arts, Shopping)

Acknowledgments

The author would like to thank his two fellow contributors for greatly lightening the load of writing this book and checking the manuscript. Other Washington friends who deserve thanks for their help, guidance and hospitality are Andrew Gray, Elisavietta Ritchie, Clyde Farnsworth and Mila Brooks. Thanks are also due to the staff of the Washington DC Convention and Visitors Association and of the International Visitor Information Center for their generous assistance.

Quotations

Extracts have been taken from the following publications: (p.18 and p.95) *Circles: A Washington Story* by Abigail McCarthy (Doubleday, New York 1977); (p.20 and p.66) *Queen Anne's Lace* by Frances Parkinson Keyes (Horace Liveright, New York 1930); (p.23) *Advise and Consent* by Allen Drury (Doubleday, New York 1959); (p.49 and p.87) *Washington, USA* by Faith Baldwin (Farrar & Rinehart Inc., New York 1942, 1943); (p.59 and p.91) *The Last of the Southern Girls* by Willie Morris (Alfred A. Knopf, New York 1973).

Few travel books are without errors, and no guidebook can ever be completely up to date, for telephone numbers and opening hours change without warning, and hotels and restaurants come under new management, which can affect standards. While every effort has been made to ensure that all information is accurate at the time of going to press, the publishers will be glad to receive any corrections and suggestions for improvements, which can be incorporated in the next edition.

Editors Leonie Hamilton and Jean Gordon
Series Editor David Townsend Jones
Project assistant Elizabeth Parks
Proof reader Sue McKinstry
Indexer Hilary Bird
Gazetteer Catherine Palmer

Art Editor Nigel O'Gorman
Design assistant Christopher Howson
Illustrator Karen Cochrane
Map Editor David Haslam
Production Androulla Pavlou

Edited and designed by Mitchell Beazley International Limited
Artists House, 14–15 Manette Street, London W1V 5LB

Produced and designed by Mitchell Beazley Publishers for the American Express Pocket Travel Guide Series

Maps in 2-colour and 4-colour by Lovell Johns Ltd, Oxford, England, based on copyrighted material of Rand McNally & Company
Typeset by Vantage Photosetting Co. Ltd, Eastleigh and London, England
Printed and bound in Hong Kong by Mandarin Offset

Contents

How to use this book

The American Express Pocket Guide to Washington, DC is an
encyclopedia of travel information, organized in the sections
listed on the previous page. There is also a comprehensive index
(pages 151–8), which is accompanied by a gazetteer (pages
158–60) of the most important streets that are shown in the full-
colour maps at the end of the book.

For easy reference, all major sections (Sights and places of
interest, Hotels, Restaurants) and other sections as far as
possible are arranged alphabetically. For the organization of the
book as a whole, see *Contents*. For places that do not have
separate entries in Sights and places of interest, see the *Index*.

Abbreviations
As far as possible only standard abbreviations have been used.
These include days of the week and months, points of the
compass (N, S, E and W), street names (Ave., Blvd., Pl., Sq.,
St.), Saint (St), rooms (rms), century (C), and measurements.

Bold type
Bold type is used in running text primarily for emphasis, to
draw attention to something of special interest or importance.
It is also used to pick out places – shops or minor museums, for
instance – that do not have full entries of their own.

Cross-references
Whenever a place or section title is printed in *sans serif italics*
(for example, *Library of Congress* or *Basic information*) in the
text, this indicates that you can turn to the appropriate heading
in the book for further information. Cross-references in this
typeface refer either to sections in the book – *Basic
information* or *Planning*, for example – or to individual entries
in the *A to Z* of Sights and places of interest, such as *Library of
Congress* or *Old Downtown*. For convenient reference, use
the headings printed at the top corner of the page (see, for

How entries are organized

Frederick Douglass House (Cedar Hill)
1411 W St. SE, DC 20020 ☎*426–5960 (house), 426–5961
(group tour reservations). Map 8K11* ☒ *¥ Open Apr–Labor
Day 9am–5pm; rest of year 9am–4pm. Closed Christmas,
New Year's Day. Tourmobile route.*
Frederick Douglass (1817–95) was the leading spokesman for
American blacks in their struggle for freedom and justice
during the 19thC. He lectured and wrote books about his own
early life under slavery, campaigned tirelessly for abolition,
helped recruit blacks for the Union army during the Civil War
and finally settled down to a distinguished old age in
Washington. He lived first in A St. (see *National Museum of
African Art*), then bought Cedar Hill, this elegant white house
on a height overlooking the Anacostia River. All the
furnishings, except for curtains and wallpaper, are original.
Douglass' library and other belongings are still *in situ*, and the
whole house is redolent of the spirit of a very remarkable man.
On arrival you are directed to the **Visitors' Center** at the foot
of the hill where a film is shown about Douglass' life and books
about black liberation, including Douglass' own, are on sale.

example, *Basic information* on pages 7–17, *Library of Congress* on pages 65–6, or *Old Downtown* on page 82).

Ordinary italics are used to identify sub-sections. For instance: see *Architecture* in *Culture, history and background*.

Floors
To conform with American usage, "first floor" is used throughout the book to refer to the floor at ground level, "second floor" to the floor above that, and so on.

Map references
Each page of the colour maps at the end of the book has a page number (2–8), and each map is divided into a grid of squares, which are identified vertically by letters (A, B, C, D, etc.) and horizontally by numbers (1, 2, 3, 4, etc.). A map reference identifies the page and square in which the street or place can be found – thus *Library of Congress* is located in Map **8G10**.

Price categories
Price categories are denoted by the symbols ☐ ▯ ▮ ▮▮ and ▮▮▮ which signify cheap, inexpensive, moderately priced, expensive and very expensive, respectively. In the cases of hotels and restaurants these correspond approximately with the following actual prices, which give a guideline at the time of printing. Although actual prices will inevitably increase, the relative price category will be likely to remain the same.

Price categories	Corresponding to approximate prices	
	for **hotels** *double room with bath; single slightly cheaper*	for **restaurants** *meal for one with service, taxes and house wine*
☐ cheap	under $50	under $10
▯ inexpensive	$50–75	$10–20
▮ moderate	$75–100	$20–30
▮▮ expensive	$100–150	$30–40
▮▮▮ very expensive	over $150	over $40

Bold blue type for entry headings.

Blue italics for address, practical information and symbols, encapsulating standard information and special recommendations. For list of symbols see page 6.

Black text for description.

Sans serif italics used for cross-references to other entries.

Bold type used for emphasis.

Entries for hotels, restaurants, shops, etc. follow the same organization, and are usually printed across a narrow measure.
In hotels, symbols indicating special facilities appear at the end of the entry, in black.

Westin
2401 M St. NW, DC 20037
☎429–2400 ☏4979800. Map
3E5 ▮▮▮ to ▮▮▮ 416 rms ⇔ ≈ AE
CB ⚫ ⚫ VISA Metro: Foggy
Bottom.
Location: N of Washington Circle.
Opened at the end of 1985, this is a luxury hotel of very attractive design, focusing on a charming garden courtyard with trees, shrubs and a stone Italian fountain in the centre. The accent throughout is on traditional elegance coupled with modern convenience.
&. ⚓ ≈ ♨

Key to symbols

- ☎ Telephone
- ⦿ Telex
- ★ Recommended sight
- ⇌ Parking
- 🆓 Free entrance
- 💵 Entrance fee payable
- ⇌ Hotel
- ☐ Cheap
- ⫽ Inexpensive
- ⫽⫽ Moderately priced
- ⫽⫽⫽ Expensive
- ⫽⫽⫽⫽ Very expensive
- AE American Express
- CB Carte Blanche
- ⦿ Diners Club
- ⦿ MasterCard
- VISA Visa

- ♿ Facilities for disabled people
- ⚘ Garden
- ⋘ Good view
- ⇌ Swimming pool
- ⚲ Tennis
- ⊱ Golf
- ⇌ Riding
- ⇌ Fishing
- ⚘ Gym/fitness facilities
- ⊏ Restaurant
- ⊏ Good wines
- ⚑ Photography forbidden
- ✗ Guided tour
- ⎁ Cafeteria
- ✻ Special interest for children

Before you go

Documents required

Canadians, Mexicans and British subjects living in Canada,
the Bahamas and the Cayman Islands need only a proof of
place of birth and residence to enter the USA, and a passport
serves this purpose. Other UK citizens must have a passport
and visa. Apply to the nearest US embassy or consulate with
your passport and one passport-sized photo. You will also need
to produce evidence that you intend to return home following
your visit. This could be a dated return ticket or a letter from
your employer. Your passport must be valid for six months
beyond the end of your visit. At present, no vaccinations are
required for entry.

To rent a car, you need a passport and a valid driving
licence. An international driving licence is not required. Some
firms ask to see your return ticket. If you are arriving by
private car from other states or countries, bring the car
registration document and certificate of insurance with you.

Travel and medical insurance

Medical care in the US is good to excellent, but very
expensive. Medical insurance is therefore strongly
recommended. UK travel agents have the necessary forms, and
tour operators frequently include medical cover in their
packages.

Money

The basic unit is, of course, the dollar ($). It is divided into 100
cents (¢). Coins are the penny 1¢, nickel 5¢, dime 10¢, quarter
25¢ and half dollar 50¢. Bank notes (bills) in general
circulation are in denominations of $1, $5, $10, $20, $50 and
$100. Some $2 bills are in circulation. Any amount of money
can be imported or exported, but when the total exceeds
$10,000 you must register with the US Customs Service.

Carry cash in small amounts only, keeping the remainder in
travellers cheques. Cash or travellers cheques in foreign
currencies are not as easily converted as in Europe. For that
reason, purchase travellers cheques in dollars, in advance, and
exchange adequate amounts of money upon arrival. Travellers
cheques issued by American Express, Bank of America,
Barclays, Citibank and Thomas Cook are widely recognized,
and MasterCard and Visa have also introduced them. Make
sure you read the instructions included with your travellers
cheques. It is important to note separately the serial numbers
of your cheques and the telephone number to call in case of
loss. Specialist travellers cheque companies such as American
Express provide extensive local refund facilities through their
own offices or agents. Credit cards are honoured by most
hotels, airlines, car rental agencies, restaurants and many
shops. American Express, Diners Club, MasterCard
(Eurocard) and Visa are the most common cards. Carte
Blanche has less coverage.

Customs

Returning US citizens present themselves and their luggage to
a single officer for inspection. All others must first clear
passport control, collect their baggage and then move on to a
customs official. Although the process has been streamlined,
the combination of three jumbo jets disgorging at once and

government concern over smuggling can slow things down to a crawl. It may take no more than 30mins from plane to street, but an hour or more is not unusual.

Non-residents can bring in any items clearly intended for personal use, duty-free, with the exceptions noted below.

Tobacco goods   200 cigarettes *or* 50 cigars *or* 4½lbs (2kg) tobacco. An additional 100 cigars may be brought in under your gift exemption (see below).

Alcoholic drinks   Adults over 18 are allowed up to 1 quart (1 litre) of spirits.

Other goods   Non-residents may also import up to $100 in gifts without tax or duty if remaining in the US at least 72hrs. Returning residents are granted a duty-free allowance of $400, if brought back personally.

Families travelling together can pool their allowances to cover joint purchases.

For more information on customs regulations, ask at the nearest US embassy or consulate for a copy of the brochure *US Customs Hints* (from Department of the Treasury, US Customs Service, Public Service & Informational Materials Division, Washington, DC 20229).

Getting there

Three airports serve the Washington area. National, the closest to the centre (15–20mins), is restricted to domestic flights of less than 1,000 miles (1,600km). International flights and additional domestic routes are served by the other two airports: Dulles (40mins to the w) and Baltimore-Washington (45mins–1hr to the NE), which lies between the two cities.

Long-distance and commuter trains arrive at Union Station, on the eastern edge of the central area at Massachusetts Ave. and North Capitol St. Many trains also stop at suburban stations, such as the Capital Beltway and Alexandria.

Two long-distance bus companies serve Washington. The Greyhound terminal is at 1110 New York Ave. NW (☎565–2662), and the Trailways terminal is at 1st and L St. NE (☎737–5800).

Washington is easily accessible by car. From New York you can go via Baltimore and then take Interstate 95 or the Baltimore-Washington Parkway; or go s from Wilmington, Delaware on US 301, across the Chesapeake Bay and on to the capital via Annapolis. From the NW you approach by Interstate 270, from the w by Interstate 66 and from the SW by Interstate 95/395. The city is encircled by the Capital Beltway at a radius of about 10 miles (16km) from the centre.

Climate

Apr, May, early June, Sept and Oct are the most pleasant months to visit Washington. The winters range from mild to bitterly cold, the average Jan temperature being 3°C (37°F). The summers are hot, humid and enervating, with an average July temperature of 28°C (82.5°F).

Clothes

However warm it is in Washington, always have something extra to put on indoors, as the almost universal air conditioning can make buildings seem positively arctic. In winter the central heating is equally extreme, so be prepared to peel off.

Washington is an informal city, and sightseers can dress as casually as they wish. In most restaurants a tie is not needed during the day, but in the evening a tie should be worn at the smarter restaurants.

Poste restante

A letter marked "General Delivery" c/o the Central Post Office (*2 Massachusetts Ave. NE, Washington, DC 20066*) should be held until collected. The office is right next to Union Station at Massachusetts Ave. and North Capitol St.

Getting around

From the airport to the city

From Dulles and Baltimore-Washington Airports there are airport buses (known as limousines or "limos") departing approximately every hour or half-hour, depending on the time of day. Taxis from both are expensive because of the distance. National Airport is a cheap taxi ride from the centre, and is also served by an airport limo and the Metro subway. At all airports you can also rent private limousines and self-drive cars. The limo service also connects with a number of downtown hotels, and the main terminal is at the Capital Hilton hotel (*16th and K St. NW*).

Public transport

The Washington Metropolitan Area Transit Authority (WMATA) runs the Metrobus system and a superb new subway system, the Metro, opened in 1973 and still being extended, with well-designed stations and sleek, quiet, comfortable trains. There are four subway lines: Blue, running from National Airport in the S to the E suburbs; Orange, running roughly E and W; Red, forming a loop to the N; and Yellow, running from Gallery Place via National Airport to Huntington station in Alexandria. A Green line is also projected and should begin running in about 1990. The trains run 6am–midnight Mon–Fri, 8am–midnight Sat, and 10am–6pm Sun. Fares depend on distance travelled, and during rush hours (6–9.30am and 3–6.30pm) they are higher. Tickets ("fare cards") are bought from a machine (there are no ticket offices); insert one-dollar or five-dollar bills and get change. A fare card valid for several journeys can be bought. Season tickets ("flash passes") are also available. When leaving the station insert your card in a machine, which computes the fare. You can change to, but not from, the buses without extra charge in DC and for a small extra charge outside. To do this, pick up a "transfer ticket", which can be obtained free from a separate machine at your station of entry.

The Metrobus system is efficient and comprehensive, but can be baffling in its size and complexity. It has about 400 city and suburban routes, many of which operate only in rush hours. Most routes run from about 5am to midnight, and a few continue until about 2am. There is one flat fare for the city and another for suburban journeys; both cost more during rush hours. If you plan to use the buses frequently a map is indispensable. Maps of each bus route and a general subway map are, in theory, available from any Metro station. In addition two comprehensive maps, for DC and Virginia and for DC and Maryland, can be bought from one of the special

Basic information

Metro sales outlets, for example at WMATA headquarters
(*600 5th St. NW*), as well as at certain stores. Be prepared to
wait some time for an answer when telephoning for bus and
subway information (☎637–2437).

Taxis
Cabs are plentiful and can be hailed easily, except in bad
weather or during rush hours. They can also be ordered by
telephone. City cabs have no meters; fares are based on a zone
system, with a surcharge during rush hours and for each
additional passenger. Suburban cabs' metered rates are
reasonable; tip 10–15 percent of the total fare. Cabs often stop
to pick up extra passengers en route.

Getting around by car
With such good public transport a visitor has little need for a
car in Washington. For trips outside the city, however, a car is
often indispensable. In Maryland and Virginia remember that
there is a strictly enforced maximum speed limit of 55mph
(90kph) on the freeways. In DC the limit is 25mph (40kph)
unless otherwise indicated. If you cannot avoid driving in the
city try to keep clear of rush hours (7–9.30am and 4–6pm)
when congestion is heavy and changes in traffic regulations can
be perplexing: for example, certain streets become one-way,
and at many intersections left turns are forbidden. Remember
that, unless otherwise indicated, you are permitted to turn
"right on red" when you come to a traffic light, but you must
give pedestrians the right of way.

Parking too is a severe problem. Some areas have meters,
which operate from 9.30am to 6.30pm. Most have a two-hour
limit. In areas with resident-only parking you may park for
2hrs, and in an unrestricted area for up to 72hrs. Visitors
staying in a private house (but not a hotel) can obtain free-of-
charge from the nearest police station a permit allowing 15
days' parking provided the car does not remain in one place for
more than 72hrs.

Renting a car
There are many car-rental firms operating in Washington, and
it is worth shopping around for the best deal. Rates vary
widely, and promotional discounts are offered at different
times of year. Certain airlines also have special-rate
agreements with particular rental companies. Rent-it-here-
leave-it-there arrangements are available, as well as unlimited-
mileage, weekend and other packages. Comprehensive
insurance is compulsory in Virginia and Maryland but
optional in DC, so make sure you are covered against accidents
with uninsured drivers.

Getting around on foot
Washington is pleasant to walk in and better suited to the
pedestrian than most other US cities. It is little more than 10
miles (16km) across at its widest point, and the main tourist
attractions are concentrated in a fairly small area; the Mall
alone has enough museums to fill a long visit. But the walker
accustomed to European cities may find it hard to adjust to the
monotonous delays at crossings, where signs flash "Walk" or
"Don't walk" alternately. Frequent intersections are a product
of Washington's grid system, but at least the grid pattern
makes it difficult to get lost.

Railway services

Washington has only one main rail terminal, Union Station, which is well served by bus routes and the Metro subway. A small centre at the station run by Travelers Aid provides tourist information and guidance in finding accommodation. AMTRAK (the Federal rail system) handles passenger inquiries (☎*484–7540*).

Domestic airlines

Domestic flights leave from all three airports. National is mainly for East Coast, Southern and Midwest routes. Other routes are served by Dulles and Baltimore-Washington. The following domestic and North American airlines, among others, serve the Washington area; telephone numbers in most cases are for central inquiry and reservation offices, and the addresses are those of ticket offices.

Air Canada   1000 16th St. NW ☎638–3348
American   Capital Hilton and Washington hotels ☎393–2345
Braniff   Dulles Airport ☎(800) 272–6433
Continental   1830 K St. NW and Dulles Airport ☎628–6666
Delta   1605 K St. NW and 1800 N Kent St., Arlington, Va. ☎468–2282
Eastern   Capital Hilton hotel ☎393–4000
New York Air   1830 K St. ☎588–2300
Northwest   Capital Hilton hotel ☎737–7333
PEOPLExpress   National, Dulles, Baltimore-Washington Airports ☎863–0960
Presidential Airways   Dulles Airport ☎478–9700
TWA   1601 K St. NW ☎737–7400
United   Offices include Capital Hilton hotel and 1725 K St. NW ☎893–3400
US Air   1611 K St. NW ☎783–4500
World Airways   918 16th St. NW ☎298–7155

Other transport

Private limousines are a de luxe way to travel but affordable if you shop around for competitive rates and special reductions, with such luxuries as a bar and colour TV available at moderate extra cost. Reputable firms include the following:
Admiral Limousine Service   1243 1st St. SE ☎554–1000
Carey Limousine   745 S 23rd St., Arlington, Va. ☎892–2000
Manhattan DC Executive Transportation   2500 Calvert St. NW ☎775–1888

Sightseeing companies are numerous (see *Useful addresses*, p.15). One of them, Landmark Services (☎*554–5100*) operates a Tourmobile service covering the city's main attractions. An all-day ticket will allow you to break your journey and catch the next Tourmobile.

River cruises on the Potomac are operated by Washington Boat Lines (*Potomac River Cruises, Pier 4, 6th and Water St. SW* ☎*554–8000*).

One of the most agreeable ways to see Washington is by bicycle. For general information contact the Washington Area Bicyclist Association (*1332 I St. NW* ☎*544–5349*). The following firms rent bicycles:
Big Wheel Bikes   1004 Vermont Ave. NW ☎638–3301 and 1034 33rd St. NW ☎337–0254
Fletcher's Boat House   4940 Canal Rd. NW ☎244–0461
Thompson Boat Center   Rock Creek Parkway and Virginia Ave. NW ☎333–4861

On-the-spot information

Public holidays

Jan 1; Martin Luther King Day, third Mon in Jan; President's
Day, a three-day weekend in mid-Feb; Memorial Day, a three-
day weekend at the end of May; Independence Day, July 4;
Labor Day, first Mon in Sept; Columbus Day, second Mon in
Oct; Election Day, first Tues in Nov; Veterans Day, Nov 11;
Thanksgiving, last Thurs in Nov; Dec 25.

Shops, schools, post offices and most public services are
usually closed on these days, although some shops stay open on
the three-day weekends.

Time zones

Washington is in the US Eastern Time Zone, 5hrs behind
GMT in winter, 4hrs behind GMT from last Sun in Apr to
last Sun in Oct during Daylight Saving. Because British
Summer Time operates almost concurrently with Daylight
Saving, the local time difference is usually 5hrs, except for a
month from the end of Mar to the end of Apr when it is 6hrs.

Banks and currency exchange

Banking hours vary widely, but average from 9am to 3pm
Mon–Fri. A few are open Sat mornings. Most will cash foreign
currency, but it is advisable to check in advance. There are
exchange offices at all three airports and in some hotels, but
rates are more favourable at banks. The main American
Express office (*1150 Connecticut Ave. NW* ☎*457–1300*) will
change foreign currency.

Shopping hours

Big department stores generally open at 10am and close at
6pm, 7pm, 8pm or 9pm, depending on the day of the week and
the season. Some are open on Sun afternoon. Otherwise,
shopping hours vary widely. Many shops, especially in smart
areas such as Georgetown's Wisconsin Ave., are open on Sun.
Some large food stores are even open 24hrs all week.

Rush hours

For ease of driving or use of public transport, avoid the periods
7–9.30am and 4–6.30pm. Rush-hour fares on the subway and
buses operate Mon-Fri 6–9.30am and 3–6.30pm.

Post and telephone services

Post offices are open 8am–5pm Mon–Fri and 8am–noon Sat,
except for the main Post Office (*N Capitol St. and
Massachusetts Ave. NE*), which is open all the time.

Telephones are everywhere, on the street, in public
buildings and in shops and restaurants. Generally they are in
working order. Lift the receiver, wait for the dialling tone and
insert the amount in coins required. The area code for DC is
202. If you are dialling within DC simply use the 7-digit
number. This also applies to most locations in suburban
Virginia and Maryland, but for some suburban numbers use
area code 703 for Virginia and 301 for Maryland. Some
numbers are "toll-free"; they are always preceded by the code
800.

Public lavatories

Washington has almost no public lavatories, except for a few in some of the parks. But there are plenty in museums, and restaurants are required to have them by law, so there will usually be one not far away.

Electric current
Current is either 110V or 220V and either AC or DC. Most sockets take either 2-pin or 3-pin plugs. Adaptors can be bought at most electrical shops and large department stores. Contact the Potomac Electric Power Company (☎872–2000) with inquiries.

Laws, regulations and safety
On all main traffic arteries you may cross only at a designated crossing and only when the "Walk" sign is lit up. Police vigilance in enforcing this rule varies, but it is best not to risk infringing it, if only for your own safety. Hitchhiking is permitted on most roads in DC and suburbs provided you keep both feet on the kerb, but is not permitted on interstate highways except at intersections.

Smoking is allowed in most public buildings and offices, but forbidden in elevators and on the subways and buses. Laws relating to drugs are strict and are getting stricter. Those caught even with marijuana face up to a year in prison.

Although mostly Washington is law-abiding, try to be accompanied by another person when walking in the city, especially at night and outside the main thoroughfares. Keep a tight hold on cameras, handbags and other items of personal equipment. Carry the minimum amount of cash and use travellers cheques instead whenever possible. Try not to leave valuables in a hotel room. Always count your change carefully, especially at souvenir stalls. In a crowd of tourists, always be on the alert for pickpockets. When driving through the city keep all your doors locked, for many snatch thefts occur at traffic lights; and when leaving your car unattended, always put valuables out of sight.

If you are attacked or robbed, do not try to resist. Memorize the appearance of the criminal and contact the police immediately (☎911 – *this is a toll-free emergency number*).

Tipping
In hotels and restaurants, tip 15–20 percent. Taxi tips should be 10–15 percent. Airport, railway and hotel porters should be tipped at your discretion; 50¢ to $1 per bag, depending on distance and service, is a fair guideline.

Disabled travellers
Provisions for disabled people are generally very good. Newer museums and galleries are fully accessible to disabled people, though some of the older ones are not. For further information contact the non-profit Information Center for Handicapped Individuals (*605 G St. NW, Suite 202, DC 20001* ☎347–4986), which publishes a special guide for handicapped people, *Access Washington*, available for a modest fee.

Local publications
The main Washington paper, the famous *Washington Post*, appears daily and has a multi-supplement Sunday edition. Another, more recently founded, daily newspaper is the *Washington Times*. *USA Today*, a colourful newcomer, concentrates on pictures rather than editorial. The *Weekend*

section of the *Washington Post* on Fri is a good source of
information for coming events and entertainment. The
monthly magazine *Washingtonian* also has a bulletin of events,
advice on dining out, and feature articles about the capital.
Similar bulletins are published in a number of free magazines
handed out in hotels. There are also a number of very lively
free newspapers appearing every two or three weeks; these
include *The Uptown Citizen*, the *City Paper*, the *Georgetowner*
and the *Northwest Current*.

Foreign newspapers such as the London *Times*, *Le Monde*,
and the *Frankfurter Allgemeine Zeitung* are not widely
distributed in Washington, but are available from the shop
called **Newsroom** (*1753 Connecticut Ave. NW, near the corner
of S St.*) and **Chronicles of Georgetown** (*3207 0 St. NW,
near Wisconsin Ave.*).

Useful addresses

Tourist information

The Washington DC Convention and Visitors Association
aims to promote the city as a convention and tourist
destination. Their Tourist Information Center (*1400
Pennsylvania Ave. NW* ☎*737–8866 for recorded information*
☎*789–7000 for specific inquiries*) will provide information on
sightseeing, hotels, restaurants, convention facilities and
general tourist matters.

The International Visitor Information Center (IVIS)
provides a comprehensive service for tourists. Their main
office and reception centre (*733 15th St. NW, Suite 300
☎ 783–6540*) has a multilingual staff. They have an office also
at Dulles Airport (☎*661–8747*).

American Express Travel Service (*1150 Connecticut Ave.
NW* ☎*457–1300*) is a valuable source of information for any
traveller in need of help, advice or emergency services.

The Travelers Aid Society (*1015 12th St. NW* ☎*347–0101*)
provides emergency help and advice to visitors in need, or
lacking accommodation. Their Union Station office
(☎*347–0101*) will also give tourist information. They have
offices also at National Airport (☎*684–3472*) and Dulles
Airport (☎*661–8636*).

Telephone services

DC Department of Recreation   Events and activities
☎673–7671
Dial-a-Museum   Smithsonian activities ☎357–2020
Dial-a-Park   National Capital Parks daily events ☎426–6975
Dial-a-Phenomenon   Things to see in the night sky
☎357–2000
General Tourist Information   ☎737–8866
Time   ☎844–1212
Voice of the Naturalist   Audubon Society information on
birds seen in Washington   ☎652–1088
Weather   ☎936–1212

Main post office

N Capitol St. and Massachusetts Ave. NE ☎523–2323 (open
24hrs)

Embassies
Australia   1601 Massachusetts Ave. NW ☎797–3000
Austria   2343 Massachusetts Ave. NW ☎483–4474
Belgium   3330 Garfield St. NW ☎333–6900
Canada   1746 Massachusetts Ave. NW ☎785–1400
Denmark   3200 Whitehaven St. NW ☎234–4300
Finland   3216 New Mexico Ave. NW ☎363–2430
France   4101 Reservoir Rd. NW ☎944–4474
Germany (West)   4645 Reservoir Rd. NW ☎298–4000
Greece   2221 Massachusetts Ave. NW ☎667–3168
Ireland (Eire)   2234 Massachusetts Ave. NW ☎462–3939
Italy   1601 Fuller St. NW ☎328–5500
Japan   2520 Massachusetts Ave. NW ☎234–2266
Netherlands   4200 Linnean Ave. NW ☎244–5300
New Zealand   37 Observatory Circle NW ☎328–4800
Norway   2720 34th St. NW ☎333–6000
South Africa   3051 Massachusetts Ave. NW ☎232–4400
Spain   2700 15th St. NW ☎265–0190
Sweden   600 New Hampshire Ave. NW ☎298–3500
Switzerland   2900 Cathedral Ave. NW ☎745–7900
United Kingdom   3100 Massachusetts Ave. NW ☎462–1340

Tour operators
American Sightseeing   519 6th St. NW ☎393–1618
DC Tours   PO Box 7028, Alexandria, Va. 22307 ☎768–5252
East Coast Parlor Car Tours   1730 K St. NW ☎783–0077
Eyre Bus Service   15910 Union Chapel Rd., Woodbine, Md.
21797 ☎854–6600
Gray Line   333 E St. SW ☎479–5900
Helicopter Sightseeing Tours   Washington National Airport
☎(703) 892–2650
Spirit of '76 Tours   1900 Kendall St. NE ☎529–2575
Tourmobile Sightseeing   1000 Ohio Dr. SW ☎554–7950
The Tourmobile is a shuttle bus service, with running
commentary, connecting the major sights of Capitol Hill, the
Mall and *Arlington National Cemetery*, which operates
continuously mid-June to Labor Day 9am–6.30pm and the
rest of the year 9.30am–4.30pm. After purchasing a daily ticket
from the driver or at one of the Tourmobile booths, you can
break your journey as often as you like. Also available are
excursions to Mount Vernon and the *Frederick Douglass
House* and a tour of Arlington Cemetery itself.

River trips
Washington Boat Lines   Pier 4, 6th and Water St. SW
☎554–8000

Major libraries
Folger Shakespeare Library   201 E Capitol St. SE ☎544–4600
Library of Congress   1st St., between E Capitol St. and
Independence Ave. SE ☎287–5000
Martin Luther King Memorial Library   901 G St. NW
☎727–1111

Major places of worship
Christian
Church of the Epiphany (Episcopal)   1317 G St. NW
☎347–2635
Church of St John the Baptist (Russian Orthodox)   4001 17th
St. NW ☎726–3000

Basic information

First Baptist Church   16th and 0 St. NW ☎387–2206
First Church of Christ Scientist   1770 Euclid St. NW
☎265–1390
Franciscan Monastery (Roman Catholic)   1400 Quincy St.
NE ☎526–6800
Friends Meeting House   2111 Florida Ave. NW ☎483–3310
Metropolitan African Methodist Episcopal Church   1518 M St.
NW ☎331–1426
*Mormon Temple (Church of Jesus Christ of Latter Day
Saints)*   9900 Stoneybrook Dr., Kensington, Md. ☎587–0144
*National Shrine of the Immaculate Conception (Roman
Catholic)*   4th St. and Michigan Ave. NE ☎526–8300
New York Avenue Presbyterian Church   1313 New York Ave.
NW ☎393–3700
St John's Lafayette Square (Episcopal)   16th and H St. NW
☎347–8766
St Matthew's Cathedral (Roman Catholic)   1725 Rhode
Island Ave. NW ☎347–3215
Saint Sophia's Cathedral (Greek Orthodox)   36th St. and
Massachusetts Ave. NW ☎333–4730
Washington National Cathedral (Episcopal)   Massachusetts
and Wisconsin Ave. NW ☎537–6200
Jewish
Adas Israel Synagogue   Connecticut Ave. and Porter St. NW
☎362–4433
Washington Hebrew Congregation   Massachusetts Ave. and
Macomb St. NW ☎362–7100
Muslim
Islamic Mosque and Cultural Center   2551 Massachusetts Ave.
NW ☎332–8343

Conversion tables

Length

cm	0		5		10		15		20		25		30
in	0	1	2	3	4	5	6	7	8	9	10	11	12

metres	0		0.5		1		1.5		2
ft/yd	0	1ft	2ft	3ft(1yd)			2yd		

Distance

km	0	1	2	3	4	5	6	7	8	9	10	11	12	13	14	15	16
miles	0		1		2		3		4		5		6		7		8		9		10

Weight

			(0.25kg)		(0.5kg)		(0.75kg)		(1kg)
grammes	0	100	200	300	400	500	600	700	800	900	1,000
ounces	0		4 (¼lb)		8 (½lb)		12 (¾lb)		16 (1lb)		20		24 (1½lb)		28		32 (2lb)

Fluid measures

litres	0	1	2	3	4	5	litres	0	5	10	20	30
imp.pints	0	1	2	3	4	5	6	7	8	imp. gallons	0	1	2	3	4	5	6
US pints	0	1	2	3	4	5	6	7	8	US gallons	0	1	2	3	4	5	6	7

Temperature chart

°C	–15	–10	–5	0	5	10	15	20	25	30	35	36.9 40	100
°F	0	10	20	30 32	40	50	60	70	80	90	98.4	105	212

Emergency information

Emergency services
Police/fire/ambulance ☎911
Medical referral service ☎466–1880
Dental referral service ☎686–0803

Hospitals with casualty departments
Ambulances called on 911 carry the patient to the nearest municipal hospital. If you wish to go directly to a hospital, the following are the main ones:
Adams-Morgan: Children's Hosp. National Med. Center, 1111 Michigan Ave. NW ☎745–4066. *Capitol Hill*: Capitol Hill Hosp., 700 Constitution Ave. NE ☎269–8000. *Georgetown*: Georgetown University Hosp., 3800 Reservoir Rd. NW ☎625–0100. *Northwest*: Sibley Memorial Hosp., 5255 Loughboro Rd. NW ☎537–4000. *Southeast*: DC General Hosp., 19th St. and Massachusetts Ave. SE ☎675–5416; Greater Southeast Community Hosp., 1310 Southern Ave. SE ☎574–6000.

For minor emergencies, treatment is available at clinics, listed in the *Yellow Pages* under "Clinics".

All-night chemist (pharmacy)
Peoples Drug Store 14th St. and Thomas Circle NW ☎628–0721

Help lines
Suicide Prevention and Emergency Mental Health ☎727–3622
Travelers Aid Society ☎347–0101

Motoring accidents
—Call the police immediately.
—If car is rented, call number in rental agreement.
—Do not admit liability or incriminate yourself.
—Ask witnesses to stay and give statements.
—Exchange names, addresses, car details, insurance companies and three-digit insurance company codes.
—Remain to give your statement to the police.

Car breakdowns
Call one of the following from nearest telephone.
—Number indicated in car rental agreement.
—Local office of AAA (if you are a member).
—Nearest garage or towing service.

Lost passport
Contact the police and your embassy (see p.15), where you will be issued with emergency travel documents.

Lost travellers cheques
Notify the local police immediately, then follow the instructions provided with your travellers cheques, or contact the issuing company's nearest office. Contact your consulate or American Express if you are stranded with no money.

Lost property
Rail ☎484–7540 (AMTRAK at Union Station)
Subway ☎637–1195
In the street ☎727–4326 (Police Communications)

Introduction

Washington in the 1980s is entering a golden age; never before has the city been so vibrant, lively, cosmopolitan and civilized. Washington retains her classical dignity, but has suddenly learned how to have fun. She still has her exquisite monuments and majestic perspectives, but she has grown sprightly of late, acquiring chic tastes, international habits and a new *joie de vivre*.

This new lease of life which Washington has assumed in the past decade or so has taken many people by surprise. Not long ago the US capital was a Cinderella among American cities, scorned by her big sisters – New York, Chicago and Los Angeles – as a "company town" dominated by the federal government and markedly lacking in culture, refinement and most of the good things of life. Now the tables have turned; Washington has become one of the most desirable American cities in which to live and one of the country's top tourist destinations.

It has taken surprisingly long for the city to achieve this transformation. The reasons lie in the multiple conflicts, anomalies and paradoxes that have marked the city's history from the beginning. The choice of site was the outcome of a deal between the northern and southern states. In the War of Independence the North, which had incurred bigger debts than the South, asked Congress to bail them out. Secretary of State Thomas Jefferson – a Southerner – struck a bargain with his northern rival Alexander Hamilton, Secretary of the Treasury, whereby the South would give way in the matter of the debts if the North would agree to a new national capital being located in the South. In due course President Washington himself chose the site, a diamond of territory 10 miles square (26sq.km) taken from Virginia and Maryland. Subsequently the area w of the Potomac seceded back to Virginia, spoiling the symmetry of the diamond.

The weather of April had been a little raw and winds had whipped the cherry blossoms early from the trees around the Tidal Basin and a week later from the sturdy trees of Kenwood in the northwest suburbs. It was a late spring, everyone agreed, but when Jeff got out of the cab that morning on the corner of C Street, the weather was Washington at its finest. A warm sun shone on the tourists streaming across the crosswalk to the Capitol, and on those standing in little groups eyeing the limousines along the curb and the secret service men already deployed at the entrance to the Old Senate Office Building on the south side.

Abigail McCarthy, *Circles: A Washington Story*

Washington appointed three Commissioners to administer this territory and to oversee the creation of the city within it, and it was they who decided to name the city Washington, after him. The man chosen by the President to lay out the city was a brilliant, irascible Frenchman called Pierre Charles L'Enfant, an army engineer who had fought for the Americans in the War of Independence. Taking his inspiration from the best examples of European town planning, L'Enfant designed a city that he considered worthy of the lofty ideals of the new nation: triumphal avenues radiating out from the President's mansion and the Capitol on its hilltop, broad streets laid out on a grid pattern, circles, squares, generous parks and imposing vistas. He drew the plan on a grand, ambitious scale, foreseeing that as the USA grew in prosperity it would be able gradually to flesh out his scheme and eventually achieve a really impressive capital. As L'Enfant put it in a letter to Washington: "It will be obvious that the plan should be drawn on such a scale as to leave room for the aggrandizement and embellishment which the increase of the wealth of the nation will permit it to pursue at any period however remote."

For its time L'Enfant's plan was astonishingly bold. He insisted, for example, on very wide streets. At that time 50ft (15m) would have been more than generous, but L'Enfant wanted 90–130ft (27–40m) for ordinary thoroughfares and 180–400ft (55–122m) for the grander ones. The capital of the United States deserved no less.

Unfortunately L'Enfant's vision was not matched by the Commissioners, nor by the local landowners, and there were bitter quarrels over the implementation of the plan. Daniel Carroll of Duddington, nephew of one of the Commissioners, built a farmhouse on a site that had been earmarked to become what is now Garfield Park to the SE of the Capitol. After writing twice to Carroll and receiving no reply, L'Enfant had the building carefully dismantled and moved away. In the ensuing outcry, L'Enfant prevailed, but in the end opposition to him became so fierce that Washington felt obliged to dismiss him a year after he had been appointed. It was the first of many setbacks suffered by the city as a result of pettiness and lack of imagination.

L'Enfant's basic scheme, however, was retained, and the construction of the city limped along. By 1800 it was sufficiently far advanced for Congress to move there, but for decades Washington remained a sorry sight. The Capitol and the White House stood out amid the chaos of sporadic housing development, farmyards and areas of swamp. The city had no proper pavements, street lighting or sanitation. To add insult to injury, the District of Columbia was made a politically neutral federal district, residence of which did not carry the privilege of a vote in congressional or presidential elections; the idea was to protect the Government from local interference. Belonging to no state, it was given short shrift by Congress, which was preoccupied with other matters.

The miserliness with which the city was treated was astounding. Oil lamps were installed in the vicinity of the Capitol and the White House, but not enough money was allocated for oil, and so the lamps became mere ornaments. Meanwhile planning control was lax. It was not until 1820 that the government ordered farmers to stop fencing in and planting areas that had been designated as streets. Periodically congressmen would agitate for the removal of the nation's capital to a more westerly location, but nothing came of it.

The city languished without proper amenities until the 1870s, when a dynamic city administrator named Alexander ("Boss") Shepherd forced through a vast scheme of public works without worrying about where the money would come from. Pavements were laid, sewers and street lights installed and thousands of trees planted. Although he bankrupted the city, posterity should be grateful to Shepherd. The response of Congress, however, was to dissolve the city council and take over the government of the District through congressional committees, thus leaving the citizens with neither federal nor

Culture, history and background

local representation – an extraordinary state of affairs for the capital of a great democracy.

During the late 19th and early 20thC the situation improved, partly owing to a steady influx of wealthy people who colonized areas such as Cleveland Heights in the NW, so-called because President Cleveland lived there. The city gained some fine buildings such as the Library of Congress and Union Station, and in the same period the Mall was laid out more or less in its present form. With World War I, the New Deal and World War II, the ranks of Washington's bureaucracy swelled, but as late as 1960 it still felt like a company town. In that year it became a black majority city, and achieved another turning point with the election of John F. Kennedy as President. Kennedy appointed his own adviser on Washington, preserved threatened historic houses, had a new code for public buildings drawn up, approved the plan for the Metro and presided over the rebuilding of the old slum area in the SW. As Kennedy put it: "the Nation's capital should represent the finest in living environment which America can plan and build".

> The trip to Washington had been everything that they both had dreamed of and hoped for and more ... to them it seemed as beautiful as a vision of a white-pillared Paradise.
>
> Frances Parkinson Keyes, *Queen Anne's Lace*

Washington since then has undergone rapid and accelerating change. Today it has its own elected mayor and city council, drawn largely from the black areas, and DC residents can at last vote in presidential elections, although they still have no full representation in Congress. The Kennedy Center, opened in 1971, has helped to fuel a cultural boom in the city. The Smithsonian Institution has expanded its already vast museum facilities. The building of the Metro, still being extended, has triggered the dramatic growth of suburban business centres such as Bethesda, Rosslyn and Crystal City, where large corporations have been rushing to set up their headquarters, bringing affluent and discriminating new customers to Washington's restaurants and night spots, which have consequently blossomed.

All over the District itself splendid new luxury hotels, office buildings and shopping malls are mushrooming, while glorious historic buildings such as the Old Post Office have been beautifully restored. At the same time a strict ban on high-rise building has kept the city's delicate skyline intact. However, not all the news is good, for large areas of deprivation and poverty remain in the predominantly black NE and SE sectors, and there are strident contrasts between rich and poor neighbourhoods – one of the contradictions that Washington has yet to overcome.

The capital of the United States is one of the most European of American cities. Its scale is human; its streets invite you to stroll rather than rush; and its unfolding vistas of townscape and its mixture of grandeur and intimacy have a distinctly European feel. Washington appropriately has been dubbed "Paris on the Potomac".

Pierre L'Enfant, whose grave is in Arlington Cemetery, would be pleased if he could see his city now, for Washington has become the gracious capital that he wanted it to be – even if it has taken nearly two centuries. For today's visitor, Washington is a rich feast.

Time chart

1608	English adventurer Captain John Smith explored the Potomac. His enthusiastic descriptions of the spot encouraged settlement.
1634	Colonization of Maryland was begun.
1749	The town of Alexandria was created on the Virginia shore of the Potomac.
1751	Georgetown was founded.
1775	American Revolutionary War, or War of American Independence, began.
1789	George Washington became the first President of the United States. Georgetown University was founded.
1790	A southern location was agreed upon for the new federal capital, and President Washington was asked by Congress to choose a site on the Potomac.
1791	Pierre Charles L'Enfant began planning the city.
1792	L'Enfant was dismissed. Work on the White House, then called the President's House, began.
1793	Work began on the construction of the Capitol.
1800	The Government moved to Washington from Philadelphia. President John Adams took up residence in the unfinished White House.
1801	Thomas Jefferson became the first president to be inaugurated in the new capital.
1802	A local government, consisting of a mayor and an elected council, was established.
1814	British forces raided Washington, burning the White House, the Capitol and other public buildings. President Madison moved temporarily to the Octagon. Congress was housed in a brick building while the original Capitol was restored.
1820	Washington residents were given the right to elect the city's mayor.
1835	The USA came into possession of the fortune bequeathed by James Smithson, which led ultimately to the creation of the Smithsonian Institution.
1846	The portion of the District of Columbia sw of the Potomac seceded back to Virginia, reducing the District to approximately 69sq.miles (179sq.km) instead of its original 100sq.miles (259sq.km).
1848	Work began on the construction of the Washington Monument on the Mall.
1861 –65	American Civil War. Washington found itself the focal point of the war effort.
1863	President Lincoln signed the Emancipation Proclamation.
1864	Arlington National Cemetery was established.
1865	President Lincoln was assassinated during a performance at Ford's Theatre.
1867	Blacks voted for the first time in local elections.
1868	President Andrew Johnson was impeached by the House of Representatives, but was narrowly acquitted by the Senate.
1871	Congress established a new form of city administration under a governor appointed by the President.
1871 –74	A public works programme under Alexander ("Boss") Shepherd turned Washington for the first time into a city with proper urban amenities.
1878	Government of DC by Commissioners appointed by

the President was re-established, leaving residents with no say in the running of the city.

1884 The Washington Monument was completed.

1896 For the first time a motor car was driven down Pennsylvania Ave.

1902 A large-scale programme of city beautification was begun.

1909 L'Enfant's remains were transferred to Arlington Cemetery.

1910 Height restrictions were imposed on buildings in the city.

1917 The USA entered World War I. In a few months the population of Washington increased by about 50 percent.

1921 The first bathing beauty contest in America was held beside the Tidal Basin. Miss Washington DC was elected Miss America in Atlantic City.

1924 Washington Senators baseball team defeated the New York Giants to win the World Series.

1926 Beginning of the Great Depression.

1931 Hunger March on Washington.

1932 Washington invaded by Bonus Marchers, veterans seeking immediate payment of their war bonuses. The marchers were dispersed by the army.

1933 Election of Franklin D. Roosevelt as President. Roosevelt introduced the New Deal, and the country began to recover from the Depression. The city population swelled as federal jobs multiplied and people were drawn to Washington by New Deal activity and lobbying.

1941 The USA entered World War II, following Pearl Harbor. War activity swelled Washington's population further.

1943 The Pentagon was completed.

1950 The black population of Washington rose from 35
–60 percent to 54 percent.

1954 Washington became the first major American city to introduce racial integration in schools.

1964 Washingtonians voted for the first time in a presidential election.

1968 The assassination of Martin Luther King Jr sparked off violent riots, blighting many areas of the city, especially Old Downtown. DC residents voted in a presidential election for the first time since 1800.

1971 Walter Fauntroy was elected DC's first representative in Congress for a century. His seat carries no vote except in committee. The John F. Kennedy Center for the Performing Arts was opened.

1974 Resignation of President Richard Nixon, following Watergate.

1975 Washington regained an elected city council, and Walter Washington, a black, was elected the first Mayor for over a century.

1976 The first stretch of the Metro subway was opened.

1980 Building of the Convention Center was begun as a key element in the revitalization of Old Downtown, a process which is now coming to fruition.

1983 The Washington Redskins football team won Superbowl XVII, watched by a record TV audience.

1987 Bicentennial of the enactment of the US Constitution.

Political Washington

Politics is the *raison d'être* of Washington, and to understand the city it is necessary to know something of the complex web of power that underlies it.

The map of Washington converges symbolically on two points: the White House and the Capitol. Between them, like a rope in a tug-of-war contest, stretches Pennsylvania Ave., as though to represent the curious link of both tension and partnership that exists between the executive and legislative branches of the government. Since the USA came into existence, power has alternated between the two, depending on the relative force and prestige of the President and Congress.

The President controls the day-to-day business of running the country's domestic and foreign affairs. He does so with the aid of a Cabinet, made up of the appointed heads of the various executive departments, and an Executive Office consisting of a large number of aides, special advisers and advisory councils. There is much coming and going between the White House and the neighbouring Executive Office Building, which is used by many of the President's advisory staff.

The President can initiate bills in Congress and veto legislation coming from Congress; but Congress can vote to override a presidential veto. Furthermore it can (and frequently does) block legislation emanating from the White House. There is a passage in Gore Vidal's novel *Washington D.C.* where a senator expresses the way Congress jealously guards the right to curb excessive presidential power: " 'You see, I think our kind of government is the best ever devised. At least originally. So whenever a President draws too much power to himself, the Congress must stop him by restoring the balance. Let him reach too far and . . . we shall . . .' The Senator's other hand, rigid as a knife, made as if to chop the tyrant's hand from its wrist." Thus Congress blocked Kennedy's Civil Rights legislation in the 1960s, and it was Kennedy's successor Johnson, the wily catcher of Congressional votes, who was able to push the legislation through.

Now in the moments before the Senate was about to begin the chamber resembled a sort of tan, marble-paneled fishbowl in which pageboys in their white shirts and black pants darted about like minnows distributing bills and copies of the legislative calendar to all the desks, whisking off stray specks of dust, shoving the spittoons carefully out of sight, checking the snuff boxes to make sure they were full, joking and calling to one another across the big brown room.

Allen Drury, *Advise and Consent*

Behind the Congress on Capitol Hill sits the gleaming marble palace of the Supreme Court, representing the third branch of government: the Judiciary. The Court, which upholds the US Constitution, has on occasions opposed both President and Congress. Some of its decisions have had epoch-making consequences, such as its famous 1954 ruling that racial segregation in the public schools was unconstitutional.

These three institutions are the most conspicuous pinnacles in the citadel of federal power, but a glance at the map of Washington reveals the extent of the government's presence. Central Washington is dominated by the names of the great departments and agencies, such as the State Department, the

23

Treasury, the Department of Commerce, the Internal Revenue Service, the National Aeronautics and Space Administration, the Department of Justice and its offshoot the Federal Bureau of Investigation. Across in Virginia is the Pentagon, housing the Department of Defense, and the Langley headquarters of the Central Intelligence Agency, which, unlike the FBI, is not open to the public. These and the other government organizations employ a total of more than 300,000 people in Washington alone – a far cry from the 130 clerks who made up the total federal workforce in 1800 when the government first moved to Washington.

There is much more to this vortex of power than the government itself, however. Take, for example, the lobbyists. Washington is continually besieged by special interest groups seeking to make the government receptive to their needs. They may be companies angling for contracts, farmers seeking bigger subsidies, environmental groups agitating for stricter pollution controls or foreign governments looking for financial aid. These groups generally employ professional lobbyists – often lawyers, former civil servants or public relations men – who frequently earn large sums of money for pleading their clients' causes over lunch or cocktails or at lavish receptions.

Another important element in Washington political life is the media: the syndicated columnists, investigative journalists and television interviewers who both reflect and monitor current events in the political sphere. The media can also influence events directly and crucially – an obvious instance was the *Washington Post*'s investigations into the Watergate scandal which led to President Nixon's resignation.

Social life too has its part to play in the political drama. Power and prestige go hand in hand, and Washington's social world acts as one barometer of prestige. Washingtonians covet invitations to White House receptions, embassy functions and private parties in the fashionable suburbs. At these events alliances are forged, deals made, gossip exchanged and reputations enhanced or diminished.

Much of America resents the size of the federal government and the growing dominance of Washington. Every so often a president, capitalizing on this resentment, sets out to reduce the federal bureaucracy, but invariably with little result. The government continues to grow in size and power, and the lure of Washington grows ever stronger.

The arts in Washington

There was a time when the cultural diet of Washington was as meagre and monotonous as its cuisine. This is no longer the case. From grand opera at the Kennedy Center to poetry readings at the Library of Congress, there is a rich menu to satisfy the culture-hungry visitor. Yet for many decades the only art that flourished in Washington was the art of politics. While the city was going through the long, slow process of transforming itself from a glorified shanty town into an effective capital, its inhabitants had little time or inclination for cultural refinements. The opening of the National Theater in 1835 at least brought regular theatrical performances, and later came Ford's Theatre (until Lincoln's assassination in 1865, after which it was closed for about a century); but still the theatrical fare was hardly impressive, and the musical fare even less so, although by the 1850s certain federal buildings were being used after office hours for concerts. Until recently, however, facilities for large musical performances were very limited.

Lovers of painting and sculpture were less deprived. In 1869 the Corcoran Gallery opened, and numerous other galleries followed, finally making Washington one of the richest cities in the world for the visual arts. Yet it was a long time before Washington had anything approaching an artists' colony; and the same was true in the literary field. It was left to Henry Adams and a tiny handful of other writers to carry the torch for literature in the US capital.

The fact is that for the first century and a half of its existence, Washington lacked the kind of social and urban fabric that makes for a thriving cultural life. In Paris and Vienna there were cafés where artists, writers and composers could gather and exchange ideas in a heady atmosphere, fuelled by the feverish energy of a great metropolis with centuries of cultural history behind it. Washington had no such milieu. Its steak-and-potatoes eating houses were no substitute for the cafés of Montmartre or the Ringstrasse.

Washingtonians eager for cultural nourishment were acutely aware of these deficiencies. One of them wrote in 1902: "What is capital life after all? Small talk and lots to eat, an infinite series of teas and dinners. Art? There is none." These were the words of the painter and society hostess Alice Pike Barney, whose Studio House on Sheridan Circle (see p.42) was, in the early years of the 20thC, one of the few centres of real cultural exchange in the city. Until she moved to Los Angeles in 1924, the house was the scene of continuous artistic activity. She herself not only painted but also taught art, wrote and produced plays, and promoted the cultural life of the city as a whole. In 1917 she was instrumental in creating the Sylvan Theater in the Washington Monument grounds, the first federally supported outdoor theatre in the USA.

Apart from valiant efforts on the part of individuals such as Mrs Barney, Washington remained culturally undernourished until long after World War II – one of the reasons why it was considered a hardship post by foreign embassy staff. The world's great orchestras and opera and ballet companies were reluctant to include Washington on their tours, mainly because the facilities for performances were so poor. The only large auditorium suitable for musical events was the Constitution Hall of the Daughters of the American Revolution. Otherwise performances had to be held in various small auditoriums dotted around the city in museums, galleries, libraries and churches. It was ironic that a city, so far ahead of its European counterparts in the grandeur and sophistication of its urban design, should lag so far behind them in its cultural life.

Clearly such a situation could not be allowed to continue, as President Eisenhower realized when in 1955 he appointed a commission to examine the feasibility of building a new auditorium in the capital. Three years later he signed the legislation for the creation of a National Cultural Center, which, after a further 13 years and much heroic battling on the part of its supporters, finally opened as the Kennedy Center in 1971. Now Washington had, under one roof, an opera house, a concert hall and a theatre, all of them large and superb in their acoustics and facilities.

Culture, history and background

The Kennedy Center has moved Washington into the top league of world cities for the performing arts, and today it features very firmly on the itinerary of the great touring companies and orchestras. Its opening was therefore a major turning-point. But it is not the only factor in the cultural efflorescence that has taken place in the capital in recent years. Before the appearance of the Kennedy, Arena Stage was already winning a reputation as one of the most vital and innovative theatres in the country, drawing audiences with its imaginative productions ranging from Shakespeare to Tom Stoppard; and a host of other small experimental theatres, such as New Playwrights and The Source, offer a consistently exciting range of drama.

Washington's small theatres have not been smothered by the Kennedy Center. On the contrary, they have benefited from the heightened cultural atmosphere that the Kennedy has created. Much the same is true in the field of music. Besides the National Symphony Orchestra, there are numerous other orchestras, large and small, performing regularly in Washington and its environs. Today Washington is possibly the richest city in the world for chamber music. Gone is the climate of musical philistinism in which President Grant could say proudly: "I know two tunes; one of them is *Yankee Doodle* and the other isn't." Likewise in opera, where in addition to the Washington Opera at the Kennedy, numerous smaller opera companies operate in less imposing premises.

The same healthy balance of great and small can be seen in the visual arts. Washington has not only the great galleries around the Mall but also a host of small private galleries, many of which can be found near Dupont Circle and in the Old Downtown area, where the work of black artists is much in evidence.

An article by Joseph McLellan in the *Washington Post Magazine* in February 1986 attributed Washington's cultural vitality partly to its lively, well-educated audiences made up of "thought-and-word people" – civil servants, lobbyists, officials of national associations, journalists, university professors and students. "The special qualities of the Washington population", McLellan says, "may account for the fact that this city has been building a major league symphony orchestra and opera company while it lacked a major league baseball team. Washington may not be the only American city where more tickets are sold for performing arts events than for sporting events, but it is certainly one of them."

The diplomatic community is an important ingredient in the cultural alchemy of Washington. As McLellan writes: "Embassies are still among the brightest cultural spots in the Washington scene. Most embassies will engage in some discreet promotion and offer a gala reception when one of their native stars is appearing in the Washington area. Quite a few embassies have also given substantial aid to Washington museums or performing arts of their countries – not necessarily financial aid, but mailing lists, refreshments and an elegant room for a reception, sometimes publicity and sometimes performing space."

One outstanding feature of Washington's culture is that so much of it is free. It would be possible to go to an exhibition, a concert and a lecture every day without paying a penny. It is no wonder that other American cities have grown envious of the capital, and little wonder that cultured diplomats no longer find Washington a hardship post.

26

Architecture

Few cities as young as Washington have spawned such an astonishingly rich variety of architecture. Included here are examples of all the great architectural styles inherited from Europe, a multiplicity of home-grown and hybrid forms, as well as buildings, such as the Islamic Mosque, which reflect an Eastern influence. In the history of Washington's architecture there are two strands, the domestic and the public, which are sometimes separate, sometimes intertwined.

18thC

Before Washington was even a twinkle in L'Enfant's eye there was already a well-established vernacular architectural tradition in Georgetown and Alexandria. The oldest house in the District, Old Stone House in Georgetown's M St., built in 1766, is a good example of the solid, unpretentious building style of the Colonial period.

The period immediately after the American Revolution is known as the Federal period and was greatly influenced by the modified Georgian style created in Scotland by the Adam brothers. It brought an increased though careful use of ornamentation to the Georgian mode, with the result that interior decorative plasterwork became a common feature of Federal houses. A striking example of this style is the Octagon, designed by William Thornton and built in 1797–1800. It is typically Federal in its beautifully balanced proportions and

Old Stone House, Georgetown, a rare example of pre-Revolutionary vernacular architecture, dating from before the founding of Washington.

The Octagon, built in the late 18thC to a design by William Thornton in the Federal style, a modified version of the Georgian idiom.

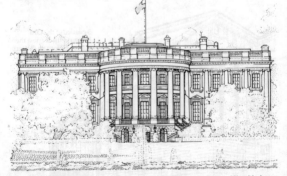

The White House, a graceful example of Federal architecture, designed by James Hoban in 1792 and lived in by every president except Washington.

27

elegant but restrained decorative features, such as the delicate wrought-iron balconies at the second-floor level.

Official buildings of the Federal period include the graceful residence designed by James Hoban as the President's mansion and now known as the White House. The Capitol, originally designed by Thornton, began in the Federal idiom, which can still be detected in the central portion of the w front, but in the hands of later architects the building developed a more grandiose aspect.

1800–50

While the Federal style continued well into the 19thC, especially for private houses, architects of public and commercial buildings increasingly favoured a Greek revival style which made every other church, bank and courthouse look as if it had been taken from the Acropolis. A typical example is the Old Patent Office (now the National Portrait Gallery and National Gallery of American Art), designed by William P. Elliott and Robert Mills and built in the years 1836–67. The s portico is a direct copy of the Parthenon in Athens. This style was in keeping with the widespread notion that, in its democratic ideals, the USA was the spiritual heir of ancient Greece.

1850–1900

This was a period of romanticism, eclecticism and experimentation in architecture. By the 1850s the growth of the nation required so many post offices, customs houses and

View from the W of the **US Capitol**, begun in 1793. William Thornton's original Federal building has been almost submerged in the more grandiose additions of later architects.

s portico of the **Old Patent Office** (now the National Portrait Gallery and National Museum of American Art), a Greek revival building constructed in the years 1836–67.

federal courthouses that a special authority called the Office of the Supervising Architect was set up within the Treasury Department to design and administer the construction of all federal buildings. It was not afraid to experiment with many different styles, provided the end results were sufficiently imposing. Examples of its work include the astounding Old Pension Building (now the National Building Museum), completed in 1885, the Old Post Office, built in the following decade in the form of a Romanesque castle, and the State, War and Navy Building (now called the Executive Office Building), completed in 1888 in the French Second Empire style, with mansard roofs, high chimneys and tier upon tier of windows, balustrades and columns. Overlapping with the Second Empire style was the Beaux-Arts style, examples of which are the Library of Congress and Corcoran Gallery. The Beaux-Arts designers developed a grandiose sensuality, using bulges, curves and wedding-cake ornamentation in their architecture.

Many other styles were employed during this period. Gothic was favoured for churches, while private houses displayed a vast range of influences. The Italianate idiom had become a national craze by the 1850s. Its houses had low-pitched roofs with markedly overhanging eaves and large decorative brackets. Then, in the last quarter of the 19thC, a style known as Queen Anne became popular, which had very little to do with the architecture of the Queen Anne era in England. This was a highly eclectic idiom, grafting together such disparate

The Neo-Romanesque **Old Post Office** on Pennsylvania Ave., built in the 1890s and typical of the romantic eclecticism of the period. Several times threatened with demolition, it has now been beautifully restored and turned into a complex of offices, shops and restaurants.

The **Renwick Gallery**, which was designed by James Renwick and originally housed the Corcoran Gallery. The style is an early example of what was called Second Empire, the high mansard roofs being a characteristic feature.

Culture, history and background

features as medieval-type gables and chimneys, Romanesque arches, turrets and heavily accented stonework. Houses built in this style can be found in many of Washington's residential districts.

1900–45

The early part of the 20thC saw a continuation of Beaux-Arts exuberance apparent in such buildings as Union Station, completed in 1908. There was, however, a general return to more sober classical forms, especially in public government buildings. Victorian eclecticism was replaced with what has been termed Late Classical Revival, epitomized by the huge Federal Triangle complex, built between 1928 and 1938, with its monumental colonnades and porticoes. A leading architect of this style was John Russell Pope, designer of the National Gallery's West Building, completed in 1941, and of the Jefferson Memorial, completed in 1943.

In domestic architecture a similar trend can be seen. The great houses built in the early 20thC in what is today the Embassy Row area (for example the Everett House, now the Turkish Embassy) still have the opulent Beaux-Arts look. But as the century progressed a Georgian revival took hold and indeed has continued to the present day. An example is the Woodrow Wilson House, designed in 1915.

More eclectic were the hotels, apartment houses and office buildings erected during this period, ranging in style from Art Deco to Neo-Romanesque.

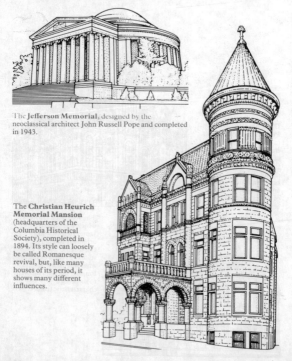

The **Jefferson Memorial**, designed by the neoclassical architect John Russell Pope and completed in 1943.

The **Christian Heurich Memorial Mansion** (headquarters of the Columbia Historical Society), completed in 1894. Its style can loosely be called Romanesque revival, but, like many houses of its period, it shows many different influences.

1945 to the present day

In the post-war years the faceless "international" style of architecture has made its mark on Washington, especially on the New Downtown business area in K St. and its environs, where glass and concrete monotony reigns supreme. The redeveloped SW has fared better with its rows of gracious new townhouses and its Arena Stage theatre, opened in 1960. A memorable example of the so-called "New Brutalist" style is the FBI headquarters, the J. Edgar Hoover Building on Pennsylvania Ave., opened in 1975. Although grim, it is not without a certain cyclopean stature. Mies van der Rohe's Martin Luther King Memorial Library, completed in 1972, has been hailed as a masterpiece, but many find it dull. By contrast, Edward Durrell Stone's Kennedy Center, which was widely vilified when it opened in 1971, has since grown in appeal. Another building which shows that modern architecture need not be boring is I. M. Pei's East Building of the National Gallery, completed in 1978.

At the time of writing, a Post-Modernist reaction against the stark functionalism that has dominated architecture for so long is evident. An exciting example of Post-Modernism in Washington is Arthur Cotton Moore's design for the huge Washington Harbour residential, commercial and leisure complex on the shore of the Potomac at Georgetown. With its profusion of domes, columns and pitched roofs, it is a dynamic combination of bold modernity and traditional forms.

Edward Durrell Stone's controversial **Kennedy Center**, opened in 1971.

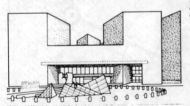

The **East Building** of the National Gallery of Art, designed by I. M. Pei and opened in 1978.

Post-modernism with a vengeance: Arthur Cotton Moore's **Washington Harbour** complex, currently nearing completion.

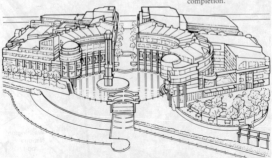

Orientation map

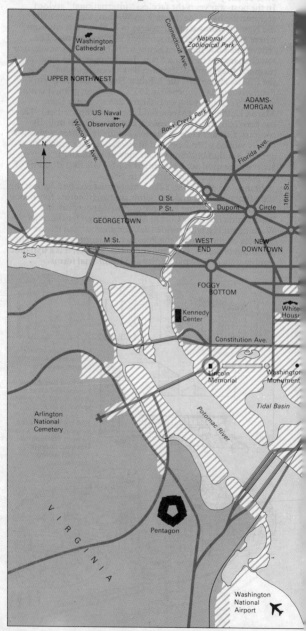

performs *1812 Overture* at Washington Monument.

Third week in July, DC National Bank Volvo Tennis Classic, Rock Creek Tennis Stadium, 16th and Kennedy St. NW.

Late July, Hispanic Festival in Adams-Morgan district.

August

Mid-Aug to early Sept, Shakespeare Festival. Free performances in grounds of Sylvan Theatre, near Washington Monument.

Mid-Aug, Middleburg Wine Festival, Middleburg, Va. (☎ *(703) 687 5528*).

Late Aug, Potomac Ramblin' Raft Race, sponsored by the WPGC radio station. A race down the Potomac on a variety of crazy crafts.

Late Aug, Redskins football exhibition season begins.

September

First Mon, Labor Day. Free National Symphony concert in Capitol grounds.

Preceding Sat and Sun, Labor Day weekend, International Children's Festival, Wolf Trap Farm Park. Performances and workshops of all kinds.

Early Sept, daylong Arts Festival in downtown DC.

Early Sept, Maryland Seafood Festival, Annapolis, Md.

Mid-Sept, Adams-Morgan Days. Ethnic festival of arts, crafts, music and foods.

Mid-Sept, Greek Festival at St Sophia's Church.

Mid-Sept, Constitution Day, band concert at National Archives.

October

First Mon, Opening of Supreme Court.

Early Oct, US Navy Band Birthday Concert, DAR Constitution Hall.

Early Oct, Washington Cathedral Open House, including extensive tours of the cathedral, organ recitals, antique merry-go-round rides and other activities for children.

Late Oct, Washington International Horse Show, Capital Centre.

Each Sun, jousting on the Mall.

November

Early Nov, Washington's Review of the Troops. Re-enactment of first commander's and president's final review of loyal colonial troops, Gadsby's Tavern, Old Town Alexandria.

Early Nov, Marine Corps Marathon. Thousands of entrants race a 26.2-mile (39.3km) course, beginning at Iwo Jima Statue.

Early Nov, Junior League Christmas shop, Mayflower Hotel. Fashionable charity sale annually opens the Capitol's holiday season.

Early Nov, Washington International Horse Race at Laurel Race Track, Md.

Nov 11, Veterans Day ceremony, Arlington National Cemetery.

Mid-Nov, DC Antiques Show, Sheraton-Washington Hotel.

Late Nov to Dec, numerous Christmas craft fairs.

December

Early Dec, YMCA International Fair including folk performances and sale of gifts from many countries, 624 9th St. NW.

Early to mid-Dec, *Nutcracker Suite* ballet at Kennedy Center.

Mid-Dec, lighting of the national Christmas tree at the Capitol. The White House Christmas tree is lit by the President.

Mid to late Dec, open house at the Corcoran.

Mid-Dec to Jan 1. Pageant of Peace. Nightly festivities and choral performances on the Ellipse and the Mall.

Late Dec, candlelight tours of the White House.

Throughout Dec, candlelight tours and carolling at many historic houses in the area.

Regular summer events

Sat and Sun in summer, artists at work, mimes, musicians and dancers performing along the Mall by the National Gallery of Art.

Every other Sun afternoon, folk and popular music concerts on C&O Canal at 30th and Jefferson St. NW.

Fri eve, Marine Corps Parade at 8th and I St. SW (*reservations necessary* ☎ *433–6060* ▣).

Tues, parade and musical tribute by the Marine Drum and Bugle Corps and silent drill team at Iwo Jima Statue.

Concerts by US Navy, Air Force, Marine and Army bands Mon, Tues, Wed and Fri eves on W Terrace of Capitol, and Sun, Tues, Thurs and Fri at Sylvan Theatre in Washington Monument grounds.

When and where to go

Each season in Washington has its own individual appeal, advantages and drawbacks. Spring, a pleasant but crowded time for sightseeing, comes to the city with a burst of cherry blossom around the Tidal Basin, bringing a fresh gaiety to the capital. The summer is slightly less crowded. The often exhausting high temperatures and humidity are mitigated by universal air-conditioning, and many special events take place during the summer months: festivals, sporting contests, open-air concerts, and, of course, the Fourth of July Independence Day celebrations. During the autumn, the crowds diminish still further, the weather is pleasantly cool, and the high cultural life of the city intensifies. The winter, however, is the richest time for the pleasures of theatre, music, opera and ballet, and is also the quietest season for visitors, with correspondingly low hotel prices. Its main disadvantage is unpredictable, often bitterly cold, weather.

The Washington metropolitan area is a cluster of communities with the District of Columbia at its centre. The District itself is an area of about 69 sq. miles (177 sq. km) stretching along the NE side of the Potomac river and incorporating a slice of land to the SE of the Anacostia river. But the main core of Washington is the area nestling in the fork of the two rivers. Originally the District was a regular diamond-shaped area straddling the Potomac, but in 1846 the inhabitants of the territory to the SW of the river opted to return to Virginia, and even a current map will show that the county boundaries on the Virginia side are still based on the old District line. Metropolitan Washington is encircled by a ring-road called the Capital Beltway.

The street plan of central Washington is essentially a grid with the Capitol at its centre. To the N and S of the Capitol, the sequence of streets runs in both directions alphabetically (but there are no J, X, Y or Z streets), while to the E and W they are numbered, again in both directions. This divides the whole city into four quadrants: Northwest (NW), Northeast (NE), Southwest (SW) and Southeast (SE). Addresses must always bear these designations or confusion will result, as there are four 1st streets, four A streets and so on. Avenues, named after states (Connecticut, Wisconsin, Massachusetts, etc.) cut diagonally across the street grid. Once you grasp the system, Washington is an easy city in which to find your way around.

The four quadrants are fairly distinct in character. NW is where the President of the United States lives, along with most of the city's middle-class population, black and white. It has the largest share of tourist attractions, hotels, restaurants and places of entertainment.

The Mall, with its numerous museums and public buildings, straddles the NW and SW sections. The small SW area, formerly a slum district, has been redeveloped on a large scale and now contains a new middle-class community. SE and NE are predominantly poor areas with a mainly black population, apart from the middle-class enclave of Capitol Hill. The suburbs contain a number of burgeoning commercial and shopping centres and many good-quality hotels. Otherwise the immediate environs have little of interest to visitors, except for isolated places such as *Arlington National Cemetery*, the old town of Alexandria and Mount Vernon (see *Excursions*).

Area planners

Washington, unlike Paris, London or Boston, is not a city of small, distinct "villages", but it does have neighbourhoods of widely differing character. The following main areas are those most likely to come within a visitor's itinerary.

The Mall (Maps 6& 7G7–8). The heart of the city, a 2-mile (3km) stretch of park from the *Capitol* to the *Lincoln Memorial*, flanked by museums and government buildings.

West End/Foggy Bottom *(Maps 2& 3E–F4–5)*. The area to the N, S and W of Washington Circle. A commercial, government, residential and academic district, it includes George Washington University, the *Kennedy Center* and the *Watergate Complex*. These surround a neighbourhood called Foggy Bottom, so-named because of the miasmic fogs that once engulfed this low-lying, formerly swampy ground. The West End area to the N of Washington Circle incorporates a cluster of big new luxury hotels.

New Downtown *(Map 3E–F5–6)*. The district to the NW of the *White House*, bounded roughly by N St., 16th St., Pennsylvania Ave. and New Hampshire Ave. This is now the focus of commercial life in Washington, and boasts many new office buildings, smart shops and expensive restaurants, but not a great deal of charm.

Old Downtown (Maps 6& 7F). This district runs E from the White House to within a couple of blocks of *Union Station*. After a period of decay it has undergone a remarkable revival. It contains department stores, museums, theatres, restaurants, smart shops, small galleries, luxury hotels and some fine old buildings that have been restored. On its N side is the *Washington Convention Center* and the emerging Techworld Trade Center.

Capitol Hill *(Maps 7& 8)*. This comprises the Capitol complex and the residential area to the E almost as far as Lincoln Park and extending roughly from E St. in the S to E St. in the N. An area of charming, tree-lined streets, much of it is still poor and crime-ridden, but is increasingly being colonized by young middle-class professional people.

Southwest *(Maps 6 & 7)*. The entire area S of the Mall, dominated by government departments, high-rise apartment blocks and new town houses. There is little to interest the visitor here, except for the Mall itself and the colourful Waterfront area.

Georgetown (Map 2). Between *Rock Creek Park* and Georgetown University. On the one hand Georgetown has picturesque charm and inflated real-estate values; on the other it is a rendezvous for young pleasure-seekers, with discos, jazz clubs, cafés and boutiques.

Dupont Circle *(Map 3D5)*. This district and Georgetown are the closest that Washington has to a Left Bank. As well as a relaxed atmosphere and a youngish residential population, Dupont Circle has some fine architecture and many small businesses: bookstores, art galleries, cafés, small bars and restaurants. This is a lively and enjoyable neighbourhood. Just to the NW of Dupont Circle is a dense colony of embassies, many of them occupying gracious former patrician houses along Massachusetts Ave., now nicknamed "Embassy Row".

Adams-Morgan *(Map 3C–D5)*. Located in NW Washington in the fork between Connecticut and Florida Ave., Adams-Morgan is a colourful Hispanic enclave with a mixture of

37

other ethnic elements and a correspondingly wide variety of restaurants.

Upper Northwest (*Map 2*). Most of the city above Georgetown and NW of Rock Creek Park. Here can be found the *National Zoological Park, Washington Cathedral*, the *US Naval Observatory*, some pleasant leafy suburbs and many interesting restaurants.

Northeast of the White House (*Maps 3D–E6–7, 6F6*). The area stretching NE from the White House to Logan Circle contains a rich pot-pourri of fine architecture in various styles. Bordering a poor district to the E, it is becoming less dilapidated as more affluent families move in and renovate, and there are now a number of recommended hotels in the area. For years 14th St. and its environs were rife with prostitution and pornography, but currently big business is redeveloping 14th St., and the sex industry is on the decline, although prostitutes still operate in the area.

When visiting Washington, it is wise, as in any other city, to plan a schedule in advance. The city's main sights are mostly concentrated in a relatively small area, and this makes sightseeing flexible. The following are suggested schedules for a two-day and a four-day visit.

Two-day visit

Day 1   Visit the White House and then climb the *Washington Monument* for an introductory bird's-eye view of the city in the morning. Have lunch in the Old Post Office Building and possibly go up the tower for another panoramic view. Spend the afternoon in Georgetown and take a boat trip on the *Chesapeake and Ohio Canal* if the season is right. Have dinner at one of Georgetown's numerous restaurants, concentrated along M St. and Wisconsin Ave.

Day 2   First visit the Capitol, then take a Tourmobile tour of the Mall, stopping off at any number of museums. After visiting the *National Gallery of Art*, try to take in the *National Archives*, immediately to the NW, then have an early supper followed by a bus tour of Washington after dark or perhaps go to the theatre or a nightclub (see *Nightlife and the arts*).

Four-day visit

Day 1   As for two-day visit.

Day 2   In the morning, see the Capitol and the *Supreme Court*. In the afternoon, visit the *Library of Congress*, then take a Tourmobile to the National Gallery of Art, National Archives and any other museums on the N Mall. In the evening, take a Washington tour by night.

Day 3   Spend the morning at the *National Air and Space Museum* and perhaps a few of the other museums on the S Mall. In the afternoon walk S to Pier 4 (at 6th and Water St. SW) and take the boat down to Mount Vernon; check beforehand if and when the boat is sailing (*Washington Boat Lines* ☎554–8000). For dinner afterwards, there are a number of recommended seafood restaurants on the waterfront.

Day 4   In the morning, take the Tourmobile to *Arlington National Cemetery* and visit *Arlington House*. Make sure you are out of the cemetery by lunchtime as no eating is allowed there. Spend the afternoon exploring the quaint old town of Alexandria, and finish up with dinner in one of its many good restaurants.

Walks in Washington

In most American cities it is regarded as highly eccentric to "go for a walk" for its own sake. Walking any distance is seen as a last resort, when you are without a car and there is no convenient public transport. This is not so in Washington, where residents as well as visitors find "shanks' pony" an enjoyable means of transport and one of the best ways to appreciate the city. Distances are manageable and the streets are hospitable to the walker. There are countless possible walks in Washington. Here are three suggested routes, diverse in character and incorporating both interesting and attractive parts of the city.

Walk 1/Getting to know central Washington
Allow 2–3hr. Maps **6** & **7**. Metro: Gallery Place.

This walk will introduce the visitor to four different aspects of the city: the *Old Downtown* area, the *Federal Triangle*, the environs of the *White House*, and finally the *Mall* and the *Washington Monument*.

Leave the Metro subway at Gallery Place, exiting at the intersection of 9th and G St. by the Old Patent Office Building, now housing the *National Museum of American Art* and the *National Portrait Gallery*. Walk along the pedestrian mall past the Martin Luther King Memorial Library at 901 G St. NW. This is the main public library of the District of Columbia, and its comprehensive collection of books, including a Washington section, can be used by any visitor for reference purposes (☎727–1111).

Turn left down 10th St. past *Ford's Theatre* at no. 511, the scene of Lincoln's assassination. Across the road at 516 is *Petersen House*, where he died. At E St. turn E past the rather forbidding, cyclopean facade of the J. Edgar Hoover Building, headquarters of the FBI, then go down 9th St. leading into

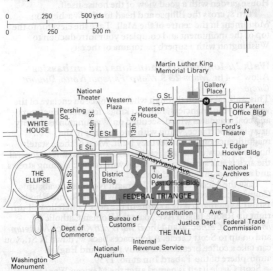

39

Pennsylvania Ave. Across the avenue and slightly to the left you will see the *National Archives*.

Now cross the avenue into what is known as the Federal Triangle. This massive government building project dates from the years 1928–38 when the triangle bounded by Pennsylvania Ave., Constitution Ave. and 15th St. was filled with a series of matching Federal buildings in an Italian Renaissance style of red-tiled roofs and imposing colonnades and porticoes. After the Department of Justice and the Internal Revenue Service, the Old Post Office Building comes as a welcome change of style – a cross between Neuschwanstein Castle and the Palazzo Vecchio in Florence, its massive clock tower vying with the Washington Monument for height. Inside, one of the most staggering interiors in the city – a huge, glass-covered atrium whose lower floors have been turned into a superb multi-purpose pavilion with shops, cafés and a stage for performances – makes a good place for a coffee break or a meal. Take a lift to the top of the tower for a superb view.

Continue up the avenue to 13th St., crossing over the Western Plaza opposite the National Theater. Set into the white paving of the plaza is a map of central Washington laid out in black stone, with the floor plan of the White House and *Capitol* in brass. There are also plaques inscribed with memorable quotations about Washington, such as Henry Adams' back-handed compliment: "One of these days this will be a very great city if nothing happens to it." Looking SE from here, another great chunk of the Federal Triangle, occupied by the Bureau of Customs, is visible. Immediately to the S across the road is the smaller but still imposing District Building, headquarters of the DC administration. Just to the W of this is the Department of Commerce, which also houses the *National Aquarium*. Immediately W of the plaza is Pershing Sq., a pleasant little oasis of greenery with an open-air café by a pool. Continue W, passing on your right the railings of the White House garden with a good view of the house itself.

Turn S, cross the Ellipse and head for the Washington Monument in the centre of the Mall. Take the elevator to the top of the monument and complete your introduction to Washington with a superb panorama of the city.

Walk 2/Monuments, mansions and embassies
Allow 3–4 hr. *Maps 2 & 3. Metro: Farragut North, Dupont Circle.*

This walk takes you through what was once an enclave of the very rich: the financiers, railroad kings, food manufacturers and coal magnates who descended on Washington as the city grew in importance, vying with one another in the magnificence of the houses they built. Most of these stately homes are now embassies, clubs or institutions, but in general the area is still strongly residential with some charming streets and a real neighbourhood flavour.

Take the Metro subway to Farragut North and walk up Connecticut Ave. to the intersection with L St. and Rhode Island Ave., marked by a statue of the poet Longfellow. Turn right up Rhode Island Ave., past the Roman Catholic *St Matthew's Cathedral* and the *B'nai B'rith Klutznick Museum* and on up to Scott Circle. A few paces back W, down N St., you can take a coffee break in the cosily rustic and English atmosphere of the Tabard Inn at no. 1739.

Scott Circle itself is named after the Mexican War General,

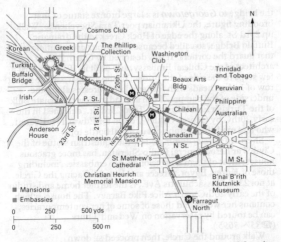

Winfield Scott, who sits astride a horse in the centre. After the statue was completed it was felt indecorous that the General should be riding a mare, so the sculptor obediently added male parts to the animal. On the W side of the Circle is a monument to the 19thC statesman Daniel Webster, while on the E is one to Samuel Hahnemann, the founder of homeopathy, whose principle, *Similia similibus curentur* (like is cured by like) is inscribed on the monument.

Now turn and walk NW up Massachusetts Ave. known as "Embassy Row". The Australian Embassy is the first, a rather unmemorable modern building on the N side, by the Circle. Next to it is the Embassy of the Philippines, and, a little farther down, on the opposite side, are the embassies of Peru, Trinidad and Tobago, and Chile. The Chilean one at no. 1732 is a rather austere red-brick building by the architect Glenn Brown, whose work is encountered again later in the walk. A little farther on is the Canadian Embassy at no. 1746, the work of a prestigious architect of French origin, Jules Henri de Sibour. Completed in 1906, it was built in the fashionable Beaux Arts style for the coal magnate and financier Clarence Moore, who died in the *Titanic* disaster after only six years of residence. On the other side a little farther on at no. 1785 is another handsome Beaux Arts building, now occupied by the National Trust for Historic Preservation.

A few steps on is Dupont Circle. Of the elegant mansions that once ringed the Circle, only two remain: 1801 Massachusetts Ave., now the Sulgrave Club, and 15 Dupont Circle, which houses the Washington Club. Both date from the turn of the century. The centre of the Circle is marked by a graceful white fountain commemorating Rear Admiral Samuel Francis Dupont (1803–65), with a bowl supported by four allegorical figures suggestive of the sea and navigation. In the little park surrounding it are some chess tables where games are often played on fine days. Now follow New Hampshire Ave. to no. 1307, a sumptuous *fin-de-siècle* mansion, currently the headquarters of the *Columbia Historical Society* with a delightful garden, entered from Sunderland Place.

From here go N up 20th St. and turn left down P St. Near

Planning

the bridge to *Georgetown* is a large bronze statue of that brooding figure, the Ukrainian poet Tara Shevchenko. Walk up 23rd St. along the edge of Rock Creek to the dramatic Buffalo Bridge, so called because of the four great buffaloes that guard the corners. It was designed by Glenn Brown, architect of the Chilean Embassy, and built in 1912–15. Just a few steps to the side of the bridge, facing along it, can be seen a row of Indian heads with feathered headdresses along the underside of the parapet. Turn around to view the ornate bulk of the Turkish Embassy at no. 1606 23rd St., designed in the early 20thC by George Oakley Totten for Edward H. Everett, who had made his fortune out of metal bottle tops.

Sheridan Circle, dominated by the equestrian statue of the Civil War hero, General Philip Sheridan, has more gracious houses, most of them now belonging to embassies, including those of Korea, Egypt, Greece and Ireland. Facing the Circle, at no. 2306 Massachusetts Ave., is the former home and studio of the early 20thC artist Alice Pike Barney. The house, which contains her works and those of some of her contemporaries, can be toured by reservation on Wed and Thurs (☎357–3095).

Walk around the Circle, then proceed SE down Massachusetts Ave. This stretch of the avenue has many remarkable mansions, each with its own story to tell. No. 2121 was built in the style of the Petit Trianon for the railroad magnate Richard Townsend, whose wife insisted, for superstitious reasons, that the building should incorporate an existing house. Sadly, this did not prevent Mr Townsend from dying of a riding injury soon after the house was completed. The building now houses the elegant and exclusive Cosmos Club. Just around the corner at no. 1600 21st St. is the mansion housing the *Phillips Collection*, austere outside but delightfully intimate inside. Across the road at no. 2118 Massachusetts Ave. is the amazing *Anderson House*, headquarters of the elite Society of the Cincinnati. Open to the public, the interior is worth a visit, being even more lavish than the exterior.

A little farther down on the same side at no. 2020 is a building of well-fed appearance, which bulges out at the corners. Like the Townsend house, its story is marked by tragedy. It was built just after the turn of the century by Thomas F. Walsh, an Irishman who had struck gold in Colorado. His son and grandson were both killed in automobile accidents, and he died a sad recluse in 1910. The house is now the Indonesian Embassy.

Continue down the avenue to return to the neighbourhood of Dupont Circle, where there is a Metro subway station. Before leaving the area a snack or meal can be had in one of the many lively cafés and restaurants along Connecticut Ave. by going NW from the Circle. At no. 1517, for example, is **Kramer Books and Afterwords**, a delightful bookshop-cum-café, while at no. 1521 is the **Café Splendide**, which has an Austro-Hungarian character.

Walk 3/Capitol Hill
Allow 2–3hr. *Maps **7**&**8**. Metro: Union Station, Eastern Market.*
This route includes not only the *Capitol* itself and the imposing buildings surrounding it, but also the charming and less well-known area to the E. As on the other walks, you will pass some striking outdoor sculptures, such as the figures on

42

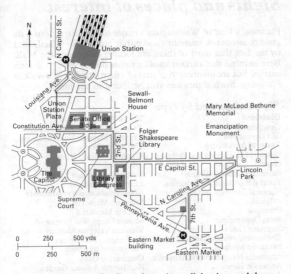

the facade of *Union Station*, where the walk begins, and the
Columbus fountain in the station plaza.

From the station, walk down Louisiana Ave. to the
intersection of N Capitol St. Turn s towards the Capitol,
passing through a park which has an elegant fountain. From
here, either continue down to the Capitol and return to the
route after your visit, or turn up Constitution Ave., passing the
two Senate office buildings. At the NW corner of 2nd St. NE
stands Sewall-Belmont House at no. 144 Constitution Ave., a
well-proportioned, red-brick town house built in 1800 and
now the headquarters of the National Women's Party. It has
been well restored and is open to the public (*open Tues–Fri
10am–3pm and noon–4pm Sat, Sun and hols* ☎ *546–1210*).

From here continue along 2nd St. past the rear of the
Supreme Court, as far as the intersection with E Capitol St.
Ahead is the *Library of Congress* on the SW corner and the
Folger Shakespeare Library on the SE corner. Notice the reliefs
on the Folger depicting scenes from Shakespeare's plays.

Proceed down E Capitol St., to Lincoln Park, passing many
attractive 19thC houses in a great variety of styles. The park
has two monuments of interest, the Emancipation Monument
showing Abraham Lincoln bidding a slave rise to freedom, and
a memorial to the black educator Mary McLeod Bethune
(1875–1955).

Return sw along N Carolina Ave. and turn s down 7th St.
Here, in the first block to the right, is the red-brick building
housing Eastern Market, one of the few genuine farmers'
markets left in the city, where anything from a side of Virginia
ham to a piece of ripe Stilton cheese may be bought. There is
also a potters' studio upstairs in the market and at the N end is
an auditorium where art exhibitions and dance performances
are held. The market (*open Tues–Thurs 7am–6pm, Fri–Sat
6am–7pm*) is liveliest on Sat mornings. Nearby are boutiques,
shops and small restaurants. The walk ends at Eastern Market
Metro Station, entered from Pennsylvania Ave.

Sights and places of interest

Planning a tour of Washington's major tourist attractions – its great monuments, museums and public buildings – is facilitated by the fact that most of them are located on or near the Mall. Bear in mind that certain smaller sights do not have their own entries, but are mentioned as part of a district entry or a walk in *Planning*. Such sights can still be found in the index.

Sights classified by type

Districts
Georgetown
Old Downtown

Federal buildings
Bureau of Engraving and Printing
Capitol
Executive Office Building
Federal Bureau of Investigation
National Archives and Records
   Service
Pentagon
State Department
Supreme Court

Galleries, museums and historic houses
Anacostia Neighborhood Museum
Anderson House
Arlington House
Arthur M. Sackler Gallery
Arts Club of Washington
Arts and Industries Building
B'nai B'rith Klutznick Museum
Capital Children's Museum
Columbia Historical Society
Corcoran Gallery of Art
Daughters of the American
   Revolution
Decatur House
Department of the Interior
   Museum
Dolls' House and Toy Museum
Dumbarton Oaks
Frederick Douglass House
Freer Gallery of Art
Hillwood
Hirshhorn Museum and Sculpture
   Garden
House of the Temple
Islamic Center
Lillian and Albert Small Jewish
   Museum
National Air and Space Museum
National Gallery of Art
National Geographic Society
   Explorers Hall
National Museum of African Art
National Museum of American Art
National Museum of Natural
   History
National Portrait Gallery
National Rifle Association of
   America
The Octagon
Old Pension Building
Petersen House
The Phillips Collection
Renwick Gallery

Textile Museum
Treasury Department Museum
Truxtun-Decatur Naval Museum
The White House
Woodrow Wilson House

Libraries
Folger Shakespeare Library
Library of Congress

Memorials and monuments
Jefferson Memorial
Lincoln Memorial
Marine Corps War Memorial
Vietnam Veterans Memorial
Washington Monument

Parks and gardens
Dumbarton Oaks
Kenilworth Aquatic Garden
Lady Bird Johnson Park and
   Lyndon Baines Johnson
   Memorial Grove
Lafayette Square
The Mall
Meridian Hill Park
National Arboretum
Potomac Park
Rock Creek Park
Theodore Roosevelt Island and
   Memorial
United States Botanic Garden

Religious buildings
Church of the Epiphany
Franciscan Monastery
Mormon Temple
National Shrine of the Immaculate
   Conception
St Matthew's Cathedral
Washington Cathedral

Theatres
Ford's Theatre
Kennedy Center for the
   Performing Arts

Other sights
Arlington National Cemetery
Chesapeake and Ohio Canal
Fort Leslie J. McNair
National Aquarium
National Zoological Park
Navy Yard
Pierce Mill
Rock Creek Cemetery
Smithsonian Institution Building
Union Station
United States Naval Observatory
Voice of America
Washington Convention Center
Washington Post
Watergate Complex

Anacostia Neighborhood Museum

2405 Martin Luther King Ave. SE, DC 20560 ☎287–3369.
Map 8K11 ▢ ▨ for certain exhibitions. Open Mon–Fri
10am–6pm, Sat, Sun 1–6pm. Closed Christmas.

Located in a black district on the SE side of the Anacostia
River, this lively museum has temporary exhibitions by black
artists or ones that reflect the culture and history of the area.
Established in 1967 as part of the Smithsonian Institution, the
museum has gained wide respect.

Anderson House

2118 Massachusetts Ave. NW, DC 20008 ☎785–0540. Map
3D5 ▢ ✗ by appt. Open 1–4pm, closed Sat in Aug, Sun,
Mon, hols. Library open Mon–Fri 10am–4pm. Metro: Dupont
Circle.

Anderson House is home to the Society of the Cincinnati,
which was founded in 1783 by a group of Washington's
officers and has remained a strictly hereditary body, with
membership restricted to male descendants of officers who
fought for three years in the Revolutionary War. It exists to
perpetuate the fraternal spirit of the original founders, to foster
American ideals and to support educational, cultural and
literary activities related to the society's aims. The name
alludes to the parallel between George Washington and the
Roman statesman Lucius Quinctius Cincinnatus, who twice
returned from his farm to assume emergency powers of
rulership – just as Washington returned from Mount Vernon –
and finally retired there declining all honours.

The house itself was built between 1902 and 1905 for Mr
and Mrs Larz Anderson with the intention that it should
eventually be given to the society. Anderson, a member of the
society, was a distinguished diplomat. The building, with its
front courtyard protected from the hoi polloi by a screening
wall, reflects the exclusive nature of the society. Both
externally and internally it is lavish and imposing.

The interior boasts a patrician elegance exemplified by the
vast **ballroom**, with its musicians' gallery. It also houses the
society's **museum** with portraits of the founders, military
relics, documents and personal memorabilia. The second floor
still has most of its original furnishings and *objets d'art*,
including an impressive collection of 18thC paintings by
Hoppner, Raeburn, Reynolds and others. The basement has a
13,000-volume **library** of works on the American
Revolutionary period.

A pleasant way to enjoy the house in leisured fashion is to
attend one of the concerts held regularly on Sat afternoons.

Arlington House ★

Arlington National Cemetery, Arlington, Va. 22211
☎557–0613. Map 4H2 ▢ ✗ Oct–Mar by reservation ◁▦
Open Apr–Sept 9.30am–6pm; Oct–Mar 9.30am–6.30pm.
Metro: Arlington Cemetery.

Also known as Custis-Lee Mansion, this house is dramatically
set on a hill within *Arlington National Cemetery*, and since
1955 has been a permanent memorial to Robert E. Lee, a Civil
War Confederate commander widely admired both N and S of
the Mason-Dixon line.

The house, with its massive Doric-columned portico, was
built between 1802 and 1817 by George Washington Parke
Custis, stepson of George Washington. Custis was a many-

faceted man: agriculturalist, painter, playwright, orator. His portrait hangs over the fireplace in the **family dining room**, and some of his own paintings are also on view; for example, his hunting scenes in the **center hall**.

Custis' daughter, Mary, married Robert E. Lee in the **family parlour** in 1831, and the house was the Lee family home from then until the Civil War. Here, wrote Lee, "my affections and attachments are more strongly placed than at any other place in the world". It was here that he took his painful decision in 1861 to leave the US Army and offer his services to Virginia. After that he never returned to the house.

During the Civil War the house was occupied by the US Army. It was later confiscated in lieu of property taxes, won back by Lee's son through the Supreme Court and finally sold by him to the Federal Government.

The original atmosphere of a gracious Virginia family home has been painstakingly re-created, complete with staff dressed in 19thC costume. Some of the original furnishings have been returned, while others are similar period pieces or copies. The servants' quarters are on the s side of the circular drive. Across the garden is a small **museum** illustrating the history of the house and the life of Robert E. Lee. From the portico be sure to take in the view E over Washington which Lafayette claimed was the "finest view in the world".

Arlington National Cemetery ★
Arlington, Va. 22211 ☎629-0931. Map **4**GHI&J2-3 ▣ **✗** *by Tourmobile* ⬟ ◁ *Open Apr–Sept 8am–7pm; Oct–Mar 8am–5pm. Metro: Arlington Cemetery.*

A serene and dignified environment for a last resting place, the cemetery is approached by the Arlington Memorial Bridge with its dramatic gold statues at either end, and through the splendid gateway, built under President Franklin D. Roosevelt's Work Project Administration (WPA). The rolling, wooded slopes have row upon row of small, simple white gravestones interspersed occasionally with larger and more imposing monuments. Burial is now restricted to certain categories of people and their dependants: members of the armed forces who have served in a foreign war, Medal of Honor recipients, and important government or political figures.

The cemetery was formerly the estate of *Arlington House*, home of Robert E. Lee, which still dominates the area. The US Government took over the estate on the outbreak of the Civil War and in 1865 began using it as a national cemetery. It now honours the dead of both armies in the Civil War. A **Confederate Monument**, in bronze and granite, surmounted by a female figure facing s, stands on the w side of the cemetery near McPherson Dr. To the s of the house, a huge granite sarcophagus marks a vault containing 2,111 unknowns of the Civil War. Anonymous victims of more recent wars are commemorated by the **Unknown Soldier's Tomb**, a chastely-carved marble block standing before the Arlington Memorial Amphitheater, watched over constantly by soldiers of the Third Infantry who, in a fine display of military drill, change guard every half hour during the day in summer and every hour in winter.

The most-visited grave is probably that of President John F. Kennedy, which lies off Sheridan Dr. on the slope below Arlington House. Marked by an eternal flame, it is approached

by a terrace with a curving wall inscribed with words from
Kennedy's Inaugural Address. The grave of his brother,
Robert F. Kennedy, is nearby. A little farther up towards the
house is the table-like gravestone of Major Pierre L'Enfant,
commanding a splendid view over the city which he planned.

Arthur M. Sackler Gallery

*1050 Independence Ave. SW, DC 20560 ☎357–2700. Map
6G7 ☺ ✈ for certain exhibitions ✗ ☎ for opening times.
Metro: Smithsonian.*
The focus of this new museum, due to open in the summer of
1987, is the art of the Near and Far East. Dr Arthur M. Sackler
is a New York psychiatrist and medical publisher who pledged
his collection of 1,000 Asian and Near Eastern works to the
Smithsonian and donated $4 million towards the construction
of an underground museum to house the collection. The
museum is part of the new Quadrangle complex behind the
Smithsonian Castle, which also houses the National Museum
of African Art. The Sackler Gallery complements the already
strong Oriental collection of the neighbouring *Freer Gallery*,
and the two will work hand in glove, sharing the same
curatorial and conservation staff, library and research facilities.
There will be major loan exhibitions as well as displays from
the museum's own collection.

Arts Club of Washington

*2017 I St. NW, DC 20006 ☎331–7282. Map 3E5 ☺ ✈
Open Tues 10am–5pm, Wed–Fri 2–5pm, Sat, Sun 1–5pm.
Closed Mon, hols. Metro: Foggy Bottom, Farragut West.*
This organization, whose aim is to support the arts in the
Greater Washington area, occupies two adjoining historic
houses. No. 2017 was built in 1802–5 and served for a time as
the Executive Mansion under President James Monroe.
No. 2015 next door was built around 1870. Apart from their
interest as period houses, the buildings house a permanent
collection of works by Washington artists as well as changing
exhibitions of work by contemporary artists from Washington
and elsewhere.

Arts and Industries Building

*900 Jefferson Dr. SW, DC 20560 ☎357–2700 (central
Smithsonian info.) Map 6G7 ☺ ✗ ⌣ Open 10am–5.30pm.
Closed Christmas. Metro: Smithsonian.*
The second oldest of the Smithsonian buildings on the *Mall*,
this quintessentially Victorian structure, with its turrets and
polychromatic brickwork, was completed in 1881 to house
objects given to the Smithsonian from the United States
International Exposition, held in 1876 to mark the centenary of
Independence. In 1980 it was extensively restored.

Its four wings, radiating out from a central rotunda,
resplendent with fountain and potted plants, contain a startling
selection of objects illustrating the wonders of 19thC
inventiveness, brought from all over America and abroad.
Pennsylvania is represented by objects as diverse as a railway
locomotive and a model of the Liberty Bell made out of sugar.
There is another Liberty Bell in tobacco from North Carolina,
a bale of cotton from Mississippi, optical instruments from
Paris and silverware from England. The growing pride in
American industrial might, felt in 1876, is reflected in the
impressive array of steam-powered machinery from pumping

engines to printing presses. There are also some fine models of ships, particularly the 45-ft (16m) model of the naval cruiser *Antietam*.

The museum has a well-stocked gift shop and a **Discovery Theater** which holds performances of films, puppetry, drama, dance, mime and singing (☎357–1500 *for details* ✱).

B'nai B'rith Klutznick Museum

1640 Rhode Island Ave. NW, DC 20036 ☎857–6583. *Map 3E6* ◻ ✉ ✗ ✱ *Open 10am–5pm. Closed hols except Christmas. Metro: Farragut North.*

This is the world headquarters of B'nai B'rith (Sons of the Covenant), an international organization existing for the purpose of "uniting Jews in their highest interests and those of humanity". Judaica of all kinds is the theme of the museum. Frequent temporary exhibitions are held on various aspects of Jewish life and history, as well as the permanent exhibition of over 400 objects: ancient Jewish pottery and coins, ritual implements, regalia, silverware and much else. The museum shop sells Jewish American craftwork. Behind the museum is the **Harold and Sylvia Greenberg Sculpture Garden**.

Bureau of Engraving and Printing

14th and C St. SW, DC 20228 ☎447–9709/9976. *Map 6G–H6* ◻ ✉ *Open Mon–Fri 9am–2pm. Metro: Smithsonian. Washington Mall Tourmobile.*

The Bureau of Engraving and Printing, the US Government security printer, is the world's largest establishment of its kind. It employs 3,500 people and operates 24hrs a day, using the most up-to-date machinery. The average life of a dollar bill is only 18 months, so the presses are kept busy replenishing the supply. As well as banknotes, the bureau also prints Treasury Bonds, postage stamps, White House invitations, government certificates and other official documents.

The self-guided tour of the building takes you along glassed-in galleries overlooking rooms where stamps and banknotes roll off huge presses and where bills are stacked ready for circulation. "This stack contains $6,400,000 in $20 bills", a recorded voice tantalizingly announces. The tour ends in an exhibit hall with a souvenir shop. Free samples are not available but a small bag containing the shreddings from $150 worth of bills can be bought. Coins are produced not here but by the Mint, whose works are in Philadelphia, Denver and San Francisco.

Capital Children's Museum

800 3rd St. NE, DC 20002 ☎543 8600 *Map 8F10* ◻ ✗ *for groups only by appt* ✱ ☞ *Open 10am–5pm. Closed major hols. Metro: Union Station.*

If your child is itching to learn how to operate a computer, write with a quill pen, run a printing press or make a radio programme, this is the place where he or she can do all of these things and many more. By having fun, the children acquire much valuable knowledge about the modern world. The computer section is a good example. Each child sits in front of a screen with a computer keyboard and, under the guidance of instructors, can learn how to make pictures on the screen using different colours and shapes. There is also a talking computer. "My name is Wisecracker", it intones in an eerie, science-fiction voice, "Come talk to me." It will then repeat whatever you type into it, even gibberish. There are also free craft activities and puppet shows on Fri–Sun for an extra fee.

Capitol ★

E End of Mall on Capitol Hill ☎224–3121. *Map* **7**G9 ◻ �⊠ *on 3rd floor* ✗ 💺 *Open June–Labor Day 9am–10pm; rest of year 9am–4.30pm. Closed some major hols. Metro: Capitol South, Union Station.*

The Capitol, seat of the Congress, was appropriately made the centre of L'Enfant's Washington plan, with all the streets numbered or lettered outward from it. Unlike the *White House*, it is unashamedly grand, standing on the hill that L'Enfant once described as "a pedestal waiting for superstructure", its vast white dome surmounted by a figure representing Liberty. Its grandeur does not intimidate but rather encourages the visitor to enter and admire the place where the supreme lawmaking body of the richest nation on earth meets, deliberates and decides. How many other legislative buildings in the world are so freely accessible? To view a session of the House of Representatives or the Senate you need a pass from your Congressman if you are a US citizen, or a passport or other identification if you are an overseas visitor (Congress is usually in session from Jan to some time between July and Oct).

Emily was staring. "The Capitol" she said, with reverence.
  Behind them Union Station, and its triumphal arches, behind them the central figures of Freedom and Imagination.
  The Capitol faced east. The dome was a massive bubble swimming in a golden heat haze.
                         Faith Baldwin, *Washington, USA*

The Capitol evolved piecemeal over many years. It was begun in 1793 to a design by the amateur architect Dr William Thornton, one of a series of nine architects who shaped the building. By 1800 it was sufficiently far advanced for the House and Senate to move there from Philadelphia. The Supreme Court and the Library of Congress also used the building in the early days. In 1814 British forces set fire to the Capitol, and, although saved from total destruction by a heavy rainfall, it needed extensive rebuilding. By 1819 it was once again ready for occupation. Since then frequent modifications have been made. In the 1860s the old copper-covered wooden dome was replaced by the present cast-iron one, and in 1962 the E side was extended by 32½ft (10m) to provide more space.

The point of departure for tours is the huge **rotunda** beneath the dome. A white marble disc in the centre of the floor marks the spot where many presidents have lain in state. Among the works of art in the rotunda are statues of American statesmen, and eight large paintings depicting scenes from American history. The four by John Trumbull of events from the Revolutionary period are particularly interesting, as the artist was present on each occasion. The centre of the dome also has a remarkable painting, *The Glorification of the Spirit of George Washington* by the Italian artist Constantino Brumidi, an immigrant who worked for 25yrs on the Capitol's interior.

To the S of the rotunda is the **Statuary Hall**, now filled with statues commemorating worthy citizens of various states. This room, formerly the House chamber, has a remarkable acoustic property called a parabolic reflection which enabled

Capitol

SECOND FLOOR
South

1
2
3
4
5

East Front

Floor plan of the US Capitol, home of the Senate and
House of Representatives since 1800. Visitors can tour
part of the main floor, with its historic paintings and
sculptures, and from the floor above there is access to the
public galleries of the House and Senate chambers.

John Quincy Adams (later President) to eavesdrop on
members of the Opposition. A brass disc marks the spot where
Adams sat, and where he died. Stand here and listen as the
guide speaks very quietly from across the room; you will be
astonished at how clearly the voice carries.

Ascend to the next floor by one of the building's four grand
staircases, and from this level enter the visitors' galleries of
both the Senate (in the N wing) and the House of
Representatives (in the S wing). The **Senate chamber** seems
surprisingly small, but there are only 100 Senators – two for
each state, irrespective of size. It is restrained in decor except
for the huge tasselled canopy over the chair of the Speaker
(who is always the US Vice-President). The much larger
House chamber has some interesting decorative features
including a frieze of medallions depicting great lawgivers of
history from Moses to Thomas Jefferson. It is here that the
President addresses the joint session of Congress. There is a
fixed number of 435 Representatives, and each represents a
given number of people rather than a state. The two houses are
equal in legislative power.

The Senate offices are in two buildings N of the Capitol: the
Russell Building, in use since 1909, and the **Dirksen
Building**, completed in 1958. These are connected to the
Capitol by a special subway train which the public can use.
The Representatives have their offices in the **Cannon**,
Longworth and **Rayburn Buildings** to the S (dating from
1908, 1933 and 1965 respectively), connected to the Capitol by
pedestrian tunnels. A special book-conveyor tunnel links the
Capitol with the *Library of Congress*. If you visit the Senate
cafeteria, try a bowl of the bean soup that has become a Capitol
institution.

The Capitol is surrounded by a fine park, superbly laid out
by the landscape architect Frederick Law Olmsted in 1872. To

1 Committee on Appropriations
2 House Chamber
3 Speaker's Office
4 Committee on Ways and Means
5 National Statuary Hall
6 House Minority Leader
7 Great Rotunda
8 Senate Minority Leader
9 Senate Majority Leader
10 Senate Chamber
11 Old Senate Chamber
12 President's Room
13 Marble (Reading) Room
14 Vice President's Formal Office
15 Senate Reception Room
16 Vice President

The Mall

West Front

North

the w the land drops away in terraces to a pool overlooked by
the dramatic bronze monument to General (and later
President) Ulysses S. Grant, showing a Civil War battle with
the intrepid Grant surveying the scene from his horse. Note
also, at the foot of the slope, just to the NW of the Capitol
building, the arched entrance to the **Grotto**, once a source of
water for thirsty travellers, now used to provide municipal
water. In the section of the park N of Constitution Ave. is an
attractively terraced area with a large fountain; immediately w
of this is a **monolith** commemorating Senator Robert A. Taft
of Ohio and designed by Douglas W. Orr in 1959. It houses 27
bells which chime every 15mins. Congressmen and public
alike enjoy the Capitol park for its beauty, serenity and charm.

Cathedrals   See *St Matthew's Cathedral* and *Washington
Cathedral*.

Chesapeake and Ohio Canal
☎ (301) 739–4200 (for info. on upper canal), 229–3614 (for
info. on canal near Metropolitan DC). Map 2E2–4. Two canal
boats, "Georgetown" and "Canal Clipper", operate mid-Apr
to mid-Oct ☎ 472–4376 (for info.), 229–2026 (for
reservations).

The C&O Canal was originally intended to connect the
Potomac with the Ohio River. Construction began in 1828 but
ceased in 1850 once the canal had reached Cumberland, Md., a

distance of 184½ miles (277km). Most of its length runs parallel to the Potomac. Although never a great financial success, it did carry goods such as grain, timber and coal before commercial traffic stopped in 1924. Today it is appreciated as one of the best-preserved of the old American canals. Now designated a National Historical Park, it has a new identity as a recreational facility, its paths used by walkers, joggers and cyclists.

At its Georgetown end, it is lined with picturesque houses, new condominiums and chic restaurants. A short distance farther on, it enters more rural surroundings. Many people, from wildlife enthusiasts to history buffs, find much to engross them along the canal's banks.

The **Monocacy Aqueduct**, near Dickerson, is an impressive piece of engineering, as is the 3,117ft (950m) **Paw Paw Tunnel** which takes the canal through a mountain. Locks, bridges, lock houses and other such remains from the canal's working heyday have been preserved.

The canal is ideal for an afternoon's excursion or a week-long hike; there are "hiker-biker" overnight campsites roughly every 5miles (8km), as well as three drive-in camping grounds. The **Great Falls Tavern** (☎ *(301) 299–3613; open 9am–5pm; closed hols*) houses a museum and a visitors' center. Other visitors' centers on the canal are located in Georgetown between Thomas Jefferson St. and 30th St. NW, and at the terminal in Cumberland, Md. These centers provide information about conducted walks and evening programmes.

Church of the Epiphany ★
1317 G St. NW, DC 20005 ☎347–2635. Map 6F7 ☺ Open 10am–2pm. Sun services 7.45am, 8am, 11am. Organ recitals Tues 12.10pm. Metro: Metro Center.

A century ago this lovely Neo-Gothic Episcopal church was attended by Washington's upper crust. Today, as the *Old Downtown* area steadily revives, the church is once again coming into its own. It has a graceful, soothing interior, lit by rich stained-glass windows, and possesses a fine pipe-organ.

Columbia Historical Society (Christian Heurich Memorial Mansion)
1307 New Hampshire Ave. NW, DC 20036 ☎785–2068. Map 3D5 ☺ for children ▨ ✗ Open Wed, Fri, Sat, 10am–4pm. Closed Mon, Tues, Thurs, Sun, hols. Metro: Dupont Circle.

Of all the great Washington houses open to the public, this is one of the most opulent. Since 1956 it has been the home of the Columbia Historical Society, founded in 1894 to record, teach and preserve the historical heritage of Washington DC. The society maintains an extensive library of Washingtonia, publishes a periodical, *Records of the Columbia Historical Society*, and holds lectures. Appropriately, the house it occupies is itself a historic monument, which the society has renovated while keeping the decor and furnishings as near to the original as possible.

The house was built in the 1890s by Christian Heurich, a German immigrant who made a fortune as a brewer. His home combined advanced technological features, such as a poured concrete shell for protection against fire, with an almost regal lavishness of decoration, carried out by German-American builders and craftsmen. The three floors of rooms open to the public include the **Dining Room**, with its rich woodwork, and the **Blue Parlor** resplendent with elaborate plaster mouldings, a delicately painted ceiling and original family furnishings. An added attraction is the charming garden entered from Sunderland Pl. and used as a park by local people.

Corcoran Gallery of Art
17th St. and New York Ave. NW, DC 20006 ☎638-3211. Map 6F6 ◙ ✗ Open Tues-Sun 10am-4.30pm. Closed Mon, some major hols. Metro: Farragut West.

The Corcoran, which is not part of the Smithsonian empire, is the city's most important private art museum and one of the major galleries of the country. Founded by the banker W. W. Corcoran in 1859, it was formerly housed in what is now the *Renwick Gallery* and later moved to its present building, an imposing edifice designed by Ernest Flagg in the palatial, classical style of the Beaux Arts school.

The collection divides into European and American sections. The former, enriched by the acquisition of the W. A. Clark collection in 1928, includes Renaissance works by Titian and others, 17thC Dutch and Flemish masters, British works of art by, among others, Gainsborough, Turner and Raeburn, and French paintings up to the Impressionists, including a particularly rich collection of Corots. There are also Greek and Egyptian figurines, Beauvais and Gobelins tapestries, majolica ware, stained glass from Soissons Cathedral, and an entire room of the Louis XVI period, complete with Marie Antoinette's harpsichord, brought from the Hôtel de la Tremoille in Paris.

The American collection is one of the nation's finest and reveals the extraordinary richness and diversity of American art. To view these works is to catch a glimmer of the soul of America. The collection embraces the stiff, amateurish portraiture of early colonial days, the romanticized Western scenes of Albert Bierstadt, the strange visionary works of Elihu Vedder, the tranquil landscapes of the so-called Luminous School of 19thC artists. All the great names of American art are here: Winslow Homer, Mary Cassatt, John Singer Sargent. A surprising inclusion is Samuel F. B. Morse, inventor of the Morse code as well as being a talented painter. His *Old House of Representatives*, an atmospheric painting of the chamber lit by candlelight, hangs in the main hallway. Contemporary American artists are well represented: Louise Nevelson, Joseph Cornell, Jules Olitski, Helen Frankenthaler among others. Temporary exhibitions are also held here.

As well as a gallery, the Corcoran is the only accredited art school in Washington, offering both full-time courses and classes for anyone of any level. Evening recitals are given in its acoustically fine auditorium. The Corcoran undeniably lives up to the inscription over its entrance: "Dedicated to art".

Custis-Lee Mansion   See *Arlington House*.

Daughters of the American Revolution (DAR)
1776 D St. NW, DC 20006 ☎628-1776. Map 6F6 ◙ ▦ for library ✗ ✱ Open Mon-Fri 8.30am-4pm, Sun 1-5pm. Closed Sat. Tours Mon-Fri 10am-3pm, Sun 1-5pm. Metro: Farragut West, Farragut North.

The DAR is an organization of women whose direct ancestors helped in the struggle for American Independence. The headquarters cover an entire city block. The address and telephone number both contain the date 1776, the year of the Declaration of Independence. Three connecting buildings occupy the site: the **Administration Building**; the **Memorial Continental Hall**, an imposing Beaux Arts edifice built in the early 1900s; and **Constitution Hall**, a 1920s neoclassical building by John Russell Pope used for conferences and cultural events.

The museum has 33 period rooms, representing various states of the Union and furnished in different styles. Their contents reflect the craftsmanship and decorative arts of America before the Industrial Revolution. They include a Californian adobe parlour of 1860, a 1775 Massachusetts bedroom, and a kitchen from an Oklahoma farmhouse complete with an assortment of 19thC kitchenware. A popular series of rooms, especially with children, is the **New Hampshire attic** with its marvellous collection of toys, dolls and games.

The museum **gallery** contains permanent and changing exhibits from the museum's extensive decorative arts collection. There is also a superb genealogical **library** open to the public for a small fee.

Decatur House ★
748 Jackson Pl. NW, DC 20006 ☎*673–4030. Map 3F6* ▣ ✗
Open Tues–Fri 10am–2pm, Sat, Sun, hols noon–4pm.
Closed some major hols. Metro: Farragut West, Farragut North.

Commodore Stephen Decatur (1779–1820), hero of the struggle against the Barbary pirates and of the War of 1812, is one of the most dashing figures in American naval history. He is also famous for his immortal and much misquoted toast: "Our country – in her intercourse with foreign nations, may she be always in the right, and always successful, right or wrong."

After coming to Washington, covered in glory, he commissioned the prominent architect Benjamin Henry Latrobe to design him an elegant, red-brick house in *Lafayette Square*, where he and his wife entertained lavishly. After Decatur's tragic death in a duel in 1820 Mrs Decatur moved to Georgetown, and subsequently the house enjoyed a succession of other distinguished tenants including diplomats and congressmen.

In 1871 it became the home of General Edward Fitzgerald Beale and his wife. They introduced Victorian features to the house, and later Beale's son and daughter-in-law lived there. Since 1956 it has been owned by the National Trust for Historic Preservation who maintain the building along with its furnishing and memorabilia of the Decatur and Beale eras. The Trust also has a fine bookshop and gift shop around the corner at 1600 H St., next to the *Truxtun-Decatur Naval Museum*.

Department of the Interior Museum
18th and C St. NW, DC 20240 ☎*343–2743. Map 5F5* ▣ ▣
Open Mon–Fri 8am–4pm. Closed Sat, Sun, hols. Metro: Farragut West.

The agencies that come under the umbrella of this department and are represented in its museum include the National Park Service, the Bureau of Reclamation, the Geological Survey, the Bureau of Land Management and the Bureau of Indian

Affairs. The exhibits range from stuffed animals, displays on endangered species and scarce, non-renewable sources of power, documents and pictures illustrating the opening of the West, to mineral samples from different parts of the country. One of the most interesting sections deals with the Indians (or Native Americans, as they are called). There is a diorama of a Navajo settlement, headdresses, bows and arrows, and other Indian artifacts.

In the same building there is a shop selling attractive but highly priced Indian craftwork – from textiles and basketwork to jewellery and pottery – and a National Park Service office which provides useful leaflets about its facilities. The department also has a comprehensive library (*open Mon–Fri 7.45am–5pm*).

Dolls' House and Toy Museum
5236 44th St. NW, DC 20015 ☎244–0024 ▨ ✖ X for 12 or more by appt. Open Tues–Sat 10am–5pm, Sun noon–5pm. Closed Mon, Major hols. Metro: Friendship Heights.

Flora Gill Jacobs, author of *A History of Dolls' Houses*, founded this entrancing museum in 1975, using her own extensive collection, only part of which is on display at any one time. The remainder is used for special and seasonal exhibitions. The emphasis is on dolls' houses, but many antique toys are also represented. Most of the objects are Victorian.

The museum provides not only nostalgic interest but also a fascinating glimpse in miniature into social and architectural history. There is a terrace of typical Baltimore row houses in bright red brick, a milliner's shop complete with minute hats, a circus tent with clowns, acrobats and performing animals, and a family house where each room is perfect in every detail from the curtain tassels to a tiny pack of playing cards on a table. The museum also sells books, toys, dolls' houses and related accessories.

Downtown See *Old Downtown*.

Dumbarton Oaks ★
1703 32nd St. NW, DC 20007 ☎338–8278. Map 2C–D3 ▨ ▨ for garden X by arrangement. Art collection open Tues–Sun 2–5pm. Closed Mon, hols. Rare book room open Sat, Sun 2–5pm. Gardens open Apr–Oct 2–6pm ▨ Nov–Mar 2–5pm. Closed hols. Bus: Georgetown routes.

This remarkable institution is the result of the vision of Ambassador and Mrs Robert Woods Bliss, who bought the house in 1920, remodelled it to contain their art collection and created around it a deliciously romantic garden. In 1944 the name of Dumbarton Oaks flashed briefly across the news headlines of the world when its Music Room was used as the venue for the conference that gave birth to the United Nations.

The museum, now a branch of Harvard University, has two main collections: one of Byzantine art, the other of pre-Columbian art. Each is linked with a research centre and library. The **pre-Columbian collection** is housed in a modern pavilion, ingeniously designed by Philip Johnson, and consisting of a cluster of eight small circular rooms. Stand and talk near the centre of any of the rooms and observe the curious reverberating sound effect. There are also other works of art that are not part of the main collections – for example, El Greco's *The Visitation*, which hangs in the Music Room. The room is still used for concerts which are open to the public.

The house also has a landscape garden department which runs a research programme and a library. Although the Dumbarton Oaks libraries are restricted to scholars, the public can view displays in the rare book room.

Don't miss the **garden** itself, built on a dramatically terraced slope and enriched by trellises, pergolas, pools, gazebos and a profusion of statuary and ornament. This undoubtedly is one of the most memorable gardens in the USA.

Executive Office Building

17th St. and Pennsylvania Ave. NW, DC 20503. Map 6F6. Closed to public. Metro: Farragut West.
This landmark lies just to the w of the White House – a vast, ornate building designed by A. B. Mullet in French Second-Empire style and completed in 1888. Its incongruity with other federal buildings bothered Washingtonians for decades, and the building narrowly escaped demolition. Now, cleaned and restored, it houses White House staff and various government agencies. The public are not allowed inside, but they can admire the exuberance of its facades which provides a refreshing change from the neoclassical mode so prevalent in Washington.

Federal Bureau of Investigation (FBI) ★

J. Edgar Hoover Building, 10th St. and Pennsylvania Ave. NW, DC 20535 ☎ 324–3447. Map 6F7 ☺ ☒ ✗ compulsory, every 15–20mins. Open Mon–Fri 9am–4.15pm. Closed Sat, Sun, hols. Metro: Federal Triangle.
Since 1975 the national crime-fighting force of the USA has occupied a rather forbidding, buff-coloured concrete building named after the formidable J. Edgar Hoover, who became head of the FBI in 1924 and ran it with an iron hand until he retired in 1972 at the age of 77. When the building was opened, a *Washington Post* writer remarked that it "would make a perfect stage set for a dramatization of George Orwell's *1984*".

Despite its austere building, the FBI does an excellent job in projecting to visitors its image of "Fidelity, Bravery, Integrity". Friendly, uniformed young guides usher you through a startling series of exhibits, such as an arsenal of criminal weapons, a rogues' gallery of famous villains, including Al Capone and John Dillinger, and a current list of the ten most wanted fugitives with their photographs (one visitor recognized his next-door neighbour). Some frightening statistics are given: a murder in the USA every 23mins, a rape every 6mins, a burglary every 8 seconds; the reassurance offered is that wherever you are in the country an FBI agent can be on the spot within an hour.

The bureau deals with a variety of offences including interstate flight, espionage, obscene telephone calls and certain types of fraud. It will also help local police forces detect such crimes as kidnapping, rape and murder. Its resources for this include highly sophisticated laboratories (seen on the tour) where anything from blood to paint samples can be analysed.

The tour ends in the firing range, with an impressive display of sharp-shooting by an FBI agent. The FBI tour is one of the most popular in the city, and no doubt helps to recruit many future agents.

Folger Shakespeare Library
201 E Capitol St. SE, DC 20003 ☎544-7077 (library), 546-4000 (theatre box office). Map 8G10 ▣ X Open mid-Apr to Labor Day 10am–4pm. Rest of year closed Sun. Closed hols. Metro: Capitol South.

Like so many other great American institutions of learning and culture, this one is the creation of a businessman with a dream: the late Henry Clay Folger, oil tycoon and Shakespearean scholar.

Its vast library of Shakespearean and Renaissance works is open to scholars only, but there is an **exhibition gallery** in the style of an Elizabethan great hall where many of Folger's treasures are displayed in rotation – books, manuscripts, portraits and relics.

There is also a **theatre**, beautifully built in the manner of a playhouse of Shakespeare's time, where a resident company performs plays by the Bard as well as some contemporary dramatists. The library is also a venue for poetry readings, concerts and lectures, and houses a shop which sells everything from busts of Shakespeare to books on the Renaissance. Note the simple elegance of the 1930s exterior, with its series of reliefs of scenes from the plays.

Ford's Theatre ★
511 10th St. NW, DC 20004 ☎426-6924. Map 6F7 ▣ X ✶ Museum open 9am–5pm. Closed Christmas. Theatre closed rehearsal days (performing season Sept–June ☎ for schedule). Metro: Gallery Place, Metro Center.

This is the place where President Abraham Lincoln was assassinated on the night of April 14 1865 while he sat watching the comedy, *Our American Cousin*. As the house exploded into laughter at the words "sockdologizing old mantrap", another explosion was heard from the box to the right of the stage, where Lincoln sat. John Wilkes Booth, noted actor and Confederate fanatic, had entered the box and shot Lincoln in the head. Booth jumped from the box, breaking a leg, and left through a back door, escaping on horseback. Some days later the cavalry caught up with him, and he was shot while attempting to defend himself.

The attractive theatre is now owned by the National Park Service. Restored in the 1960s to its original appearance, it once again functions as a theatre as well as a museum. During the day visitors can view the auditorium and the fateful box and hear a short lecture on the assassination. In the basement are two exhibitions. One, focusing on Lincoln's life and career, has memorabilia, documents and a taped commentary. The other, relating to Booth and the other conspirators, includes the murder weapon, a small Derringer pistol. (See also *Petersen House*.)

Fort Leslie J. McNair ★
4th and P St. SW, DC 20319 ☎693-8214. Map 7J8 ▣

Founded in 1791, this is the oldest functioning military post in America. It now houses the prestigious National War College, the Industrial College of the Armed Forces, the Inter-American Defense College and the headquarters of the US Army Military District of Washington. On a peninsula between the Washington Channel and the Anacostia River, it contains some impressive buildings, notably the War College – a somewhat forbidding red-brick structure with a vast portico, incongruously overlooking a little golf course for military personnel. Although the public cannot enter the buildings, the fort is worth a quick drive around if you happen to be in the area.

Franciscan Monastery

1400 Quincy St. NE, DC 20017 ☎526–6800 ▢ *✗ Church and gardens open 8am–5pm. Tours 9am–4pm approx. every 45mins. Metrorail to Brookland station; Metrobus to monastery gates.*

Also referred to as Mount St Sepulchre or the "Holy Land of America", this place has more than a touch of Hollywood kitsch about it – which is not to denigrate the spirit of reverence in which it is visited by Catholics and non-Catholics alike. The monastery's Byzantine-style **church**, consecrated in 1899, contains reproductions and impressions of a number of Holy Land shrines and sacred places, such as the Holy Sepulchre, the Stone of Anointing, the Grotto of the Annunciation and the Grotto of the Nativity. Visitors can also walk through a small-scale version of the Roman Catacombs. Outside in the attractive grounds are more re-creations of shrines: the Grotto of Gethsemane, the Tomb of the Blessed Virgin and the Grotto of Lourdes.

Frederick Douglass House (Cedar Hill)

1411 W St. SE, DC 20020 ☎426–5960 (house), 426–5961 (group tour reservations). Map 8J11 ▢ *✗ Open Apr–Labor Day 9am–5pm; rest of year 9am–4pm. Closed Christmas, New Year's Day. Tourmobile route.*

Frederick Douglass (1817–95) was the leading spokesman for American blacks in their struggle for freedom and justice during the 19thC. He lectured and wrote books about his own early life under slavery, campaigned tirelessly for abolition, helped recruit blacks for the Union army during the Civil War and finally settled down to a distinguished old age in Washington. He lived first in A St. (see *National Museum of African Art*), then bought Cedar Hill, this elegant white house on a height overlooking the Anacostia River. All the furnishings, except for curtains and wallpaper, are original. Douglass' library and other belongings are still *in situ*, and the whole house is redolent of the spirit of a very remarkable man. On arrival you are directed to the **Visitors' Center** at the foot of the hill where a film is shown about Douglass' life and books about black liberation, including Douglass' own, are on sale.

Freer Gallery of Art ★

1200 Jefferson Dr. SW, DC 20560 ☎357–2104. Map 6G7 ▢ *✗ Open 10am–5.30pm. Closed Christmas. Metro: Smithsonian.*

This is first and foremost a superb museum of Oriental art, founded by the refined railway-car manufacturer, Charles Lang Freer, who in 1906 donated his collection to the nation. The building, opened in 1923, is a low, grey structure in the style of a Florentine palace, surrounding a tranquil little courtyard. The exhibition galleries are all on one floor. On a lower level are offices, conservation laboratories and a resear library.

The Freer, a Smithsonian Institution gallery, ranks as one of the finest Oriental collections in the world. Here you can immerse yourself in the floating world of a Japanese screen; admire the meticulous craftsmanship of a *netsuke*, a lacquer box or a Chinese tomb figure; and contemplate the tranquillity of a Buddhist statue from India or the strange form of an ancient Egyptian animal god.

The **Peacock Room**, decorated by Freer's friend James McNeill Whistler to house the latter's stunning painting *The Princess from the Land of Porcelain*, is the museum's most astonishing room. Its furnishings originally belonged to the London dining room of Whistler's patron Frederick R. Leyland, but were purchased by Freer in 1904 and brought to the USA, complete with the portrait. This is a room straight out of an Aubrey Beardsley drawing, dripping with *fin-de-siècle* sensuality: dark green walls with huge, swirling peacocks highlighted in gold.

This room forms a link with the rest of the Freer collection, which consists of American paintings. Not surprisingly, Whistler dominates, but there are many works by other distinguished American artists such as Winslow Homer and John Singer Sargent.

Georgetown
Map 2C,D&E2–4.

Georgetown is one of those urban villages, like Montmartre in Paris, that are almost as famous as the cities they belong to; and in fact Georgetown predates Washington. It was founded in 1751 and named after George II of England. In common with its Paris counterpart, it is elegant and gracious in parts, while fraying to brash commercialism in others.

Her imagination in those early days fastened itself on certain of these Georgetown dwellings. As the first dying leaves of October swirled on the rusty brick sidewalks and streets and the lamplights flickered in the dusk, she walked down the hill from Rock Creek Park toward her own apartment, admiring those mansions and quaint old town-houses and the clapboards with coach lamps and gabled roofs and dormers and brightly colored doors which to her seemed touched, ever so fragilely, with age and influence.
Willie Morris, *The Last of the Southern Girls*

The best way to approach Georgetown is over the P St. Bridge into the prettiest part of the district, an area of tree-lined, brick-paved streets with rows of neat houses that have more than an echo of Georgian London. Solidly residential, save for the occasional recherché little shop, these hushed streets seem to wait perpetually for the twilight hour when congressmen, lawyers, heiresses and ex-ambassadors gather in softly lit rooms to take pre-dinner cocktails and talk the gossip of power. No. 1607 28th St. was once the home of Senator Edward Kennedy. His brother John lived at 3307 N St., farther up to the w, before he became President.

Walk uphill to the N and you will pass many large, gracious mansions. Most of these are private homes, but an exception is **Dumbarton House** (*2715 Q St.* ☎ *337–2288* ✉ *but donations welcomed; open Mon–Sat 9.30am–12.30pm; closed July, Aug, Christmas–New Year, Sun, hols*), not to be confused with nearby *Dumbarton Oaks*. A fine early Federal

house of about 1799, it is now headquarters of the Colonial
Dames of America, who preserve it as a museum with 18thC
and 19thC furnishings, domestic objects and memorabilia.

Farther uphill, with its entrance in R St., is **Oak Hill
Cemetery**, a serene place with a romantic atmosphere
reminiscent of Père Lachaise in Paris. Next to the cemetery is
the quiet oasis of **Montrose Park**, on the w side of which is
Lover's Lane, leading down to the even more secluded
Dumbarton Oaks Park. Dumbarton Oaks estate, with its
museum and glorious gardens, is immediately to the w of
Montrose Park.

In the opposite direction is the southern part of Georgetown
and the environs of the *Chesapeake and Ohio Canal*. One of
the most interesting historical buildings in this area is **Old
Stone House** (*3051 M St. NW* ☎ ✗ *open Wed–Sun
9.30am–5pm; closed some major hols*). Now supervised by the
National Park Service, it is believed to be the only surviving
pre-Revolutionary building in DC. Once a cabinetmaker's
home and workshop, it has five rooms furnished in typical
18thC manner and a spacious garden at the back. The guided
tours are given by docents (trained guides) in period costume.

On leaving this cosy haven you enter the commercialized
environs of M St., a thoroughfare which, together with the
intersecting Wisconsin Ave., represents the bustling, pleasure-
seeking side of Georgetown. These streets are lined with
boutiques, bars, discos, cafés and restaurants with French
names. At 3222 M St., backing onto the canal, is **Georgetown
Park**, which is not a park but a multi-level modern
development with shops and restaurants surrounding a central
skylit atrium. Its prolonged construction, involving the
demolition of several elderly buildings, aroused much
controversy, but there is no denying that it is a stylish and
lively place.

w of Wisconsin Ave. are more quiet, residential streets, and
on the western fringe of the district is the Jesuit-run
Georgetown University, the oldest Catholic university in
the USA and a prestigious place of learning. The main
building, Healy, with its soaring Victorian Gothic spires, is
one of the landmarks of western Washington.

Hillwood ★
4155 Linnean Ave. NW, DC 20008 ☎*686–0410* ▨ ✈ ✗
compulsory ▣ ⬤ ◁€ *Tours at 9am, 10.30am, noon, 1.30pm
(reservations required). Closed Tues, Sun, hols. Children
under 12 not admitted. Metro: Van Ness.*
Hillwood is a dazzling museum that was once the home of a
dazzling woman. Marjorie Merriweather Post's life was the
stuff of which Hollywood films are made. Daughter of Charles
William Post, founder of the Postum Cereal Company, she
inherited a fortune, beauty and a taste for high living and high
art. One of her four husbands, Joseph E. Davies, was
Ambassador to the Soviet Union from 1937 to 1938. During
their stay in Moscow she started to buy Russian *objets d'art*
and thus laid the foundation for her great collection, which
focused mainly on the art of Imperial Russia and that of 18thC
France. She acquired Hillwood in 1955 and enlarged it so that
her collection could be installed there. After her death in 1973
the house became a museum, as she had intended.

Tours of the house, lasting about 2hrs, are limited to 25
people at a time, and there is often a waiting list, so book well

in advance. The tour begins at the Visitors' Center, where a film is shown about the collection and its creator, then proceeds through the house itself. The rooms on show include: the **Pavillon** where Marjorie Post used to hold square dances and show movies to her dinner guests; the **French Drawing Room**, in Louis XVI style, with Beauvais tapestries, a chair from the household of Marie Antoinette and a charming portrait of the Empress Eugénie by Winterhalter; the **Porcelain Room**, containing dinner services used by Catherine the Great; and the **Icon Room**, which has a staggering display of icons, chalices, Fabergé jewelled Easter eggs and other treasures. The more domestic rooms are still redolent of the privileged life that was lived here. The collection contains a number of portraits of Marjorie Post herself, a striking woman even in old age. The whole house is lavish, elegant, impressive, fascinating; but such an *embarras de richesses* can be cloying, and the general atmosphere somehow lacks warmth.

The museum has three annexes in the grounds. One is a copy of a Russian dacha containing more Russian works of art. The second houses the paintings, sculptures and furnishings collected at the turn of the century by C. W. Post. The third, added in 1983, contains American Indian artifacts formerly exhibited by Mrs Post at Topridge, her camp in the Adirondacks. There is also a gift shop and a greenhouse where plants can be bought.

The 25 acres (10ha) of beautifully-landscaped grounds are a delight. There is a French formal *parterre*, a rose garden, a Japanese garden, a pet cemetery and many meandering paths and secluded corners. The gardens alone can be seen for a reduced fee (*open 11am–4pm; closed Tues, Sun, hols*).

Hillwood is more than an art museum: it is a museum of an era and a monument to the remarkable woman who created it.

Hirshhorn Museum and Sculpture Garden

Independence Ave. and 8th St. SW, DC 20560☎357–2700. Map 7G8 ⬛ 🎫 with flash and tripod ✗ 🍴 summer only. Open 10am–5.30pm; extended summer hours announced annually. Closed Christmas. Metro: L'Enfant Plaza.

There are few more exciting places in the world than this in which to look at modern art. The collection, one of the largest ever assembled by a private individual, was a gift to the US Government from the late Joseph Hirshhorn, a Latvian immigrant who made a fortune in uranium. A ravenous and independent-minded collector, he ignored fashion and stuck to gut reaction as his criterion. The result is a collection of rare breadth and impact.

The building housing the collection, which opened to the public in 1974 under the umbrella of the Smithsonian Institution, is a daring piece of work: a great concrete drum standing on four massive legs. Some said it spoiled the *Mall* but, as the Smithsonian's Secretary S. Dillon Ripley pointed out: "If it were not controversial in almost every way it would hardly qualify as a place to house contemporary art. For it must somehow be symbolic of the material it is designed to encase."

Only about 900 out of the many thousands of works in the collection can be shown at any one time. These are displayed in the galleries on the second and third floors – paintings in the artificially-lit outer circle, sculptures in the inner circle looking onto the courtyard. The emphasis is on American and contemporary art. There are works by Milton Avery, Stuart Davis, Robert Henri, Edward Hopper, Sol Le Witt, Richard Estes, Frank Stella and Kenneth Nolan, among others. Many are by immigrant artists such as Josef Albers, Willem de Kooning and Max Weber. But European artists are not under-represented. They include Balthus, Francis Bacon, Jean Dubuffet, Georg Grosz, René Magritte and Joan Miró.

The outside of the building is windowless, save for a 70ft (21m) balcony and window commanding a superb view to the N over the Mall. On the museum's plaza are some monumental works of sculpture, including a huge, brightly coloured, angular metal creation by Mark di Sivero entitled *Isis*, 42ft (13m) high and weighing 30 tons/tonnes. The plaza also has an outdoor café which is open in the summer.

Other less gigantic works of sculpture, many of them figurative bronzes, are displayed in the delightful sunken **Sculpture Garden**, opposite the museum on the other side of Jefferson Dr. This quiet oasis, with its lawns, pool and greenery, is a marvellous environment in which to contemplate such works as Rodin's *Burghers of Calais*, Matisse's series of *Backs* and a number of Henry Moore's *Reclining Figures*.

Joseph Hirshhorn's gut reactions have served us well, and this important collection continues to expand.

House of the Temple

1733 16th St. NW, DC 20009 ☎232–3579. Map 3D6 ⊡ ✗ compulsory. Open Mon–Fri 8am–3pm. Closed Sat, Sun, hols. Metro: Dupont Circle.

The richly symbolic world of freemasonry is powerfully exemplified in this building, headquarters of the Supreme Council of the 33rd Degree of the Scottish Rite of Freemasonry for the Southern Jurisdiction of the United States (to abbreviate an even longer title). The building was designed by the brilliant neoclassical revivalist John Russell Pope and is based on the Mausoleum at Helicarnassus in Asia Minor, one of the Seven Wonders of the ancient world, and thus complements the **George Washington Masonic Memorial**, which is inspired by another of the Seven Wonders, the Pharos Lighthouse. Pope's building is the more distinguished of the two (in fact he received a medal for it): a great square stone structure, surrounded by 33 Ionic columns and rising to a pyramidal roof. The imposing bronze door is approached by a long flight of steps guarded by two sphinxes representing Wisdom and Power.

The interior is equally impressive, especially the main **Temple Room**, a soaring chamber decorated with immense lavishness; the windows, for example, are glazed not with glass but with alabaster. There is a series of museum rooms containing masonic memorabilia, and a superb library of books on masonry and related subjects. More unexpected is one of the world's greatest collections of books on and by the Scottish poet (and freemason) Robert Burns.

Islamic Center

2551 Massachusetts Ave. NW, DC 20008 ☎332–8343. Map 2C4 ⊡ ✗ Open 10am–5pm. Closed Fri to non-Muslims. Metro: Dupont Circle.

Amid the discreet opulence of Massachusetts Ave. with its many embassies, there stands a corner of the Middle East, marked by a slender minaret. This is the Islamic Center, comprising a mosque, library, study centre and bookshop, which was built between 1949 and 1953 on the initiative of the ambassadors from certain leading Muslim nations. The construction was overseen by the Egyptian Ministry of Works, and the designer was an Italian expert on Islamic architecture, Mario Rossi, who himself became a Muslim late in life. Every Muslim country contributed money and objects.

In the magnificent **mosque room** itself there are carpets from Iran, tiles from Turkey, and a superb brass chandelier from Egypt. When entering the mosque, visitors must remove their shoes, and women must dress so as to expose only their hands and faces. The staff of the centre are friendly and always pleased to inform visitors about their religion.

Iwo Jima Statue See *Marine Corps War Memorial*.

Jefferson Memorial ★
Tidal Basin, W Potomac Park ☎426–6821. Map *6H6* 🖼
Closed Christmas. Metro: Arlington Cemetery.
This attractive monument was a *cause célèbre* at the time it was built. When in the 1930s it was decided to erect a memorial to America's third president, the site chosen was a point on the Tidal Basin directly s of the White House, forming the lower point of a cross whose other points were marked by the Lincoln Memorial, the White House and the Capitol. The architect was John Russell Pope, designer of the w wing of the *National Gallery of Art* and of the masonic *House of the Temple*. His elegant design for a shallow-domed neoclassical rotunda immediately aroused opposition. The Commission of Fine Arts condemned both site and design, and modernist architect Frank Lloyd Wright called it an "arrogant insult to the memory of Thomas Jefferson", and a group of female conservationists threatened to chain themselves to the cherry trees that stood in the way of construction. But the project had the strong support of President Roosevelt who admired Pope's building and wanted it in exactly that spot. If a tree was in the way, he said, "we will move the tree and the lady and the chains and transplant them to some other place". And so the building went ahead, although Pope did not live to see its completion in 1943.

The monument is a delight, with its ring of Ionic columns and its airy interior dominated by Rudolph Evans' vast bronze statue of Jefferson, that Renaissance man who, among other things, was architect, statesman, inventor and botanist. Around the inner frieze are his words: "I have sworn upon the altar of God eternal hostility against every form of tyranny over the mind of man."

Works on Jefferson are available at a small bookstall in the basement, along with postcards and memorabilia. On summer evenings, regular military band concerts are given on the steps of the monument. There can be few more serene places in the entire city.

Kenilworth Aquatic Garden
Kenilworth Ave. and Douglass St. NE, DC 20019
☎426–6905 🖼 *Open 7am–sunset. Metro: Deanwood.*
Located on the edge of the Anacostia River opposite the National Arboretum, this remarkable nature reserve consists of a series of ponds divided by paths. Waterlilies, water

hyacinths, lotuses and a variety of other aquatic and waterside plants grow here in abundance, producing glorious blooms in the summer months. It is best to go in the early morning, as many of the tropical flowers close during the day. The wildlife includes fish, turtles, frogs, muskrats, opossums and racoons.

Kennedy Center for the Performing Arts

New Hampshire Ave. and Rock Creek Parkway, DC 20566
☎*254–3600. Map 5F4* ◻️ ▦ *for performances* ✗ ▆ ⇌ ⬤
Open 10am–11pm. Metro: Foggy Bottom.

The most surprising thing about this great cultural complex overlooking the Potomac is that it was not built many years earlier. Until it was opened in 1971, Washington had no major centre for the performing arts and was regarded as something of a backwater when it came to music, opera and drama – an extraordinary state of affairs for a great world capital. To remedy the situation a scheme for a national cultural centre was initiated under Eisenhower in 1958 and received active support from John F. Kennedy. But, initially lacking congressional funding, the project progressed painfully slowly, until Kennedy's assassination in 1963 and the decision to turn the centre into a memorial to him finally spurred Congress into voting the money to finish it.

The building was designed by the prominent architect Edward Durrell Stone and built on a grand scale. Two vast transverse halls connect with an even vaster **Grand Foyer** opening onto the river terrace and with access to the three main auditoriums: the **Eisenhower Theater**, the **Opera House** and the **Concert Hall**. The **American Film Institute Theater** is on the ground floor, and the top floor has a 500-seat auditorium called the **Terrace Theater** and a library of the performing arts.

Two companies, the National Symphony Orchestra and the Washington Opera, are based here. But the centre is also host to many great companies and orchestras from other parts of the country and abroad. Materials, decorations and fittings were donated by various countries: marble for the walls from Italy, chandeliers from Sweden and Austria, mirrors from Belgium, curtains from Japan, tapestries from France. The overall design of the building is a huge rectangle in plain white marble, surrounded on all sides by an immensely broad colonnade of slender metal pillars. It has the austere monumentality of a design by Albert Speer, but with a lightness of touch that saves it from being forbidding. From the roof terrace, there is a stunning view over the city and across the Potomac.

Some cynics still scoff at the centre and its design. Its furnishings and decorations undoubtedly do have a touch of department-store gaudiness; and the great rough-cast bronze head of Kennedy that dominates the Grand Foyer is not to everyone's taste. But these are minor quibbles. The Kennedy Center is a triumph, not least in the way that it has brought Washington into the major league of world cities in the fields of music, opera and drama.

Lady Bird Johnson Park and Lyndon Baines Johnson Memorial Grove

George Washington Memorial Parkway. Map **4&5***G,H,I 3–5*
◻️ ⬤ *Open 8am–sunset.*

Sited on a long, narrow island running parallel to the shore of the Potomac near Arlington Cemetery, this park was dedicated

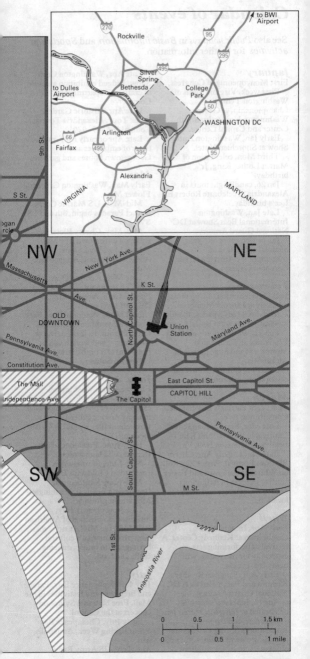

Calendar of events

See also *Public holidays* in *Basic information* and *Sports and activities* for further information.

January

First Mon, opening of Congress.

First week, Virginia Slims of Washington Tennis Championship, at George Washington University Smith Center and Capital Centre.

Early Jan, Washington Antique Show at Shoreham Hotel.

Third Mon, celebration of Martin Luther King, Jr's birthday.

Jan 26, candlelight tours in Alexandria to celebrate Robert E. Lee's birthday.

Late Jan, Washington International Boat Show at DC National Guard Armory.

Jan or Feb every odd year, biennial exhibition of contemporary American art at Corcoran Gallery.

February

Feb 12, celebration of Lincoln's birthday at Lincoln Memorial.

Mid-Feb, Ice Capades. Family ice-skating show at Capital Centre.

Feb 22, Washington's birthday. Festivities at Washington Monument and huge parade in Alexandria.

Late Feb, Chinese New Year celebrations in Chinatown.

March

Mar 17, St Patrick's Day Parade, Constitution Ave.

Late Mar, Smithsonian Kite Carnival in the Mall and Kite Festival at Gunston Hall, Va.

Late Mar or early Apr, Cherry Blossom Festival, Easter Egg Roll on White House Lawn and Easter sunrise services in Arlington National Cemetery and other locations.

April

Early Apr, Imagination Celebration at Kennedy Center. A festival of performing arts, especially for the young, with many free events.

Early Apr, Ringling Brothers/ Barnum and Bailey Circus at DC National Guard Armory.

Apr 13, Jefferson's birthday celebrated at Jefferson Memorial.

Late Apr, Smithsonian Institution's Spring Celebration including clowns, mimes and many other attractions for children.

Late Apr, Washington Craft Show. Judged exhibition and sale of crafts at Department of Commerce.

Late Apr, Historic Garden Week Tour, Alexandria Tourist Council (☎549–0205).

Late Apr or early May, public tours of embassies and Georgetown houses and gardens.

May

Early May, Washington Cathedral Flower Mart.

Mid-May, US Marine Corps Sunset Parades begin, 8th and I St. SW.

Mid-May, Cherry Blossom Rugby Tournament, the Mall.

Late May, Boat Show, Annapolis Harbor, Annapolis, Md.

Late May, Kemper Open PGA Golf Tournament, Tournament Players Club, Avenel, Md. (☎(301) 983–4052).

Last Mon, Memorial Day. Free National Symphony concert in Capitol grounds, jazz festival at Alexandria, and wreath laid by President at Tomb of the Unknown Soldier.

June

First weekend, Washington International Arts Fair. Series of exhibitions of contemporary work in many private galleries throughout the city (☎547–1080 for details).

Early June, President's Cup Regatta, off Hains Point.

Mid-June, Smithsonian Institution Children's Day.

Mid-June, Smithsonian Boomerang Festival, Washington Monument grounds.

Late June or early July, Smithsonian Festival of American Folk Life, the Mall. A rich cross-section of America's cultural heritage, with music, dancing, crafts and food.

July

July 4, Independence Day. Parade and fireworks and festivities in the Mall. Free National Symphony concert at the Capitol.

Early July, Chesapeake Bay Yacht Racing Week, Annapolis, Md.

Mid-July, US Army Band

to Mrs Johnson, a lover of the countryside, in 1968. Despite the noisy George Washington Memorial Parkway that runs through the island, this is a refreshing place which blazes every year with daffodils and flowering dogwood.

At the southern end of the park is a memorial grove named after Lyndon Baines Johnson. In the centre is a monument to LBJ in the form of a pink granite monolith, large and rough-hewn like the man himself.

Lafayette Square
Map 3F6. Metro: McPherson Square, Farragut West.

With the White House on its southern side, this square or park is one of the focal points of Washington. The equestrian statue in the centre of the park is not of Lafayette but of Andrew Jackson, hero of the War of 1812 and later the first "log-cabin" president. Lafayette himself is portrayed in one of four statues, at the corners of the square, of foreigners who fought in the American Revolution. The others are: Comte de Rochambeau, another Frenchman; Baron von Steuben, a Prussian; and Koscinszko, a Pole. The park is a pleasant, leafy oasis in the busy heart of the city where office workers picnic and chess games are played.

The square was once the centre of high social life in Washington, but is no longer residential, and only its western side retains its facade more or less intact, thanks to President Kennedy who prevented its demolition. The *Decatur House*, at the NW corner, is open to the public. Its architect, Benjamin Latrobe, also designed **St John's Episcopal Church** on the N side, which was completed in 1816 and is known as the "Church of the Presidents". Pew 54 has been reserved for worshippers from the White House since President Madison started the tradition. With its crisp, classical design, delicate wooden belltower and serene white interior, St John's is one of the most pleasing churches in the city.

Another building worth noticing, though not open to the public, is **Dolley Madison House** at the corner of Madison Pl. and H St. The widow of the President lived here from 1837 to 1849, a tireless socialite to the last.

Library of Congress ★
10 1st St., DC 20540 ☎287–5000. Map 8G10 ▣ ⊀ ▣ in Madison Building. Open (main reading room) Mon–Tues, Thurs–Sat 9am–5.30pm, Wed 9am–9pm; (exhibit halls) Mon–Fri 8.30am–9.30pm, Sat 8.30am–6pm. Closed Sun and hols. Tours Mon–Fri 9am–4pm every hr on the hr. Metro: Capitol South.

This wonderfully frothy building stands just to the E of the US Capitol. A foretaste of the building itself is the superb **Fountain of the Court of Neptune**, which faces onto 1st St. below the entrance and is reminiscent of the Trevi Fountain in Rome. But the fountain is overshadowed by the amazing **foyer**, a huge hall with a great double marble staircase lit by a stained-glass skylight high above. There is a profusion of stone cherubs, garlands of fruit, bronze figures holding torches, balustrades, Corinthian columns, a floor inlaid with the signs of the zodiac, and acres of beautifully-painted frescoes. The richness is breathtaking. But a closer examination of the frescoes will reveal that one series shows the colophons of the great printers of the past, and at the back of the hall a pair of glass display cases contain a Gutenberg Bible and a contemporary handwritten Mainz Bible. This is indeed a library, probably the greatest library in the world, and, more than that, one of the most civilized institutions of learning ever created.

The library was built when the collection of books became too large for the Capitol. It was designed by two mid-European architects, Smithmeyer and Pelz, who produced a richly eclectic mixture of styles. Much of the credit for the success of the main building, the **Thomas Jefferson**, goes to the army engineers who completed the job, which they did with military thoroughness. One officer, for example, was appointed to co-ordinate the colour scheme, and the result is certainly pleasing. The building was finished in 1897, 24yrs after the plans were originally chosen.

Even more impressive than the foyer is the **main reading room** with its great soaring dome. The cupola is painted with a fresco of figures representing the nations and cultures that have most advanced the cause of learning. The figure for Germany is a portrait of General Casey, the engineer who supervised the construction of the building (and also, incidentally, that of the *Washington Monument*).

They crossed the green park to the new Library of Congress recently opened, glittering with mosaic, gorgeous with Pompeian red . . . hour after hour passed, and still they had not seen it all, the endless corridors, the wide, shallow-stepped staircases leading on and on to new wonders.

Frances Parkinson Keyes, *Queen Anne's Lace*

The conducted tour, which begins with an introductory slide and sound presentation, takes you to the most imposing parts of the building, but some of the less prominent areas are also worth seeing: for example, the **Hispanic Division** with its striking 1940s' murals by the Brazilian artist Candido Portinari.

The Library of Congress has two more recent buildings which were necessitated by the continued growth of its collection. The **John Adams Building** to the E, dating from the 1930s, is a complete contrast, but a fine specimen of its time, with rich Art Deco ornamentation. The **James Madison Memorial Building** to the S, completed in 1980, is the largest library building in the world, although its architecture is less memorable than that of the other two buildings. The severity of the interior is broken only by the **James Madison Memorial Hall**, which contains a statue and exhibits. In all three of the buildings, manuscripts, rare books, prints, drawings and maps are exhibited in the hallways and on the walls of many of the corridors.

The library was originally only for the Congress but has long since been open to the public. Anyone above school age pursuing serious research may use its vast facilities. It contains not only 20 million books and pamphlets and over 35 million manuscripts, but also nearly 4 million maps and atlases, 10 million prints and photographs, and copies of 1,200 different newspapers. Its **music department** has a vast number of scores and a fine collection of musical instruments. The **Motion Picture, Broadcasting and Recorded Sound Division** has, among other things, more than 250,000 reels of motion pictures which researchers can arrange to view. An outpost of the Performing Arts Library is situated on the roof terrace of the *Kennedy Center*.

In the library's **Coolidge auditorium** and the adjacent **Whittall Pavilion**, frequent concerts, poetry readings, lectures and symposia are held. Once a month, from May to Oct, folk music and dancing groups from various traditions perform on the plaza in front of the Jefferson Building.

The Library of Congress is more than just a library, and it is not surprising that the staff who work here are passionately devoted to it.

Lillian and Albert Small Jewish Museum
3rd and G St. NW, DC 20001 ☎881–0100 ⊡ ✗ compulsory. Open Sun 11am–3pm, other days by appt. Closed Aug, Jewish hols. Metro: Judiciary Square.

The building housing this museum is the original Adas Israel Synagogue, the first synagogue in Washington, built in the 1870s and originally at 6th and G St. NW. After the congregation moved away, the building became a Christian church, then a grocery store. Saved from demolition in the late 1960s, it was towed in a precarious condition to its present site and lovingly restored. Apart from a small permanent exhibition on the building itself, the museum mounts temporary exhibitions focusing on the life and history of Washington's Jewish community.

Lincoln Memorial ★
W End of Mall ☎426–6895. Map 5G5 ⊡ ✗ of crypt. Open 8am–midnight. Closed Christmas. Metro: Foggy Bottom, Arlington Cemetery.

Abraham Lincoln, 16th President of the United States and saviour of the Union in the Civil War, has acquired a uniquely cherished place in the memory of the American people, and his memorial has become the most prestigious of the city's monuments. It is significant that it appears on both the penny and the $5 bill. It looks so congruous where it stands at the w end of the Mall that it is surprising to learn of the controversy surrounding its planning.

A commission to plan the monument was set up two years after Lincoln's death in 1865, but it was many years before any agreement was reached on the design or position of the memorial. At that time the present site was an unattractive marsh at the edge of the Potomac, and Joseph ("Uncle Joe") Cannon, Speaker of the House of Representatives, declared that he would "never let a monument to Abraham Lincoln be erected in that God-damned swamp". But the swamp was drained and became a worthy setting for the design by Henry Bacon that was finally chosen, a Parthenon-like structure surrounded by 36 Doric columns representing the 36 states that existed at the time of Lincoln's death. The design employs the same sleight-of-hand technique used by the ancient Greeks, whereby the walls and columns tilt slightly inward, the rows of columns bend outward and each one bulges a little around the waist. Without these tricks, the building would appear top-heavy and the rows of columns concave. The monument was completed in 1922.

Dramatically mirrored in the reflecting pool, it now forms a key element in the superb parkscape of the *Mall*. The seated statue of Lincoln inside, 19ft (6m) high, was carved out of white marble by Daniel Chester French, who has captured powerfully the massive yet accessible personality of the man.

On the wall to the left is the Gettysburg Address, to the right is Lincoln's Second Inaugural Address, while behind the statue are the words: "In this temple as in the hearts of the people for whom he saved the Union the memory of Abraham Lincoln is enshrined forever."

The word "temple" is significant, for that is what this monument is. There was a time when visitors had to wear ties and speak in whispers in the presence of the statue. Now the atmosphere is less formal, but the mystique of the place is as powerful as ever.

At certain times of year there are conducted tours of the **crypt** below the monument, where the seepage of water from above has created curious formations of stalactites and stalagmites. Reservations can be made in advance by telephone, but these tours are so popular that there is often a waiting list of two months or more.

Malcolm X Park See *Meridian Hill Park*.

The Mall ★
Maps 6 & 7G. Metro: Smithsonian.

The Mall today is one of the finest town parkscapes in the world, but the effect was achieved with much toil and over a period of many years. Pierre L'Enfant saw its possibilities when he planned it in 1791, but the Mall remained more or less a visual mess until the early 1900s when Senator James McMillan, chairman of the Senate District Committee, launched a plan to landscape the Mall in a way that incorporated many of L'Enfant's original proposals. Even then it took a long time to evolve to its present state.

Gradually the clutter disappeared. A railway was removed; a canal along the N side was filled in (though a former lock-keeper's cottage still remains); and a number of unsightly shacks were demolished. The *Washington Monument* was finished in 1888, the *Lincoln Memorial* and the reflecting pool were added in the 1920s and the *Jefferson Memorial* in 1943. In the 1960s and 1970s further improvements were made. The ugly temporary office buildings from the two world wars were removed, as well as the parking lots. In their place walkways and lawns were added. In 1976 **Constitution Gardens** were opened, with a lake and 50 acres (20ha) of tree-shaded parkland. The gardens contain a memorial to the veterans of the Vietnam War.

Today the Mall forms a splendid, green triumphal way extending for some 2 miles (3.5km) from the *Capitol* in the E past the great buildings of the Smithsonian on either side, past the Washington Monument and on down to the Lincoln Memorial and the Watergate Steps by the Potomac. The w end of the Mall is known as **West Potomac Park**. There are playing fields here, where you can watch polo, rugby, soccer and other sports, depending on the time of year (see *Sports and activities*).

One of the most beautiful features of the Mall is the **Tidal Basin**, overlooked by the Jefferson Memorial and surrounded by cherry trees given to Washington by Japan in 1912, which make a dazzling array when in blossom. The occasion is celebrated by the Cherry Blossom Festival. Another splash of colour is provided by the "floral libraries" to the E of the Tidal Basin, a series of flowerbeds planted with a variety of species. The Mall is the scene of many other public events besides the

Cherry Blossom Festival: Washington's birthday celebration, the Festival of American Folk Life, concerts and theatrical performances (see *Calendar of events* in *Planning*).

The Mall is much more than just a park: it is an arena, a forum, an outdoor room of vast proportions. To obtain the most dramatic vantage point, stand on the steps of the Lincoln Memorial and look past the Washington Monument towards the Capitol. Here the spirit of L'Enfant's vision is triumphantly realized.

Marine Corps War Memorial ★
Fort Myer Dr., Arlington, Va. Map 4G2 ⬚ ⬤ *Metro: Rosslyn, Arlington Cemetery.*

In a commanding position just N of Arlington National Cemetery, this striking sculpture honours the men of the US Marine Corps who have died for their country since 1775. It illustrates one of the most glorious moments in the history of the Marines: the capture of the Pacific island of Iwo Jima from the Japanese in 1945. The work is based on the famous photograph by Joe Rosenthal showing six men raising the US flag on the island. It was designed by Horace W. Peaslee and sculpted by Felix de Weldon, who took nine years to complete the job. Four times life-size, it is the largest sculpture ever cast in bronze. (There is a performance by the Marine Drum and Bugle Corps and Silent Drill Platoon mid-May to Labor Day every Tues at 7.30pm.)

A stone's throw to the S of the monument is the **Netherlands Carillon**, a tower with 49 bells presented to the US by the Netherlands in thanks for American aid in World War II. Free concerts are given there Apr–Sept Tues, Sat, Sun, hols (☎426–6700 *for details*).

Meridian Hill Park
16th and Euclid St. NW, DC. Map 3B–C6.

About 1½ miles (2.5km) up 16th St. from the White House is an area that might have been one of the most fashionable in the city. That was the hope of a rich senator's widow named Mrs John B. Henderson who lived here in a now demolished mansion in the early part of this century. Her dream was not realized, but the 12-acre (5ha) park built by the Government as a result of her agitation still remains. It is part French, part Italian in character, with a water cascade, a pond, terraces with balustrades, formal promenades and statues of Dante, Joan of Arc and President James Buchanan.

The park has become somewhat faded and melancholy, and in recent years it has been a haunt of vagabonds and drug addicts. But there are hopes that it will regain its former charm and beauty. The DC Government has tried, with limited success, to rename it Malcolm X Park, but the old name is more appropriately romantic.

Mormon Temple ★
9900 Stoneybrook Dr., Kensington, Md. 20795 ☎587–0144 ⬚ ⬤ *Temple closed to non-Mormons. Visitors' Center open 10am–9.30pm.*

Approached along the Capital Beltway, this building gives a first impression of a science-fiction illustrator's creation: a soaring white edifice with six needle-sharp spires made of a gold and steel alloy, one of them surmounted by an 18ft-high (5.5m) figure of the Angel Moroni covered in gold leaf. In the sunlight, spires and angel gleam dazzlingly. The temple, completed in 1971, is built of Alabama marble. Even the windows are marble planed to a thickness of ⅝in (16mm), so that they are translucent. Around the building, 57 acres (23ha) of grounds have won awards for their landscaping.

In the Mormon faith, or the Church of Jesus Christ of Latter-Day Saints, a temple, as distinct from a church, exists for marriage (for eternity) and for the baptism of ancestors by proxy. Only Mormons in good standing may enter the temple. Others, however, are given a cordial welcome at the **Visitors' Center**, where they are given a short talk on Mormon beliefs, then shown a series of dramatic life-size tableaux featuring the prophets Isaiah and Mormon, Christ and his Disciples, and Joseph Smith, the founder of the Church. Finally there is a film in which Mormons in different walks of life explain their beliefs.

National Air and Space Museum ★

*6 Independence Ave. SW, DC 20560 ☎357–2700. Map **7**G8 ▨ ▨ for Langley Theater and Planetarium ▨ except with special permission ✗ free highlight tours and for groups by arrangement ▣ ✱ ▭ ⇌ Open 10am–5.30pm, extended summer hrs announced annually. Closed Christmas. Metro: L'Enfant Plaza.*

It would be hard to imagine a more compelling testament to man's age-old dream of flight than this dazzling museum with its unique array of flying machines, spacecraft and exhibits relating to all aspects of air and space travel and technology. The museum is housed in a crisp white building on the Mall, opened in 1976, with 23 galleries, each devoted to a single subject or theme. All the aircraft are genuine, and most of the spacecraft, although occasionally a replica has been used where the craft was not brought back to earth.

From the Mall side, the first gallery is **Milestones of Flight**, containing such epoch-making craft as the Wright brothers' 1903 Flyer, Lindbergh's Spirit of St Louis and the Apollo 11 Command Module. Galleries to the w contain other historic aeroplanes of various periods: gliders, passenger airliners, cargo carriers and helicopters. Turn left from the Mall entrance into the **Space Hall**, with examples of space boosters, guided missiles and manned spacecraft. Exhibits here include the Skylab Orbital Workshop, America's first space station, which visitors can walk through. Other displays on this floor include: **Looking at Earth**, **Flight Testing**, **Stars** and **Lunar Exploration Vehicles**. Also on the ground floor is the **Langley Theater**, which shows four aviation- and space-related films daily. The films were produced using a large-format projection system and are shown on a screen the height of a five-storey building. So convincing is the illusion of reality in such films as *To Fly* that you will literally want to hold on to your seat as you hurtle over a clifftop or swoop just above the surface of a river as it plunges into a waterfall. The Langley Theater is also used for free evening lectures.

Also well worth the small entrance charge is the **Albert Einstein Planetarium** on the second floor, one of the most advanced planetariums in the world, which creates startling images of the sun, moon, planets and stars by the use of a Zeiss model VI projector. After visiting the Planetarium, you can continue your imaginary space journey by going to the **Exploring the Planets** gallery, where the moving surface of

Mars is visible through a porthole. If you want to go back to the early days of flight, visit the **Balloons and Airships** gallery, where the exhibits include the original Zeppelin, a model of the ill-fated Hindenburg and a model of the Montgolfier balloon. The third floor of the building houses a library, offices and a restaurant.

If, having seen the museum, you are still eager to see more aircraft and spacecraft, take a trip out to the **Paul E. Garber Facility** (*3904 Old Silver Hill Rd., Suitland, Md.* ☎ *357–1400* ▣ ✗ *Mon–Fri 10am, Sat, Sun 10am, 1pm, reservations must be made two weeks in advance*). The facility is the storage, restoration and preservation centre of the museum, where you can see 90 aircraft as well as many spacecraft, engines, propellers and other flight-related objects. Take a look also at the restoration workshop. Note, however, that this is a "no-frills" museum with no heating or air-conditioning in the exhibit areas – it is strictly for the keenest air and space buffs.

National Aquarium

Department of Commerce Building, 14th St. and Constitution Ave., DC 20230 ☎*337–2826. Map **6**F6–7* ▣ ▣ *Open 9am–5pm. Closed Christmas. Shark feedings: Mon, Wed, Sat 2pm; piranha feedings: Tues, Thurs, Sun 2pm. Metro: Federal Triangle.*

This is a strange place in which to find an aquarium – tucked away in the basement of the Department of Commerce, one of the sober government buildings in the Federal Triangle. It is in fact the oldest aquarium in the country, dating from 1873, though it has only been at its present location since 1932. Originally run by the US Fish and Wildlife Service, it is now operated by a private, non-profit-making group, the National Aquarium Society.

It has about 1,000 specimens representing 225 different species, half freshwater and half saltwater. There is plenty to marvel at: the archer fish (*Toxotes jaculator*), for instance, which shoots small jets of water to dislodge insects from overhanging vegetation, or the blue damselfish, a tiny, darting sapphire, as well as turtles, sharks, horseshoe crabs, eels and many other creatures of the deep. There are also recordings of the sounds made by marine animals.

On your way out stop in the lobby to catch a glimpse of a typical Federal Triangle interior with its neoclassical expanse of marble. And observe the meter which continually records the growth of the US population – every 16 seconds it clocks up another American.

National Arboretum

24th and R St. NE, DC 20002 ☎*475–4815, 475–4857 (tour reservations for 10 or more)* ▣ ✗ *Open Mon–Fri 8am–5pm, Sat, Sun 10am–5pm. Closed Christmas. Metrorail or Metrobus to Stadium-Armory Station.*

An idyllic Arcadia incongruous among the bleak surroundings of E Washington, this park boasts a herb garden, *bonsai* collection, aquatic gardens, lakes, a nature trail and over 400 acres (162ha) of hilly countryside containing many varieties of trees, shrubs, and flowering plants. The arboretum is particularly proud of its azaleas, a glorious panoply in springtime. You can drive around and there is a designated picnic area. A visit to this park is well worth the journey to the eastern fringes of the city, but is awkward without a car.

National Archives and Records Service ★
*Constitution Ave. and 8th St. NW, DC 20408 ☎523–3000.
Map 7G8 ☷ ☙ ✗ by arrangement. Exhibition hall open
Apr–Labor Day 10am–9pm, Sept–Mar 10am–5.30pm.
Closed Christmas. Research rooms open Mon–Fri
9am–10pm, Sat 9am–5pm. Closed Sun, major hols. Metro:
Federal Triangle.*

"We hold these Truths to be self-evident, that all Men are
created equal, that they are endowed by the Creator with
certain unalienable Rights, that among these are Life, Liberty
and the Pursuit of Happiness . . . ." These words, which most
American schoolchildren learn by heart, are part of the
Declaration of Independence of 1776, written principally by
Thomas Jefferson. The Declaration of Independence, the
Constitution and the Bill of Rights are known together as the
Charters of Freedom, and the original documents are the most
treasured possessions of the National Archives. They are
displayed in a great domed, semi-circular temple in which the
public files reverently past a kind of altar where the charters
are kept in helium-filled bronze cases that descend at night or,
in states of emergency, into a bomb- and fire-proof vault.
Facsimiles of the charters, as well as pictures, books and
postcards, can be bought at the sales desk.

The Charters of Freedom are only a tiny part of the vast
collection of US government records housed in the archives,
from Acts of Congress to applications for federal jobs. A
selection of some of the more interesting documents is
displayed in the corridors of the building, but access to the
main files is reserved for serious researchers. The public can,
however, listen to the Watergate tapes. Portions of these are
played Mon–Fri from 10.15am. From the Pennsylvania Ave.
entrance you will be directed to the appropriate room. Don't
overlook the building itself. Designed by John Russell Pope, it
is an imposing classical-style edifice approached by immense
flights of steps.

National Building Museum   See *Old Pension
Building*.

National Gallery of Art ★
*Constitution Ave. NW, between 4th and 6th St., DC 20565
☎737–4215. Map 7G8 ☷ ☙ for temporary exhibitions only
✗ ═ ▆ Open Mon–Sat 10am–5pm, Sun noon–9pm. Metro:
Archives.*

This is a relative newcomer to the major league of art galleries,
yet it is now ranked among the top dozen in the world. In
paintings it outstrips most other galleries in North and South
America, especially in the field of European Old Masters and
Impressionists. The gallery owes its existence to the financier
and statesman Andrew W. Mellon, who formed the nucleus of
the collection, partly by buying from the Soviet government in
the 1930s when it was selling art treasures to pay for tractors
and other necessities. Mellon bequeathed the collection to the
nation and provided funds for the construction of the West
Building. The daily running of the gallery is now funded by
the Federal Government, but the acquisition of works of art is
financed privately.
West Building
It is hard to believe that the massively neoclassical West
Building, designed by the indefatigable John Russell Pope

(*National Archives*, *Jefferson Memorial*, *House of the Temple*) was opened as recently as 1941. Unlike the Louvre and many other great galleries, it was purpose-built as a museum. It houses works of art from the 10thC up to the mid-20thC.

Tours of the West Building start in the great rotunda, which has a fountain to Mercury in the centre and is encircled by massive pillars of green Tuscan marble. The works are divided by nationality and subdivided by time period. The following are the ten groups into which they are arranged.

Florentine and Central Italian art The range extends from the highly stylized paintings of the Byzantine period, with their deliberately stiff figures and lack of perspective, to the more naturalistic paintings of the Renaissance, when art had begun to free itself from religious constraints. The star item is the gallery's single Leonardo da Vinci, a small painting of about 1474 portraying the young Florentine noblewoman Ginevra de'Benci, so accurate in its detail that even the subspecies of tree in the background is identifiable – a kind of juniper, which is a pun on the subject's name. Its acquisition in 1967 helped to make this one of the most comprehensive collections of Italian medieval and Renaissance paintings in the world. Another remarkable item is the ceremonial shield with Andrea del Castagno's painting *The Youthful David* from about 1450, one of the few shields of this kind to have survived.

Venetian and North Italian art The lavish art in this collection reflects the prosperity of the great maritime city of Venice in its heyday. Typical of this period is Giovanni Bellini's elaborate *Feast of the Gods*, reworked by his pupil Titian. Other Titians, such as the arresting portrait of *Doge Andrea Gritti*, fill an entire room. Giorgione's peaceful *Adoration of the Shepherds* and Jacopo Sansovino's enchanting bronze figure of *Venus Anadymone* are also noteworthy.

Italian art of the 17th–18thC Visual drama and complexity of technique were the hallmarks of the Baroque era. One of the best examples is *The Lute Player*, painted by Orazio Gentileschi in about 1610, a masterly composition of abruptly contrasting light and shadow. By the 18thC view-painting had come into vogue to satisfy the demands of travellers who took the Grand Tour of Europe. Giovanni Paolo Panini's interiors of the Pantheon and of St Peter's, Rome, are good examples of this genre. There are also some Canalettos, including a typical example: *Venice, the Quay of the Piazzetta*.

Spanish art During the 15th and 16thC Spanish art was dominated by foreign immigrants such as El Greco, represented here by *Laocoön, Saint Martin and the Beggar* and a cadaverous *St Jerome*. But from the 17thC Spain produced its own great artists: Zurbarán, Murillo, Velásquez and Goya. All are included here. Note Velásquez' penetrating study for a portrait of Pope Innocent X – "All too true", said the Pontiff when he saw the finished work. Goya has a room to himself, whose highlights are his famous portrait of the beautiful *Señora Sebasa Garcia* and one of his paintings of the Duke of Wellington.

Flemish, German and Dutch art This is a particularly rich and extensive part of the collection. Here are encountered the austere, meticulous works of such early Flemish painters as Van Eyck and Rogier van der Weyden. Among the German works is a small *Crucifixion* by Matthias Grünewald, the only one of his paintings in the USA. This section also includes a great galaxy of Dutch artists of the 17thC. Among many fine Rembrandts, note particularly the *Self-Portrait* with its troubled expression, painted when the artist was 53, after his fortunes had begun to decline. Rubens is here too: see, for example, his huge and dramatic *Daniel in the Lion's Den*. So too are Van Dyck, Vermeer and other painters of the Dutch golden age. Look closely at the *Vase of Flowers* by Jan de Heem. Not only does it show an impossibility, since in nature none of the flowers depicted bloom concurrently, but it is full of symbolism: a butterfly at the top to indicate the spiritual life; moths, snails and faded flowers at the bottom to stand for worldly decay.

French art of the 17th, 18th and early 19thC   The age of Louis XIII and XIV produced an art that looked towards classical and Renaissance models for inspiration. The masters of this era include Claude Lorrain (*Landscape with Merchants* and *The Judgment of Paris*) and Nicolas Poussin, with his serene colours and geometric harmony (*Holy Family on the Steps* is a fine example). In the late 17th and early 18thC French art became more light-hearted, developing into the delicate, sensual style known as Rococo. The tone was set by Antoine Watteau whose work is here exemplified by his *Italian Comedians* and by *Ceres*, an oval panel with the four summer months of June, July, August and September symbolized astrologically by a pair of twins, a crayfish, a lion and the goddess Ceres herself representing Virgo. Paintings by Boucher (*Allegory of Painting*) and Fragonard (*A Young Girl Reading*) illustrate how this style was continued until well into the 18thC. Gradually, however, it gave way to the more severe and earnest style of neoclassicism. This section ends with the great neoclassical masters, notably Ingres (Portrait of *Madame Moitessier*) and David (*Napoleon in His Study*).

British art   Portraiture was one of the great fortes of British art in the 18thC, and this collection contains some choice examples. The two supreme masters of the "Grand Manner", Gainsborough and Reynolds, are here. So are Romney, Hoppner, Raeburn and Lawrence. There are works by both of the great early-19thC English landscape artists, Constable and Turner. Typical of Turner's genius is his *Keelmen Heaving Coals by Moonlight*, where the port of Newcastle is transformed into a glowing, dreamlike vision.

American art   Portraiture, much influenced by English models, dominated American art in the 18th and early 19thC. Benjamin West, one of the greatest American painters of this era, lived and worked in London, where he significantly influenced visiting compatriot artists. His masterly *Self-Portrait* hangs here, together with other great portraitists such as Charles Wilson Peale and Edward Savage. Pride of place, however, goes to Gilbert Stuart, unofficial "court portraitist" of the young republic. The gallery possesses 41 Stuarts, including his famous set of the first five presidents. A total contrast is the large amount of naive or primitive art by untrained painters of the 19thC, much of it charming and fresh.

The late 19th and early 20thC saw a notable flourishing of American art. The spirit of rural America at this time is vividly captured in the work of Winslow Homer. In his sea painting *Breezing Up* you can almost feel the wind and the spray. One of the greatest American artists of all time, James McNeill Whistler, also has many paintings here, ranging from his exquisite portrait, *L'Andalouse, Mother-of-Pearl and Silver*, to his typically hazy view of the Thames, *Chelsea Wharf, Grey and Silver*.

French art of the 19thC   Think of this period and you think automatically of the Impressionists, who are here in full force: Renoir, Cézanne, Monet, Pissarro, Seurat – a feast of liberated light and colour. Note the curiously untypical Van Gogh, *Flowerbeds In Holland* (*c*.1883), a tranquil little scene quite unlike the feverish paintings of later years. The Post-Impressionists, such as Gauguin, are here too, as are the Symbolists: see Puvis de Chavannes' matching pair *Le Travail* and *Le Repos*. These artists pave the way for the full impact of 20thC art housed in the East Building of the gallery.

Lower-level galleries
A new set of galleries has recently opened on the lower floor. There is a print gallery devoted to rotating exhibitions from the National's rich collection of prints and graphics. Another has exhibits of Chinese porcelain and small bronzes; yet another contains French furniture. Before leaving the West Building it is also worth taking a look at the large and well-stocked shop on the ground floor, which sells books, cards and reproductions.

East Building
The East Building can be approached via an underground tunnel which, halfway along, opens out into a spacious restaurant, verdant with indoor plants and with a huge window looking dramatically onto a falling wall of water. The passage continues with a moving sidewalk to the East Building. Alternatively, approaching from the outside, you will cross a plaza with a fountain and pass a great bronze sculpture by Henry Moore, *Knife Edge Mirror Two Piece*, as you enter.

The East Building, designed by I. M. Pei and opened in 1978, looks like an iceberg with edges so sharp you could almost cut your finger on them. Inside, the iceberg impression continues, as if the ice had been hollowed out to create an immense space bathed in pale light. The Central Court is dominated by a vast Alexander Calder mobile in red, blue and black, while around the courtyard are other impressive works such as Joan Miró's tapestry *Woman*; Anthony Caro's steel *Ledge Piece* looms over the entrance to the s part of the building housing the library, the Centre for Advanced Study in the Visual Arts, the graphics collection and the administrative offices.

From the Central Court, there are stairs, escalators and bridges which lead up, down and across to the various exhibition areas and provide a constantly changing spectacle of the building and its contents. Few works of art are permanently on view, and the building is primarily used for temporary exhibitions, either on loan or from the gallery's own collection. The emphasis is by no means entirely on contemporary art, and the temporary shows include work from many periods.

Free lectures (*Sun afternoons*) and film shows are held in the Auditorium, and these are often linked to exhibitions. These are among the best free events in the city. The museum will supply a programme upon request.

One word of advice: do not try to see all of the National Gallery in one visit, especially if you want to include both buildings. As one of the richest collections in the world it merits two or even three visits.

National Geographic Society Explorers Hall

National Geographic Society Explorers Hall
17th and M St. NW, DC 20036 ☎857–7000. Map 3E6 ◧ ✻
Open Mon–Sat 9am–5pm, Sun 10am–5pm. Closed
Christmas. Metro: Farragut North, Dupont Circle.

The National Geographic Society, through its monthly
magazine and other publications, effectively conveys the
exciting and unique character of our planet earth. It does the
same here in the Explorers Hall in its headquarters. The
introductory video presentation about man's earliest ancestors
is followed by a tour through simulated Neanderthal and Cro-
Magnon caves, emerging by a pool over which is suspended a
vast globe. Nearby stands a giant basalt head from Mexico.
Mementoes of exploration include the binoculars carried by
Admiral Byrd on his polar flights in 1926 and 1929, under the
sponsorship of the society. Other displays include a specimen
of the giant Goliath frog from Cameroun, a film of underwater
exploration, a working model of the solar system and many
beautiful photographs of the natural and animal world.

Related temporary exhibitions are also held here, and there
is a stall selling the society's publications. This is a great place
to take children, and an eye-opener for adults too.

National Museum of African Art
950 Independence Ave. SW, DC 20560 ☎357–2700. Map
6G7 ◧ ✿ for certain exhibitions ✗ ✻ Open Mon–Fri
10am–5pm, Sat, Sun, hols noon–5pm. Metro: Smithsonian.

Finding its old premises on Capitol Hill too cramped, this
museum has moved house and is due to re-open in the summer
of 1987 in underground quarters in the new Quadrangle
complex behind the Smithsonian Castle. The only museum in
the USA devoted to the visual arts of sub-Saharan Africa, it
has a collection of about 6,000 objects ranging from Benin
bronze figures to vibrant woven textiles. Apart from a small
number of objects on permanent display, the museum is
devoted to temporary exhibitions, either of a thematic nature
or dealing with particular regions or ethnic groups. The
entrance to the museum is a striking pavilion with six shallow
domes.

National Museum of American Art
8th and G St. NW, DC 20560 ☎357–2700. Map 7F8 ◧ ✗ ▣
Open 10am–5.30pm. Closed Christmas. Metro: Gallery
Place.

There are some 32,000 works in this collection, illustrating the
development of American painting, sculpture and graphic art
from the 18thC to the present day. A large and representative
selection is on permanent display, and temporary exhibitions
are also held. The museum is strong on the 19th and early
20thC. Take a look at the works by Winslow Homer: limpid
paintings bathed in a golden glow of fresh innocence that is
quintessentially American. Albert Bierstadt, though a German
immigrant, is American in another way, with his poignant
evocations of the wild expanses of the West. Less typical are
the works of Albert P. Ryder: eerie, dream-like scenes
reminiscent of the French Symbolists.

Other great names of the period in this collection include
George Catlin, Elihu Vedder, Thomas Moran, Frederic
Church, Thomas Cole, James Whistler, Mary Cassatt and the
sculptor Hiram Powers. The modern period is also well
represented by such artists as Franz Kline, Willem de

Kooning, Robert Rauschenberg, Stuart Davis and Edward Hopper. A particularly striking modern work is James Hampton's visionary creation, *The Throne of the Third Heaven of the Nations' Millennium General Assembly*, consisting of 177 objects sheathed in glittering aluminium and gold foil (seen in the first-floor lobby).

The museum shop on the first floor sells books, catalogues, posters and reproductions. The museum organizes periodical concerts, symposia, lectures and other public programmes.

The building, which it shares with the *National Portrait Gallery*, is the Old Patent Office, a massive 19thC Greek revival structure. The two museums share a fine library and a good cafeteria which in summer spills out on to the attractive inner courtyard. A branch of the museum is the smaller *Renwick Gallery* near the White House. It also administers the **Barney Studio House**, built in 1902 on Sheridan Circle as artist Alice Pike Barney's home, studio and salon (*open for guided tours by appointment* ☎*357–3111*). See also *Walk 2* in *Planning*.

National Museum of American History

Constitution Ave. and 13th St. NW, DC 20565 ☎*357–2700. Map 6G7* ☒ ✗ ▐ ✤ *Open 10am–5.30pm. Closed Christmas. Metro: Federal Triangle.*

This museum will save archaeologists of the future a great deal of work when they come to study the civilization known as the United States of America. It is as though someone had cut a trench through the whole of the country's history and from it had taken objects that reflect and have shaped the changing patterns of life. In this immense collection, housed in an austerely elegant 1960s building on the *Mall*, you can learn how Americans of different eras worked, played, tilled the soil, travelled, dressed, shopped, communicated, entertained themselves and coped with the technical problems that confronted them. Originally known as the National Museum of History and Technology, the collection is very strong on technological matters, and the scope of it extends beyond America.

The first-floor lobby, entered from Constitution Ave., is dominated by a Foucault pendulum, a 240lb (108kg) brass bob suspended on a 70ft (21m) wire, which demonstrates the rotation of the earth. The lobby area has a bookstore, an auditorium and a complete country post office-cum-general store, where you can buy stamps, including special issues, and post a letter that will receive a "Smithsonian Station" postmark. On the same floor the electricity section has Edison's light bulb; the motor vehicle room has the famous Model T Ford; and the railroad collection has a majestic 1926 Pacific-type locomotive. Other displays include physical sciences, medicine, folk art, typewriters, clocks and farm machinery.

On the second floor, which can be entered from the Mall, there is a souvenir shop and a lobby dominated by the original (though much restored) Star Spangled Banner. The galleries on this floor contain a more intimate kaleidoscope of American life: for example, a collection of First Ladies' gowns, a display of the life of George Washington, a remarkable set of original interiors from different periods, and a permanent exhibition called "After the Revolution: Everyday Life in America, 1780–1800" which illustrates the lives of three actual families.

The third floor has even more riches, among them displays of firearms, military history, photography, news reporting, money and medals, philately and musical instruments. There is an auditorium where the instruments are played (*Mon–Fri 11am*). Other free demonstrations are given of spinning and weaving, printing and typefounding, and operating machine tools. In addition to the permanent displays, temporary exhibitions also cover aspects of American life and history.

National Museum of Natural History
*10th St. and Constitution Ave. NW, DC 20565 ☎357–2700, 357–2627 (guided tours). Map **6**G7 ⌧ ✗ by arrangement ▣*
▰ Open 10am–5.30pm. Closed Christmas. Metro: Smithsonian.

The great stuffed African bush elephant that stands in the huge central rotunda of this museum seems calculated, like the museum itself, to inspire the visitor with awe at the onward march of evolution, the vast multiplicity of life on our planet, and the complex phenomenon of man himself. There is plenty to marvel at here – first of all, the scope of the collection. The natural history part of the museum traces back to the earliest signs of life in the form of fossil ammonites 160 million years old. There are skeletons and models of prehistoric monsters and stuffed specimens of more recent origin: mammals, birds, sea life and reptiles. A special section is devoted to bones, and another to the "Dynamics of Evolution". For a change, the **Insect Zoo** houses live specimens.

Moving on to inorganic material, there are sections of the earth, moon and meteorites, minerals and gems. The dazzling display of gems always draws a crowd; its primary attraction is the famous **Hope Diamond**, the largest blue diamond in the world. Other startling exhibits include the world's biggest star ruby and a topaz the size of a goose egg.

This museum also doubles as the **Museum of Man**, housing a vast range of anthropological material from many different periods and cultures: Stone Age North American axe heads, Inca artifacts, ancient Egyptian coffins. There are also life-size dioramas; the one in which a South American Indian on a pony chases an ostrich across the grasslands is particularly effective.

The museum's special facilities include a **Naturalist Center** (*open Mon–Sat 10.30am–4pm, Sun noon–5pm*) for the use of amateur researchers, with books, scientific instruments and specimens that can be handled and examined. There is a **Discovery Room** (*☎357–2747 for group reservations; open Mon–Thurs noon–2.30pm, Fri–Sun 10.30am–3.30pm*), where children can handle a variety of objects from the world of nature. Youngsters also enjoy climbing on Uncle Beazley, a life-size model of a triceratops dinosaur outside the Mall entrance.

The museum's café is relatively expensive for indifferent food. Next door, an excellent shop sells books and museum-related objects. On the ground floor there is an auditorium for lectures and an area for temporary exhibitions.

National Portrait Gallery ★
*8th and F St. NW, DC 20560 ☎357–1300. Map **7**F8 ⌧ ✗ ▣*
Open 10am–5.30pm. Closed Christmas. Metro: Gallery Place.

This gallery shares the splendid Old Patent Office building

with the *National Museum of American Art*. Its collection consists of paintings, prints, drawings, photographs and sculptures of "men and women who have made significant contributions to the history, development and culture of the people of the United States". The presidents have a hall to themselves, with an anteroom devoted solely to George Washington. Most of the presidential portraits are predictably reverential, except for the most recent ones – Nixon, Ford, Carter and Reagan – which are sharply penetrating. The same is not true, however, of the fascinating room devoted to famous portraits from the covers of *Time* magazine. Here is Nixon, haggard and harrassed, in September 1974; John Wayne against the background of a gunfight scene; Bob Hope captured in a block of wood, half-carved, half-painted; Raquel Welch sculpted in epoxy resin.

Altogether the National Portrait Gallery has some 4,500 portraits in its collection. It also holds loan exhibitions. There is a museum shop on the first floor, and the gallery shares a library and cafeteria with the National Museum of American Art.

National Rifle Association of America
1600 Rhode Island Ave. NW, DC 20005 ☎*828–6000. Map 3E6* ▣ *Open 10am–4pm. Closed hols. Metro: Farragut North, Dupont Circle.*

With some 2½ million members, the NRA is one of the largest voluntary organizations in the USA. It defends fanatically the right of all Americans "to keep and bear arms" and employs five full-time lobbyists to ensure that no law obstructs this objective. The **Museum of Firearms** covers a remarkable range, including old flintlock pieces, duelling pistols, Civil War guns, sporting and competition rifles and commemorative firearms. Many of them are superb works of craftsmanship, however deadly. For some this museum will be fascinating, for others, chilling.

National Shrine of the Immaculate Conception ★
Michigan Ave. and 4th St. NE, DC 20017 ☎*526–8300* ▣ *☓ Open May–Oct 7am–7pm, Nov–Apr 7am–6pm. Metro: Brookland.*

A glimpse of this building from the train is reminiscent of the view of the Sacré Coeur on leaving the Gare du Nord in Paris. There is the same dominating, hilltop position and the same echo of Byzantine splendour. Located next to Catholic University, the church was begun in 1914 and built in two stages: first the enormous crypt, completed in 1926; then the upper church consecrated in 1959. Despite its imposing size, this is not a cathedral, nor does it serve a parish. It is primarily a shrine to the Virgin Mary in her capacity as Patroness of the USA, and it is filled with Marian imagery.

Descriptions of the church abound in superlatives. It is the biggest Catholic church in the Western hemisphere and possesses one of the largest church organs in the world (☎ *for details of recitals*). Its many splendid mosaics include the world's largest one of Christ (67ft/20.5m high), and others reproducing such works as Murillo's *Immaculate Conception* and Titian's *Assumption*. The whole interior, with its magnificent soaring central dome, coloured marble pillars and domed baldaquin over the altar, combines richness, serenity and dignity.

National Zoological Park

3001 Connecticut Ave. NW, DC 20008 ☎673–4717. Map 2&3A–B4–5 ☺ ✗ by arrangement (☎673–4955) ◪ ✳ ☂ Open May to mid-Sept, grounds 8am–8pm, buildings 9am–6pm; mid-Sept to Apr, grounds 8am–6pm, buildings 10am–4.30pm. Metro: Woodley Park-Zoo.

Before the zoo was established in 1889 the Smithsonian Institution had only rudimentary facilities for gifts of live animals. Early records indicate that animals presented to the Smithsonian were sent to the Philadelphia Zoo and to the US Insane Asylum (now St Elizabeth's Hospital), where they were used as a harmless diversion for patients.

By the late 1880s animals donated to the Smithsonian formed a menagerie in the shadow of the Smithsonian Castle. Finally in 1889 a proper home for the animals was created when 163 acres (66ha) of then-surburban NW Washington were set aside for a National Zoological Park, to be run as part of the Smithsonian.

Conservation and preservation of endangered animals has been a central concept throughout the zoo's history. The threatened extinction of the American bison and the diminishing number of other native North American species helped focus public interest and support for the founding of the zoo. Today the preservation of such endangered animals as the panda and the golden lion tamarin monkey remain a major concern.

The zoo is one of the finest in the world. Many of the exhibits have been skilfully laid out to resemble different types of habitat. Polar bears, for example, can be seen basking on simulated icebergs or watched through underwater windows as they swim in their pool. Some of the animals here, such as the rare Bongo antelope of central and western Africa, and the endangered Indian rhinoceros, are virtually impossible to see in the wild. Always popular are the two giant pandas, Ling-Ling and her male companion Hsing-Hsing, presented by the People's Republic of China in 1972. These are most active at feeding times: around 11am and 3pm. All the creatures that traditionally belong to zoos can also be found here: lions, tigers, giraffes, monkeys, exotic birds and many more.

The zoo is continually being modernized and restructured, but the old **Reptile House** remains, its exterior reminiscent of a Byzantine cathedral. It contains a **Herplab** (*open Tues–Sun noon–3pm, winter Fri–Sun*), where children can explore the world of herpetology (the study of reptiles and amphibians). They will also enjoy the **Zoolab** (*same opening times as Herplab*) in the **Education Building**, where they can draw, read, or handle skulls, eggs, crocodile skins and other animal materials. Films about animals and the workings of the zoo are shown in the Education Building at weekends and all week in the summer. The building contains a bookstore and gift shop.

The zoo is mapped with a colour-coded system of six different trails, named after types of animal. The zebra trail, for example, colour-coded black, takes you past hoofed mammals as well as kangaroos and pandas. By following all six trails you will see the entire collection.

Navy Yard

9th and M St. SE, DC 20024 ☎433–4882. Map 8I10–11 ☺ ✗ available for groups ◪ ✳ ☂ US Navy Memorial Museum open Mon–Fri 9am–5pm (winter 9am–4pm), Sat, Sun, most hols

10am–5pm. Closed major hols. US Marine Corps Museum open Mon–Sat 10am–4pm, Sun noon–5pm. Closed Christmas. Metro: Eastern Market.

This yard, the oldest naval facility in the country, was opened in 1799. It no longer functions as a gun factory, which it did for a century, but is worth a visit, especially for children with nautical leanings. They can explore the dock area along the Anacostia River and climb on the old guns and other military objects exhibited in the grounds. There are two museums and an art gallery in the yard as well as the destroyer *John Barry*, which can be toured.

The **US Navy Memorial Museum**, in Building 76, illustrates the history of the Navy from 1775 to the present. There are dioramas of battles, model ships, displays of weaponry and technology, flags and uniforms. Children can sit behind guns and train them on imaginary targets, or enter a submarine room and operate a periscope. Nearby is the **Navy Art Gallery**, which contains naval art.

The **US Marine Corps Museum**, in Building 58, is smaller but also interesting, explaining the history of the Corps with similar exhibits of weapons, uniforms, portraits, flags and memorabilia. A series of dioramas re-creates great actions by the Corps.

A popular event at the Navy Yard during the summer is the public presentation (*June–Aug Wed 8.45pm*), which consists of a band concert and a historical review of the Navy with slides and films on a wide screen. Advance reservations must be made (☎433–2678).

The nearby Marine Corps Barracks (*8th and I St. SE*), the nation's oldest marine post, offers a spectacular sunset parade with marching band and precision drill teams (*mid-May to mid-Sept Fri 8.20pm*). Reservations must be made at least three weeks in advance (☎433–4073).

The Octagon ★

1799 New York Ave. NW, DC 20006 ☎638–3105. Map 6F6
▦ 𝕏 Open Tues-Fri 10am–4pm, Sat, Sun 1–4pm. Closed Mon, major hols. Metro: Farragut West.

This is a house with a curious shape and a colourful history. Built between 1797 and 1800, it was designed by Dr William Thornton, first architect of the Capitol. His design copes ingeniously with the awkward corner site, but it is really a heptagon rather than an octagon, unless the bow at the front qualifies as an extra side.

The house was occupied by President Madison while the *White House* was under repair after being set on fire by the British in the War of 1812. It was here, in what is now called the **Treaty Room**, that Madison signed the Treaty of Ghent which ended the war. The dispatch box that contained it remains, as well as the table on which the signing is believed to have been done.

Owned by the American Institute of Architects, the house has been well restored and furnished in the Federal style. Portraits include one of John Tayloe, the original owner, as well as those of Dolley Madison and Dr and Mrs Thornton. There is an interesting basement kitchen, complete with early-19thC implements, and on the second floor are galleries for changing exhibitions relating to architecture. The new AIA headquarters next door also holds occasional exhibitions.

Old Downtown
Maps 6 & 7F

The word "downtown" once suggested a magic and glamour that inspired songwriters. That was before an epidemic of inner city decay affected most of the northeastern USA. In many cities deteriorating conditions were further aggravated by the riots that swept the country in 1968. After years of blight the tide has turned, and many inner cities, including Washington, are undergoing urban revival.

Symbolic of this renaissance is the **Willard Hotel** at the w end of Pennsylvania Ave. An Edwardian byword for elegance and style, it was home to President Calvin Coolidge and provided guest accommodation to many foreign dignitaries, but was driven to closure by the 1968 riots. Now, however, its lavish renovation is one of the central elements in a huge scheme for the revitalization of the entire Downtown area, from the White House to Union Station and from Pennsylvania Ave. to M St., a joint venture between the DC Government and private enterprise.

Downtown Washington is now poised to become the city its founders promised through their planning two centuries ago. The biggest single development is the *Washington Convention Center* occupying an entire block bounded by 9th, 11th and H St. and New York Ave. Opened at the beginning of 1983, it acts as a catalyst, bringing other forms of new life to the area: hotels, restaurants, shops, places of entertainment. On the block adjacent to it another huge complex is taking shape. Called **Techworld**, it will be a technological conference and exhibition centre incorporating two new hotels.

The rebirth of Old Downtown includes 7th St., which bisects the area. Designated in the redevelopment plan as an "Arts Spine", it links the Old Patent Office (containing the *National Portrait Gallery* and *National Museum of American Art*) with the *National Gallery of Art* to the s. Smaller galleries are opening along this street. The remainder of the area can be divided into three sections: Downtown, E Downtown and Pennsylvania Ave. The western part, concentrated around F and G St. between 9th and 15th St., has a burgeoning new "Retail Core", dominated by the three largest stores: Woodward and Lothrop, Garfinkel's and the recently relocated Hecht's flagship store (see *Shopping*).

A pedestrian mall stretches along G St. by the Martin Luther King Memorial Library, and pedestrian access will be made easier by the widening of pavements. Although many new buildings are springing up, older ones of quality are not being neglected. *Ford's Theatre* at 511 10th St. was restored in the 1960s and functions once again as a stage as well as a museum. The graceful *Church of the Epiphany* at 1317 G St. has likewise been restored. The **National Press Club**, at 14th and F St. has re-opened its refurbished doors to the club, to office suites and to a shopping arcade on the three lowest levels. The old Masonic temple at New York Ave. and 13th St. is currently being transformed into the **National Museum of Women in the Arts**, due to open in spring 1987.

The area E of 7th St. similarly contains a mixture of fine buildings which are gradually coming into their own again as the surrounding areas are redeveloped. **Judiciary Sq.**, for example, is an attractive townscape, surrounded by municipal and federal buildings, with the splendid *Old Pension Building* (now the National Building Museum) on its N side. The axis of the square has been extended to the S with the creation of **John Marshall Park** leading down to Pennsylvania Ave. Farther to the E a new park and a cluster of office and hotel developments are planned for the area along New Jersey Ave. **Chinatown** (roughly 6th to 9th St. at H and I St.) is a tiny enclave of Chinese restaurants and businesses. At the time of writing it is poised for a much-needed facelift.

The S boundary of Downtown, Pennsylvania Ave., is a noble thoroughfare connecting the White House with the Capitol. Like the Champs-Elysées in Paris, it seems expressly designed for parades and has often been used for this purpose. Unfortunately, however, the earlier decay of Downtown had left it rather moth-eaten on the N side, in contrast to the somewhat monotonous neoclassicism of the Federal Triangle to the S. For years it had been barren of restaurants and places to linger on a sunny day. As with the rest of Downtown, however, this condition has almost completely changed.

Travelling E down the avenue from 15th St. you will pass **Pershing Sq.**, with its sunken park, pool and outdoor café. Facing the National Theater is Western Plaza, which has been lovingly and expensively restored to its Federal period elegance. (Notice the plan of Washington set into the paving of the plaza.) A little farther E, on the S side, contrasting strikingly with the Federal Triangle buildings surrounding it, is the **Old Post Office**, a splendid piece of Victorian Romanesque, resembling a cross between Neuschwanstein Castle and the Palazzo Vecchio in Florence, whose 315ft (96m) clocktower is the third tallest structure in the city. This fine building, saved from demolition by a vigorous conservationist campaign, has been remodelled to serve two functions. The seven upper floors house the **National Endowment for the Arts** and its twin the **National Endowment for the Humanities**. The focal point of the three lower floors, known as **The Pavilion**, is a dramatic skylit atrium; here there are shops, restaurants, bars, cafés and a stage for everything from ballet to jazz.

At the front of the building the cafés spill out onto Pennsylvania Ave., adding a Parisian touch to the environment. Another feature of the building is the dramatic view of the city from the top of the tower. The Pavilion has given a tremendous boost to the new spirit of Downtown and to Washington as a whole.

Across the avenue, and a little farther E, is the FBI headquarters. The remainder of the avenue, on its Downtown side, is in a state of flux, with new parks and plazas being created, new buildings constructed and old ones, such as the twin-towered, red sandstone **Apex Building**, restored. If all continues to go according to plan, Pennsylvania Ave. and all of Downtown, for too long prospering only in political promises, should emerge as one of the liveliest parts of the whole city – as L'Enfant himself envisaged.

Old Pension Building (National Building Museum) ★
G St. between 4th and 5th St. NW, DC 20001 ☎*272–2448.
Map* **7F8** ⊡ ✗ *Open Mon–Fri 10am–4pm, Sat, Sun, hols noon–4pm. Closed major hols. Metro: Judiciary Square (F St. exit).*
Despite its rather sober name this is one of the most astonishing buildings in the city. Based on the Palazzo Farnese

in Rome and completed in 1885, the exterior is imposing in its own right, with a ¼ mile-long (500m) encircling frieze in low relief of Civil War scenes added in 1887. But the interior is yet more impressive – rather the product of a Roman emperor's *folie de grandeur* than, as it was, the creation of an army engineer named General Meigs. Once inside you are dwarfed by a vast courtyard divided by eight columns the size of giant redwood trees. A fountain dominates the centre and around the sides several storeys of arched galleries rise to a row of windows high above. This spectacular hall, as it was intended, is used for grand festivities and has been the venue for several presidential inaugural balls, including Reagan's second in January 1985. It would take the length of a waltz to dance once around the floor!

In 1926 the building ceased to house the Pension Bureau, and at one time was threatened with demolition. Now, securely protected as a National Historic Landmark, it houses the **National Building Museum**, a privately funded organization founded to commemorate and encourage the American building arts. The museum mounts temporary exhibitions on architectural and building themes.

This is one of the many Washington buildings reputed to be haunted; a number of strange apparitions have been seen including a transparent horseman and malevolent skulls hovering around the pillars.

A museum shop sells books and items of architectural interest.

Pentagon

Department of Defense, DC 20301 ☎695–1776. Map 5I–J4
▣ ✿ ✗ ⬤ Open Mon–Fri 8.30am–3.30pm. Closed Sat,
Sun, hols. Metro: Pentagon.

Headquarters of the Department of Defense, the Pentagon is one of the world's largest office buildings, with three times the floor space of New York's Empire State Building. The architects who designed it seem to have measured its dimensions by the fingers of one hand. It has five sides, five floors and five concentric rings, and the centre courtyard covers 5 acres (2ha). It was all built with incredible speed in 16 months and completed in 1943 to meet the sudden expansion of the armed forces caused by World War II. Intended as a temporary solution, the Pentagon has instead become a permanent fixture, and its design is now recognized as brilliant. Although there are 17½ miles (26km) of corridors and nearly 4 million sq.ft (372,000sq.m) of office space, it takes no more than 7min to walk from one side to the other – if you know the quickest route. There are some surprising statistics; for example, 23,000 people work here, drinking 30,000 cups of coffee and making 200,000 telephone calls every day.

Guided tours of the building are very popular, so it is advisable to book in advance. Following a film presentation, the walking tour begins; it takes approximately 1½hrs and is conducted by a guide who walks backwards so that he can keep an eye on his group. Exhibited in the corridors are examples of war art and photography, militaria such as army banners, and memorabilia of army, navy and air force heroes. The **Hall of Heroes** commemorates recipients of the Medals of Honor.

The building has a shopping mall but no restaurant or café open to the general public. There is, however, a bakery in the mall, which sells sandwiches, drinks and snacks.

Petersen House
516 10th St. NW, DC 20004 ☎426–6830. Map 6F7 🏛
*Open 9am–5pm. Closed Christmas. Metro: Gallery Place,
Metro Center.*

After President Lincoln was shot in *Ford's Theatre* on April 14
1865, he was carried across the street to a modest house built in
1849 by a Swedish tailor named William Petersen, who used
the basement for his business and rented out the other rooms.
The house, like the theatre, is now owned by the National Park
Service, and the ground floor is open to the public. The
present furnishings are not original but are based on a study of
contemporary inventories. Between visits to her husband's
bedside, Mrs Lincoln spent the anguished night, consoled by
her son and friends, in the front parlour. In the back parlour,
Edwin M. Stanton, Secretary of War, launched an
investigation into the shooting. The room where Lincoln died,
nine hours after the shooting, is a small, low-ceilinged back
bedroom. The only original object is one of the blood-stained
pillows from his bed, now reverentially glassed over.

The Phillips Collection
1600 21st St. NW, DC 20009 ☎387–2151. Map 3D5 🏛 ▣
*Open Tues–Sat 10am–5pm, Sun 2–7pm. Closed Mon, most
major hols. Metro: Dupont Circle.*

This gallery bears the highly personal stamp of its founder,
Duncan Phillips (1886–1966), a remarkably individual
collector who refused to operate through dealers and followed
only his personal judgment. The works he collected were
"modern" in the broadest sense, including great innovative
artists of the past as well as those of the 20thC. In 1921 he
opened his collection to the public on three afternoons a week
in the Neo-Georgian house he had inherited off Massachusetts
Ave. This, the first permanent museum of modern art in the
country, was such a popular success that Phillips and his wife,
who was herself a painter, turned the whole house into a
gallery and moved to another home.

In his book *A Collection in the Making*, Phillips described
his type of gallery: "We plan to try the effect of domestic
architecture, of rooms small or at least livable, and of such an
intimate, attractive atmosphere as we associate with a beautiful
home. To a place like that I believe people would be inclined to
return once they have found it and to linger as long as they can
for art's special study and its special sort of pleasure."
Although many extensions have been added to the house, it
retains this intimate, private atmosphere.

In keeping with the eclectic scope of Phillips' taste, there are
works here by artists as early as Giorgione and as avant-garde
as Robert Cartwright. A highlight of the collection is Renoir's
supremely joyful painting, *Luncheon of the Boating Party*.

Temporary exhibitions, concerts and poetry readings are
also held here. As Phillips intended, his gallery is a place where
you will want to linger.

Pierce Mill
Beach Dr. and Tilden St., DC 20008 ☎426–6908 🏛 ⚘
*Open Wed–Sun 8am–5.30pm. Closed Mon, Tues, hols.
Grinding Sat, Sun 1pm. Lectures second Sat of each month
11am. Metro: Van Ness.*

This simple stone building, nestling snugly in a leafy dip in
Rock Creek Park, is the only survivor of eight water mills that

operated on the Creek during the 18th and 19thC. Completed in about 1829, Pierce Mill was advanced for its time, using conveyor belts and other labour-saving machinery. It ceased functioning in 1879 and is now run by the National Park Service. Milling has been revived, and visitors can buy corn, whole-wheat, rye, buckwheat and oat flour in traditional cloth sacks from a miller in authentic dress. The millstones, chutes and machinery are still here, and a friendly miller will always be happy to tell you about the mill's history.

There are regular authentic craft demonstrations given by artisans in period costumes, and monthly lectures on the techniques and economics of 18thC milling.

The **Art Barn** is just across the road from here (see *Rock Creek Park*). The setting of these buildings is tranquil and rustic, a delightful place in which to stroll on a fine day and perhaps picnic by the creek.

Potomac Park

s of Independence Ave., w of 14th St., DC ☎*426–6700. Map* **5&6***. Tourmobile.*

This park is divided into two sections: **West Potomac Park** has the *Lincoln Memorial* and reflecting pool, playing fields and landscaped areas; **East Potomac Park**, extending in a long peninsula between the Potomac and the Washington Channel, has a golf course and facilities for swimming and tennis. **Hains Point**, at the southern tip of the park, is a great place to take the kids; it has a playground, picnic tables and a startling piece of outdoor sculpture entitled *The Awakening*, a metal figure of a giant struggling up out of the earth from a horizontal position with only his head and part of his limbs visible. Between the two parks is the **Tidal Basin** (where paddle boats can be rented in season), overlooked by the *Jefferson Memorial* and ringed by cherry trees which also extend down the side of E Potomac Park. Access to the latter is difficult unless you have a car. From both parks there are splendid views across the Potomac.

Renwick Gallery ★

17th St. and Pennsylvania Ave. NW, DC 20560 ☎*357–1300 (info.), 357–2531 (guided tours). Map* **3F6** ☒ ☜ *temporary exhibitions only* ✗ *by arrangement. Open 10am–5.30pm. Closed Christmas. Metro: Farragut West.*

Amid the bustle of Pennsylvania Ave. this branch of the Smithsonian's *National Museum of American Art* comes as a delightful surprise. The building, originally constructed to house the Corcoran collection, is in the French Second Empire style with a high mansard roof and an ornate brick and sandstone facade. Named after the architect, James Renwick, it was saved from demolition in 1965 and beautifully renovated. Frequent temporary exhibitions are organized here, the emphasis being on American design, crafts and decorative arts.

A permanent display of painting and sculpture can be seen in the second-floor **Grand Salon** and **Octagon Room**, both exquisitely furnished in opulent Victorian style with padded velvet sofas. Luxuriously seated on one of these you can admire works by such artists as G. F. Watts, Pierre Puvis de Chavannes and William Sartain.

Films, concerts, lectures and craft demonstrations are held at the National Museum of American Art (apply there for the calendar of events).

Rock Creek Cemetery
Rock Creek Church Rd. and Webster St. NW, DC 20007.
A tranquil place on rolling terrain, farther E than Rock Creek
itself. **St Paul's Church**, within its grounds, is the oldest in
DC. The cemetery contains some fine sepulchral art, notably
the figure by Augustus Saint-Gaudens called *The Peace of
God*, or *Grief*.

Rock Creek Park
Map 2&3&5F4.
The Washington equivalent of Hampstead Heath or the Bois
de Boulogne, this park consists of 1,754 acres (710ha) of
beautiful woodland. There are many different things to see and
do: riding stables, tennis courts, a golf course, 30 picnic areas,
playing fields, and an extensive system of routes for walking,
jogging, riding and cycling. The **Carter Barron
Amphitheater** (*16th St. and Colorado Ave. NW
☎829–3200*) is a 4,000-seat outdoor theatre which offers a
variety of performing arts in an attractive rural setting during
the summer months.

Washington weather, in the early autumn, blew hot and cold.
On the cool days people went horseback riding in Rocky Creek
Park and tired gentlemen, strangulating in red tape, took a new
lend lease of life. The multitudes . . . found that they could
walk to work without frying. The crowded buses seemed less
crowded, somehow, when there was more air to breathe. And
in a mellow, more benevolent sunlight the working boys and
girls of Mecca-on-the-Potomac went outside in the luncheon
hour and ate their sandwiches under a pale blue sky.

Faith Baldwin, *Washington, USA*

Other attractions of the park include *Pierce Mill*; **Art Barn**
(*2401 Tilden St. NW ☎426–6719*), formerly a carriage house
and now a lively gallery showing the work of local artists,
where classes and artists' demonstrations are also held; and
Rock Creek Nature Center (*5200 Glover Rd. ☎426–6829
▣ ✗ open Tues–Fri 9.30am–5pm, Sat, Sun noon–6pm,
Dec–Apr Sat, Sun noon–5pm; closed Mon*). Information on
Rock Creek Park can be obtained from the Park Headquarters
(*☎426–6832*), and a useful leaflet on the park is published by
the National Park Service.

St Matthew's Cathedral ★
*1725 Rhode Island Ave. NW, DC 20005 ☎347–3215. Map
3E6 ▣ ✗ Sun 2.30–4.30pm. Open 6.30am–6.30pm. Metro:
Farragut North.*
This is the Roman Catholic church that President Kennedy
attended and where his funeral mass was held on November 25
1963. In Oct 1979, during his American visit, Pope John Paul
II celebrated the Eucharist here. Designed in the Renaissance
style with a central dome, the cathedral has a remarkably rich
interior, vibrant with coloured marble, mosaics and murals.

Smithsonian Institution Building
*1000 Jefferson Dr. SW, DC 20560 ☎357–2700. Map 6G7
▣ Open 10am–5.30pm. Closed Christmas. Metro:
Smithsonian.*
On the S side of the Mall stands a many-turreted, red
sandstone building in a vaguely Romanesque style, which was

built in 1849 to a design by James Renwick. Popularly known as the **Castle**, this is the headquarters of the Smithsonian Institution, the largest complex of museums and art galleries in the world. Its empire includes not only a dozen museums in Washington as well as the *National Zoological Park* but other facilities elsewhere in the USA and abroad. It also conducts and sponsors research in science and the arts and issues a wide range of publications. An introductory slide presentation and talk, giving a bird's-eye view of all the Smithsonian museums in Washington, is held daily in the **Great Hall** on the first floor of the Castle. (Check at the information desk in the Great Hall or telephone in advance for the schedule.)

This extraordinary institution owes its existence to the English scientist James Smithson, who died in 1829 and left a large fortune to the USA to found an institution in Washington bearing his name, "for the increase and diffusion of knowledge among men". Today, James Smithson's tomb rests in a little room off the entrance lobby to the Castle, along with his portrait and a few mementoes. The **Visitors' Information and Reception Center** offers information on all parts of the Smithsonian.

In the space behind the Castle an exciting addition to the Smithsonian is taking shape. Known as the **Quadrangle**, the new museum complex includes the *National Museum of African Art*, the *Arthur M. Sackler Gallery*, devoted to Asian and Near Eastern Art, and the **International Center**, which will sponsor research, hold symposia and mount large exhibitions on themes that embrace many countries and cultures, especially those of the non-Western world. These three facilities, due to open in the summer of 1987, will be located underground. At ground level is the **Enid A. Haupt Garden**, 4.2 acres (1.7ha) beautifully planted and laid out in the manner of a Victorian garden and in keeping with the style of the Castle.

The Castle's main tower looks like a good home for owls and that is exactly what it is – a colony was introduced there some years ago by Dr Ripley, Secretary of the Smithsonian.

State Department

Tour Office FMAS/GS, Room 7493, 2201 C St. NW, DC 20520 ☎*647–3241. Map* **5***F5* 🎦 *🎥 by appt only 4–6 weeks in advance. Mon–Fri, tours at 9.30am, 10.30am, 3pm. Closed Sat, Sun, hols.*

One of the less widely advertised attractions of Washington is the collection of art objects and furniture housed in the sumptuous reception rooms on the eighth floor of the State Department, the federal agency that handles foreign policy and relations. Most of the antique furnishings and decorative objects were given to the government in lieu of tax and they are beautifully displayed in a series of interiors created in the 1960s in the gracious style of old American stately homes. One of the most attractive rooms is the **John Quincey Adams State Drawing Room** with its portraits of Adams, Jefferson, Washington, Benjamin Franklin and others. The room also contains the desk on which the Treaty of Paris, which ended the War of Independence, was signed.

Supreme Court ★

1st and E Capitol St. SE, DC 20543 ☎*479–3000. Map* **8***G10* 🎦 *🎥 by appt only* 🚇 *Open Mon–Fri 9am–4.30pm. Closed*

Sat, Sun, hols. Hearings 10am–noon, 1–3pm, first come first seated. Courtroom lectures when Court is not in session every hr on the half hr. Metro: Capitol South, Union Station.

The function of the Supreme Court is to prevent infringements of the US Constitution by reversing any unconstitutional laws or decisions that are referred to it. There are nine members: a Chief Justice and eight Associate Justices. The court sits on alternate fortnights from the first Mon in Oct until May or June. Sessions are 10am–3pm with a lunch break noon–1pm. These are open to the public on Mon, Tues and Wed; Mon is the most popular day for observing as the court's decisions are usually pronounced then.

Proceedings are carried out with great solemnity in an imposing room, ringed with Ionic columns, the black-robed justices sitting in a row behind a raised bench against the backdrop of a red velvet curtain – a formidable array for the counsel who stand facing them to argue their cases. Certain quaint traditions are cherished by the court; for example, white quill pens are placed, in crossed pairs, on the counsel tables every day. It is legal theatricality at its most fascinating.

As befits the highest court in the land, the building is extremely imposing. Completed in 1935, it is a gleaming, white marble, Corinthian-columned temple, approached by an apparently endless flight of steps, with the words "Equal Justice Under Law" inscribed over the portico. The interior is equally splendid and has two unusual self-supporting spiral staircases, rising through five storeys in an elegant ellipse.

On the ground floor is a **museum** illustrating some of the Court's history, and a film about the Court and how it works is shown in the small auditorium.

Textile Museum

2320 S St. NW, DC 20008 ☎667–0441. Map 2D4 ▩ ✗ Sat 1–3pm. Open Tues–Sat 10am–5pm, Sun 1–5pm. Closed Mon, hols. Metro: Dupont Circle.

Founded by George Hewitt Myers in 1925, this museum, occupying two handsome early-20thC brick houses in the Embassy Row area, contains more than 1,000 rugs and over 10,000 other textile items from South American ponchos to Indian shawls. In addition to the permanent displays, there are three major temporary exhibitions each year. If, after seeing the collection, you want to buy textiles, the museum shop has some lovely examples, as well as books on the subject. The museum also has a library and offers lectures, demonstrations and courses.

Theodore Roosevelt Island and Memorial

George Washington Memorial Parkway, Mclean, Va. 22101 ☎285–2601. Map 4F–G3 ☒ ✗ by appt a week in advance ⇒ Open 9.30am–sunset.

This island in the Potomac is appropriately dedicated to Theodore Roosevelt, President of the USA from 1901 to 1909 and early champion of wildlife and nature conservation. The 88 acres (36ha) of swamp, marsh and forest contain a rich variety of native plants and provide a refuge for kingfishers, turtles, frogs, muskrats, squirrels, chipmunks and many other fauna. The island boasts 2½ miles (4km) of trails and an impressive memorial to Roosevelt: a 17ft (5m) bronze statue of him, larger than life, like the man himself.

Treasury Department Museum

Treasury Department Museum
15th St. and Pennsylvania Ave. NW, DC 20220 ☎*566–2000.
Map* **6***F6* 🖸 🖵 *Open Mon–Fri 9am–6pm. Closed Sat, Sun,
hols. Metro: McPherson Square, Metro Center.*

The US Treasury Department is a huge empire whose
branches include Internal Revenue, the Mint, the *Bureau of
Engraving and Printing*, Customs, the Bureau of Alcohol,
Tobacco and Firearms, and the Secret Service – surprisingly,
those "heavies" protecting the President are Treasury men,
not police or FBI. In the basement of this impressive Greek
revival Treasury Building is a small museum illustrating some
aspects of the department's work; for example, displays
explain how medals are made, and a small cinema screens films
about some of the jobs done by the Treasury, from the
investigation of a bombing to the use of dogs to sniff out
illegally imported drugs. There are sales counters at both the
Treasury and the Mint.

Truxtun-Decatur Naval Museum
1610 H St. NW, DC 20006 ☎*842–0050. Map* **6***F6* 🖸 *Open
10am–4pm. Closed hols. Metro: Farragut West.*

A small museum in the former carriage house of the *Decatur
House*, around the corner. The exhibits relate to naval history
and include models, relics, photographs, paintings, prints and
other memorabilia, which are of particular interest to naval
buffs.

Union Station
Massachusetts and Delaware Ave. NE ☎*484–7540 (Amtrak
info.). Map* **7***F9. Metro: Union Station.*

Designed by Daniel H. Burman, this station was completed in
1908 when rail journeys between big cities were rituals that
began and ended in temples of awesome magnificence. This
one has, as its main entrance, a portico based on the Arch of
Constantine in Rome, surmounted by allegorical figures
sculpted by Louis Saint-Gaudens (son of the more famous
Augustus). The plaza in front is dominated by a great white
marble fountain, its focal point a 15ft-high (4.5m) figure of
Christopher Columbus standing in the prow of a ship.
   In the 1970s the interior of this magnificent building was
turned into the short-lived National Visitor Center, an
expensive failure which, due to leaks and other structural
deterioration, was closed in 1981. In the interim the tracks had
been moved, and travellers now use an alternative modern
concourse. Currently, however, the main hall, with its fine
statuary and decorative detail, is undergoing comprehensive
renovation and, when the tracks are back in their old position,
will once again serve as the station concourse, complete with
restaurants, cinemas and shops. The reopened building
promises to be a vibrant and exciting place – a superb foretaste
for rail travellers to Washington.

United States Botanic Garden
1st St. and Maryland Ave. SW, DC 20024 ☎*225–8333. Map*
7*G9* 🖸 𝓚 *by arrangement* ☎*225–7099. Open June–Sept
9am–9pm, Oct–May 9am–5pm. Metro: Federal Center.*

There is something irresistibly romantic about plant houses.
In their steamy greenness it is easy to imagine once again
playing a childhood game of jungle exploration where snakes
and crocodiles lie hidden in the shadows. The central palm

house in this building, complete with stream, lends itself to such flights of fancy. There are also sections for orchids, cycads, ferns, cacti, bromeliads and other types of plant. And there are areas for temporary flower shows, notably the **Easter Show** (Palm Sun–Easter Sun), the **Summer Terrace Display** on the patio in front of the building (late May–Sept), the **Chrysanthemum Show** (mid-Nov to Thanksgiving), and the **Poinsettia Show** (mid-Dec through the Christmas hols).

> There is a bustle to Washington at the approach of autumn, the Indian summer briskness that slowly sheds the torpid layers of August and deepens somehow the hopes and renewals of the official city, as if the health of the Republic itself depends on such simple cycles. Washington at the first touch of fall was like the new school years of one's childhood, when even the most perfunctory rituals are for a time fraught with possibility.
> Willie Morris, *The Last of the Southern Girls*

The building, just to the sw of the Capitol, is in the grand manner of the great Victorian conservatories, but, surprisingly, it was built in the 1930s. The Botanic Garden also administers a public park on Independence Ave. opposite the rear entrance to the conservatory, which is used as a display garden for spring and summer flowering plants. The focal point of the park is the **Bartholdi Fountain**, named after its creator, the French sculptor Frederic Auguste Bartholdi, who also designed the Statue of Liberty.

United States Naval Observatory
34th St.and Massachusetts Ave. NW, DC 20390
☎*653–1543 (tour info.), 653–1541 (public affairs). Map*
2B–C3 🔳 *✗ compulsory by appt Mon night only.*
When glancing at' your watch or dialling the speaking clock you probably forget that all measurement of time is ultimately determined by astronomical observations. The US Naval Observatory is the source of all standard time used in the country. Special telescopes monitor the positions and movements of the heavenly bodies, while some 30 atomic clocks record an average time reading which is acccurate down to one trillionth of a second. In addition, the observatory has conventional telescopes for astronomical research. It also publishes the official almanacs for astronomers and navigators.

A visit to the observatory for one of the Mon night tours is a fascinating experience. The scientific complexities are well explained by the guides, and a slide show illustrates the work of the observatory. The 26in (65cm) refracting telescope and the 6in (15cm) transit circle telescope are available for celestial viewing.

Walking up the driveway from the observatory gates, you can see, behind a railing to the left, the official residence of the US Vice-President.

Vietnam Veterans Memorial
Constitution Gardens, W end of Mall. Map **5**G5 🔳
Tourmobile.
This memorial, in Constitution Gardens to the w of the Lincoln Memorial, aroused much controversy when it was unveiled in 1982. Designed by Maya Ying Lin, it consists of a long tapering cliff of black polished stone set into a bank and

91

inscribed with the names of all dead or missing combatants (some 58,000). There are alphabetical directions to help visitors find the names they seek. In 1984 a more traditional statuary group was added. The memorial is a simple and grimly effective testimony to a traumatic episode in American history.

Voice of America

330 Independence Ave. SW, DC 20547 ☎485–6231. Map 7G8 ☎ ⚿ last tour 2.45pm ▣ Open Mon–Fri 8.30am–5.30pm. Closed Sat, Sun, hols. Metro: Federal Center.

The Voice of America is a broadcasting division of the United States International Communication Agency. Its radio programmes, designed to convey a positive image of the USA, are listened to by approximately 75 million people, a large proportion of them in the Soviet Union and Eastern Europe. The station broadcasts 24hrs a day in English and some 35 other languages. Visitors touring the building are shown staff at work and can hear a programme being transmitted.

Washington Cathedral

Mount Saint Alban, DC 20016 ☎537–6200. Map 2A2 ☎ ⚿ ⟲ ⚔ Open Mon–Sat 10am–4.30pm, Sun 8am–4.30pm. Metro: Woodley Park–Zoo, then a stiff walk.

Washington Cathedral (officially the Cathedral Church of St Peter and St Paul and also known as the National Cathedral), seat of the Episcopal Bishop of Washington, is a glorious anachronism: a great medieval Gothic church built in the 20thC, indeed probably one of the last of its kind that will ever be constructed. The foundation stone was laid in 1907, and completion is now in sight. The principal architect was Philip Hubert Frohman, who worked on the building from 1921 until his death in 1972.

Superbly located on Mount St Alban in NW DC, it is laid out in the traditional form of a cross. At the intersection of nave, choir and transept rises the **Gloria in Excelsis Tower**, 676ft (206m) above sea level and with the unique feature of two sets of bells, one above the other. At the W end of the church are the two smaller towers of St Peter and St Paul. The **observation gallery** below these twin towers affords a good view of Washington and its environs, as well as some of the building's exterior stonework – pinnacles, gargoyles and grotesques. Notice also from here the beautiful geometry of the flying buttresses. Not only for show, they structurally balance the outward thrust of the walls, so that no steel reinforcement was necessary anywhere in the building.

Stand in the vast interior where the nave meets the transepts, and the illusion of Chartres or Canterbury is powerful. Three superb rose windows blaze from W, N and S, and the proportions of column, arch, clerestory and soaring ribbed vaulting sing out in exhilarating harmony. The cathedral does have at least one advantage over its medieval counterparts: central heating under the marble floors – so there is no need to freeze while your spirit is nourished.

Other details also indicate that this is a 20thC cathedral: for example, the **Space Window**, halfway along the S side of the nave, commemorating the Apollo XI flight. It depicts the spaceship's trajectory and contains a sliver of moon rock brought back from the flight. The next bay to the E houses the tomb of President Woodrow Wilson and has another striking window, depicting war and peace, by Ervin Bossanyi. Notice the quality of fine detail throughout the building. Every boss and decorated column has been as lovingly carved as the great pulpit, made of French limestone from Caen, or the high altar with its assembly of prophets and saints.

Downstairs on the crypt floor is a Visitors' Center, a shop selling books, souvenirs and gifts, a brass rubbing centre, and four small chapels, including the **Chapel of the Good Shepherd** which is open for private prayer 24hrs a day. Services in the cathedral are memorable for their music and choral singing; choirs from all over the country come here to sing. There are also Sun afternoon organ recitals following evensong. The carillon in the main tower is played on Sat at 4.30pm, and a ten-bell peal is rung after the 11am service on Sun.

In the extensive **grounds** of the cathedral you can linger in the Bishop's Garden, buy plants from the Greenhouse and visit the Herb Cottage, where not only dried herbs are on sale, but also books, souvenirs and a variety of gifts.

Washington Convention Center

900 9th St. NW, DC 20006 ☎*789–1600, 371–4200 (events). Map 6E–F7* ☷ *but* ☷ *for events* ☎ *events line for opening times. Metro: Metro Center, Gallery Place.*
Convention centres have become a popular way for cities to attract business and revenue. This one, opened at the beginning of 1983, boasts an impressive range of facilities for conferences and exhibitions: 378,000sq.ft (35,000sq.m) of exhibition space; 40 meeting rooms, capable of holding between 50 and 14,000 people; sophisticated security; closed-circuit television; and computerized air-conditioning and heating. Its Downtown location is convenient for access and the centre is planned as part of the massive revival scheme for the area that is being implemented (see *Old Downtown*).

Washington Monument ★

Centre of the Mall, Constitution Ave. and 15th St. NW ☎*426–6839. Map 6G6* ☷ 𝄞 *three times a day in summer, once a day in winter. Open Mar 20–Labor Day 8am–midnight, rest of year 9am–5pm. Metro: Federal Triangle, Smithsonian. Tourmobile.*
The gleaming marble obelisk that rises from the centre of the *Mall* has become as much a symbol of Washington as the Eiffel Tower has of Paris. It is strong, simple, majestic and exquisitely proportioned. It positively sings out over the skyline, sounding a clear note of classical beauty which resonates powerfully with the rest of the city. So perfect is it as a visual focal point of the capital that it is impossible to imagine Washington without it.

When Pierre L'Enfant designed the city he intended to have a Washington Monument occupying the point at the intersection of the western axis of the Capitol and the southern axis of the White House. But the ground was too marshy, and another site had to be chosen some 360ft (110m) to the E and 120ft (36.5m) to the S. A stone marking the original site was placed there in 1884 by Thomas Jefferson and replaced in 1889.

Although a monument to George Washington had been mooted even before his death in 1799, it was not until 1833

Washington Post

that a National Monument Society was set up, largely by
Washington's fellow freemasons. A competition was held, and
the winning design by Robert Mills was for a great colonnaded
circular mausoleum with an obelisk projecting from the centre.
Gradually, under financial pressure, the concept was whittled
down until only a simple obelisk remained. The cornerstone
was laid in 1848, but by 1865 only about a quarter of the
monument had been built, and the Corps of Engineers of the
US Army took over the construction, with the help of federal
funds. The able officer-in-charge, Lt.-Col. Casey (who also
built the *Library of Congress*), reinforced the base, corrected a
tilt, and altered the proportions to conform to those of the
ancient obelisks. When Casey took over, a slightly different
marble was used, and it is evident how the colour changes
about a quarter of the way up the shaft. The monument was
finally finished in 1885 and opened to the public in 1888,
equipped with a steam-driven elevator that took about 10mins
to reach the summit.

Today you are whisked to the top in 70 seconds. Despite the
rather small windows, there is a magnificent view of the city in
all directions, and from here the full, formal grandeur of
L'Enfant's town plan is revealed. Come here on a summer
night when all the monuments and the great public buildings
are floodlit. (During the day you may have to queue for 40mins
or so to get in.)

At 555ft 5⅛in (169.29m), the monument was once the tallest
building in the world. It has long since lost that title, but it
remains an impressive tribute to the man who has been called
"first in war, first in peace, and first in the hearts of his
countrymen".

Washington Post

1150 15th St. NW, DC 20007 ☎*334–7969. Map* **3E6** 📷 ☼
✗ *by arrangement Mon–Fri 10am–3pm every hr. Metro:
McPherson Square, Farragut North.*

The public can tour the offices of this famous newspaper,
known worldwide for the journalistic investigation into the
Watergate scandal which led to President Nixon's resignation
in 1974. The conducted tour, which includes the newsroom
and printing presses, gives a fascinating insight into the
workings of a modern newspaper. Be sure to reserve in
advance.

Watergate Complex

Virginia and New Hampshire Ave. NW, DC 20037. Map **5F4**.
Metro: Foggy Bottom.

In June 1972, five men working for the re-election of President
Nixon were caught burgling the headquarters of the
Democratic National Committee in the Watergate complex.
Since then the name "Watergate" has been associated with the
ensuing scandal that ultimately led to Nixon's resignation in
1974. To most Washingtonians, however, the Watergate is
primarily a big shopping, residential and office complex near
the Kennedy Center, with some smart boutiques and a high-
class hotel. The sweeping curves of the building are striking.
The sixth-floor offices, where the burglary took place, are no
longer occupied by the Democratic National Committee.

The Watergate Complex is not to be confused with the
Watergate itself, which is a broad flight of steps leading down
to the Potomac near the Lincoln Memorial.

The White House ★
1600 Pennsylvania Ave. NW, DC 20500 ☎*456–2323. Map 6F6* 🅿️ ♿ 🚇 ✗ *through congressional offices only, 8am–9am. Open Tues–Sat 10am–noon, rest of year queue for ticket on day of visit 8–10am. Closed Mon, Sun, major hols. Metro: McPherson Square.*

The most striking thing about the President's official residence is that it is rather modest. It is elegant, distinguished but unostentatious – and all the better for that. For this we have to thank George Washington; he chose the site in 1791, and approved the simple dignity of the design by the Irish architect James Hoban. But George Washington never lived here, and President John Adams was the first to move into the house referred to as the "President's Mansion" or "President's Palace" in 1800, while it was still unfinished.

In 1814, during the War of 1812, the British burned the house, leaving only the shell. It was rebuilt, and the Virginia sandstone exterior walls were painted white to obliterate the fire marks. By the 1940s it was discovered to be so unsound that it had to be almost completely reconstructed around a new steel skeleton. During the rebuilding, from 1949 to 1952, President Truman and his family lived across the street in Blair House at 1651–3 Pennsylvania Ave. NW. The house you see today is therefore largely a skilful reproduction, altered and added to over 132 years.

It was a beautiful May evening and the cars came and went before the embassy overlooking the park. Inside, the ambassador and his wife stood saying goodbye to the hundreds of people they had come to know in Washington. Outside by the pool, guests eddied around each other and smiled and nodded, investigator and investigatee meeting on common ground.

Abigail McCarthy, *Circles*

President Theodore Roosevelt rechristened the mansion "The White House". It is the only residence of a head of state, anywhere in the world, that is open to the public regularly and free of charge, and is one of the most visited stately homes in the country, with more than 1½ million visitors each year. This makes for some long queues. In summer, tickets must be obtained from a booth on the Ellipse. Make sure you arrive early, as the daily quota of tickets often disappears quickly. During the rest of the year, go straight to the E gate of the building and queue for admittance. The **gardens** are open to the public on certain days during the year (*telephone for details*).

A normal visit includes a tour of the five main public rooms of the house. The family apartments are not shown to the public; nor is the Oval Office, tucked away at the end of the small W wing and well screened by trees from the outside. There are many fine portraits, pieces of furniture and *objets d'art*, accumulated over the years as each president and his family added their own stamp to the presidential home. Here is the approximate order in which the rooms are viewed.

Entering via the E wing lobby, built in 1942 and hung with portraits of First Ladies, you will first pass through the light **Garden Room** overlooking the **Jacqueline Kennedy Garden**, down a corridor (with more First Ladies) flanked by rooms which can be glimpsed in passing. To the right is the

The White House

cosy **library**, the room where the President traditionally gives his televised fireside broadcasts. On the other side are the **Vermeil Room**, where a Monet hangs above the fireplace, the **China Room**, with its fine display of ceramics, and the oval **Diplomatic Reception Room**, decorated with superb panoramic wallpaper and a carpet woven with the seals of the 50 states.

Up on the next floor is the largest room in the house, the **East Room**, used for dances, concerts, press conferences and

WHITE HOUSE FLOOR PLAN

1 Vermeil Room
2 Library
3 China Room
4 South Portico
5 Diplomatic Reception Room
6 Ground Floor Corridor
7 Curator
8 White House Staff Office
9 Map Room
10 Doctor's Office
11 Housekeeper's Office
12 Kitchen
13 President's Oval Office and
   Executive Offices

14 East Room
15 Green Room
16 Truman's Balcony
17 Blue Room
18 Cross Hall
19 North Portico
20 Red Room
21 Usher's Office
22 State Dining Room
23 Family Dining Room
24 Lincoln Bedroom
25 Queen's Bedroom
26 Treaty Room
27 Yellow Oval Room
28 First Family's Private Quarters

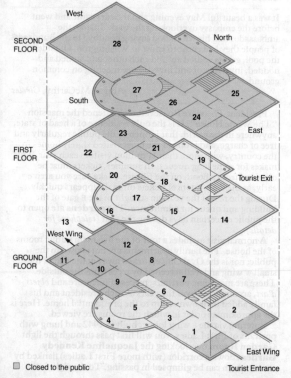

☐ Closed to the public

96

ceremonies of various kinds, none more awesome than the lying-in-state of seven assassinated presidents. The portrait of George Washington by Gilbert Stuart was daringly saved by Dolley Madison when the house was under attack in 1814. This room was not always as elegant as it is now. When John Adams was president, his wife Abigail used it to dry laundry, and, over a century later, President Theodore Roosevelt's children roller-skated here in bad weather.

The next three rooms are designated by their colours: green, blue and red. They face s over the garden and are filled with fine furniture and interesting portraits, such as that of the ornithological artist John James Audubon on the w wall of the **Red Room**. The last room to be visited is the **State Dining Room**, which is white with yellow curtains, and features a portrait of Abraham Lincoln over the fireplace. The inscription on the marble mantlepiece is from a letter by John Adams, written on his first night in the mansion to his wife Abigail, who was still in Massachusetts: "I pray heaven to bestow the best of blessings on this house and all that shall hereafter inhabit it. May none but honest and wise men ever rule under this roof." Here sometimes as many as 140 guests sit down to dinner. Passing the long Cross Hall and Entrance Hall, hung with portraits of recent presidents, you emerge from the house on the N side under the great portico of the main entrance.

Although Abigail Adams, first of the First Ladies to attempt to make a home out of the White House, was most concerned simply to see the structure completed, other presidential wives have made the improvement of their executive residence a national priority. (It was not until 1902 that the First Families could enjoy total privacy in their second-floor quarters, although they continued to take their meals in the first-floor dining room for another 60yrs.) Mary Todd Lincoln spent compulsively (criminally, her critics said) on lavish French furnishings for the mansion while the nation was on the brink of the Civil War. A century later, Jacqueline Bouvier Kennedy spearheaded a worldwide campaign for private and public contributions to return to the White House those historically accurate and original furnishings that had been looted, loaned or moved during 34 administrations.

This massive restoration has been carried on by successive First Ladies, so that today the White House is a treasure trove of significant American furnishings and decorative objects, as well as the stately home of the nation's highest statesman.

Woodrow Wilson House

2340 S St. NW, DC 20008 ☎673–4034. Map 2D4 ▨ ✗ compulsory. Open Feb Sat, Sun 10am–4pm, Mar–Dec Tues–Sun 10am–4pm. Closed Jan, Feb Mon–Fri, Mar–Dec Mon. Metro: Dupont Circle.

"An unpretentious, comfortable, dignified house, fitted to the needs of a gentleman's home" is how Mrs Woodrow Wilson described the house that she and her husband settled into in 1921, following his retirement from the Presidency. The handsome brick Georgian revival house, designed in 1915, is preserved much as it was when the Wilsons lived there. Mementoes include the typewriter on which Wilson drafted the League of Nations proposal, and the projector and screen that enabled him to enjoy silent films at home. There is also a small gift shop.

Where to stay

Hotels are concentrated in various parts of town. After a period of decline, the area near Union Station has, with the revival of rail travel, once again become a thriving hotel district. In Old Downtown the burgeoning new hotels around the Convention Center compete with the gracious establishments of the **Willard** and the **Washington**, both recently renovated. New Downtown has such *grande dame* hotels as the **Hay-Adams**, **Sheraton-Carlton** and **Mayflower**. In the West End and Foggy Bottom there is a colony of new luxury hotels: the **Grand**, **Westin**, **Park Hyatt**, **Bristol**, **Ramada Renaissance** and **Watergate**. The embassy area is catered for by the **Embassy Row** and **Ritz Carlton**.

Bear in mind that most hotels in the greater Washington area offer reduced rates at weekends and often during holiday periods, for example in July and Aug, and for special occasions such as New Year's Eve. These packages frequently carry bonuses ranging from free parking to complimentary breakfast (the price does not usually include breakfast). For further details of such offers or for general hotel information, contact the **Washington Convention and Visitors Association** (*1575 I St. NW, DC 20005* ☎*789–7000*) or the **Hotel Association of Washington** (*1219 Connecticut Ave. NW, DC 20036* ☎*833–3350*).

Bed and breakfast arrangements in private homes or small guest houses are becoming increasingly popular in Washington, and the following referral services have lists of available rooms: **Bed 'n' Breakfast** (*PO Box 12011, DC 20005* ☎*328–3510*) and **Sweet Dreams and Toast Inc.** (*PO Box 4835–0035, DC 20008* ☎*483–9191*).

Many hotels have sprung up in the immediate suburbs of Washington, including the big new commercial colonies at Rosslyn and Crystal City. Prices are generally lower than in the District, and there is usually quick and easy Metro access.

The following list of hotels is a selective one, covering a broad spectrum with regard to size, price, area and character. In the major hotels all rooms have private bathrooms.

Hotels classified by area

Capitol Hill
Bellevue Hotel ☐
Holiday Inn Capitol ▥▥
Hyatt Regency Washington on Capitol Hill ▥▥ to ▥▥
Phoenix Park
Quality Inn Capitol Hill ▥▥
Sheraton Grand on Capitol Hill ▥▥ to ▥▥

Dupont Circle
Canterbury ▥▥
Embassy Row ▥▥ to ▥▥
Highland ▥▥ to ▥▥
Holiday Inn Connecticut Avenue

Omni Georgetown Hotel ▥▥
Ritz Carlton ▥▥

Embassy District
Normandy Inn ☐
Washington Hilton and Towers ▥▥ to ▥▥

Foggy Bottom
Watergate Hotel ▥▥

Georgetown
Four Seasons Hotel ▥▥
Georgetown Inn ▥▥ to ▥▥
Georgetown Marbury House ▥▥

Maryland
Bethesda Marriott ▥▥
Hyatt Regency Bethesda ▥▥

New Downtown
Capital Hilton ▥▥ to ▥▥
Dolley Madison Hotel ▥▥
Hampshire ▥▥
Hay-Adams ▥▥ to ▥▥
Governors House Holiday Inn ▥▥ to ▥▥
Jefferson ▥▥
Madison ▥▥
Mayflower ▥▥ to ▥▥
Ramada Renaissance ▥▥
Sheraton Carlton ▥▥
Tabard Inn ☐ to ▥▥

Northeast of the White House
Holiday Inn Central ▥▥

Holiday Inn Thomas Circle ▢ to ▥

Radisson Henley Park ▥
Vista International Hotel ▥ to ▦
Old Downtown
J. W. Marriott ▥
Hotel Washington ▥
Willard Inter-Continental ▦
Southwest
Channel Inn ▥
Loews L'Enfant Plaza ▦
Upper Northwest
Holiday Inn Georgetown ▢
Howard Johnson's Wellington Hotel ▢
Omni Shoreham ▥ to ▦
Rock Creek ▢
Sheraton Washington ▥ to ▦
Virginia
Best Western – Rosslyn Westpark ▢

Hyatt Regency Crystal City ▥
Marriott – Key Bridge ▥
Morrison House ▢
West End
Hotel Bristol ▥
Grand ▦
Washington Marriott ▥
Westin ▥ to ▦

Bellevue Hotel
15 E St. NW, DC 20001
☎638–0900. Map **7F9** ▢
140 rms ━ *night only* ━ AE CB
Ⓓ Ⓓ VISA *Metro: Union Station.*
Location: Near Union Station. A quiet, intimate little hotel. The lobby has the atmosphere of a London gentleman's club.

Best Western – Rosslyn Westpark
1900 North Fort Myer Dr., Arlington, Va. 22209
☎527–4814. Map **4F2** ▢
308 rms ━ ━ AE CB Ⓓ Ⓓ
VISA *Metro: Rosslyn.*
Location: Across the river from Georgetown. A very friendly hotel whose 17th-floor dining room commands an exciting view over Washington.
& ⟨⟨ ⇌

Bethesda Marriott
5151 Pooks Hill Rd., Bethesda, Md. 20814 ☎228–9290 ▥
407 rms ━ AE CB Ⓓ VISA
Metro: Medical Center.
Location: 6 miles (10km) NW of the city centre, off the Beltway. Set in 18 acres (7.3ha) of attractively landscaped grounds, this hotel has three restaurants in addition to extensive sports facilities. There is a complimentary shuttle service to the Medical Center Metro station a mile away.
& ⌄ ⇌ ⟨⟨ ⟨⟨

Hotel Bristol
2430 Pennsylvania Ave. NW, DC 20037 ☎955–6400
Ⓥ292024. Map **2E4** ▥ *240 rms*
━ ━ AE CB Ⓓ VISA *Metro: Foggy Bottom.*
Location: In the West End, a 5min walk from Georgetown. As the name suggests, this elegant hotel has adopted an English style, right down to the mahogany four-poster bed in every room. Each room also has a kitchen attached. The excellent **Bristol Grill** is famous for its mesquite-grilled dishes.

Canterbury
1733 N St. NW, DC 20036
☎393–3000 Ⓥ892669. Map
3E6 ▥ *99 rms* ━ ━ AE CB Ⓓ
Ⓓ VISA *Metro: Dupont Circle.*
Location: Near the lively Dupont Circle area and six blocks from the White House. A fairly small, attractive hotel, where the amenities are modern, with kitchenettes in every room, though the overall style is old-world with paisley fabrics and some four-poster beds.

Capital Hilton
1001 16th St. NW, DC 20036
☎393–1000 Ⓥ7108229068.
Map **3E6** ▥ to ▥ *533 rms* ━
━ AE CB Ⓓ Ⓓ VISA *Metro: McPherson Square, Farragut North.*
Location: Three blocks N of the White House. Built in 1943, this de luxe hotel with its marvellous art deco finery was recently totally renovated at a cost of $44 million and the rooms reduced from 800 to 533, making them among the most spacious in Washington. The hotel is a pick-up point for airport buses.
& ⟨⟨ ⟨⟨

Channel Inn
650 Water St. SW, DC 20024
☎554–2400 ⓉCHNLINN
6971708. Map **7I8** ▥ *100 rms*
━ ━ *Metro: L'Enfant Plaza.*
Location: On the SW waterfront. A modern hotel with an excellent seafood restaurant, **Pier Seven**.

Dolley Madison Hotel
1507 M St. NW, DC 20005
☎862–1600 Ⓥ64245. Map **3E6**
▥ *42 rms* ━ ━ *closed dinner*
AE CB Ⓓ VISA *Metro: McPherson Square.*
Location: Six blocks N of the White House. Small sister hotel to the nearby Madison, serving breakfast and lunch only, with a more intimate atmosphere but the same individual touch in the furnishing.

Hotels

Embassy Row
*2015 Massachusetts Ave. NW,
DC 20036* ☎*265–1600*
📞*892650. Map 3D5* ▮▮▮ *to*
▮▮▮ *194 rms* 🚗 AE CB ⓘ ⓒ VISA
Metro: Dupont Circle.
*Location: In the embassy district, a
stone's throw from Dupont Circle.*
Hungarian-born Gabor Olah, the
original manager of the Watergate
Hotel, was lured out of retirement
in Florida to manage this hotel in
the embassy district. He has
brought great polish to the hotel,
and his staff have been carefully
trained in the European tradition
of courteous and efficient service.
≋

Four Seasons Hotel
*2800 Pennsylvania Ave. NW,
DC 20007* ☎*342–0444*
📞*904008. Map 2E4* ▮▮▮ *197 rms*
🚗 *Metro: Foggy Bottom.*
*Location: On the edge of
Georgetown, backing directly onto
the C&O Canal.* Recently one
rating placed this hotel as the best
in the Americas. For enormous
prices, you get impeccable service.
♿

Georgetown Inn
*1310 Wisconsin Ave. NW,
DC 20007* ☎*333–8900*
📞*4970926. Map 2E3* ▮▮▮▮ *to* ▮▮▮▮
95 rms 🚗 ➡ AE CB ⓘ ⓒ VISA
*Location: In the heart of
Georgetown.* A small brick
building decorated in attractive
Colonial style with four-poster
beds in all the rooms.
♿

Georgetown Marbury House
3000 M St. NW, DC 20007
☎*726–5000. Map 2E4* ▮▮▮▮
164 rms 🚗 ➡ AE CB ⓘ ⓒ
VISA
Location: Central Georgetown. A
pleasant, comfortable hotel in the
liveliest part of Georgetown. The
building is new but the decor and
furnishings are in Colonial style.
♿ ≋

Grand
2350 M St. NW, DC 20037
☎*848–0016* 📞*904282. Map
3E5* ▮▮▮▮ *265 rms* 🚗 ➡ AE CB
ⓘ ⓒ VISA *Metro: Foggy Bottom.*
*Location: West End, a 10min walk
from Georgetown.* The serene,
circular, domed lobby sets the tone
for this luxury hotel. The overall
style is elegantly European with
attractive touches such as a
secluded little courtyard.
♿ ⚓ ≋

Hampshire
*1310 New Hampshire Ave. NW,
DC 20036* ☎*296–7600*
📞*7108229343. Map 3E5* ▮▮▮▮
82 rms 🚗 ➡ AE CB ⓘ ⓒ
Metro: Dupont Circle.
*Location: Two blocks sw of Dupont
Circle.* A former apartment block
converted into a small hotel with a
good reputation for comfort and
service. Guests have free use of a
health centre nearby. The
restaurant, **Lafitte**, is known for
its New Orleans Cajun and Creole
cooking.

Hay-Adams
*1 Lafayette Square NW,
DC 20006* ☎*638–6600*
📞*7108229543. Map 3F6* ▮▮▮▮ *to*
▮▮▮▮ *155 rms* 🚗 ➡ AE CB ⓘ
ⓒ VISA *Metro: McPherson
Square, Farragut West.*
*Location: Directly across Lafayette
Park from the White House.* A
Rolls-Royce of a hotel, fairly small,
quiet, intimate and elegant in an
old-world way. The handsome
building occupies the site of two
earlier houses, one lived in by the
historian Henry Adams, the other
by John Hay, diplomat, statesman
and author of a biography of
Lincoln.
◁€

Highland
*1914 Connecticut Ave. NW,
DC 20009* ☎*797–2000*
📞*4941795. Map 3C5* ▮▮ *to* ▮▮▮▮
140 rms 🚗 ➡ AE CB ⓘ ⓒ
VISA *Metro: Dupont Circle.*
*Location: Three blocks N of Dupont
Circle.* A handsome former
apartment block in ornate turn-of-
the-century style, beautifully
renovated in 1979. The rooms are
stylishly furnished in the
European manner.

Holiday Inn Capitol
550 C St. SW, DC 20024
☎*479–4000. Map 7G8* ▮▮▮
530 rms 🚗 ➡ AE CB ⓘ ⓒ
VISA *Metro: L'Enfant Plaza.*
♿ ≋

Holiday Inn Central
*1501 Rhode Island Ave.
DC 20005* ☎*483–2000. Map
3E6* ▮▮ *214 rms* 🚗 ➡ AE CB
ⓘ ⓒ VISA *Metro: Farragut North.*
♿ ≋

Holiday Inn Connecticut
Avenue
*1900 Connecticut Ave. NW,
DC 20009* ☎*332–9300. Map
3C5* ▮▮▮ *149 rms* 🚗 ➡ AE CB
ⓘ ⓒ VISA *Metro: Dupont Circle.*
⚓ ◁€ ≋

Holiday Inn Georgetown
2101 Wisconsin Ave. NW,
DC 20007 ☎*338–4600. Map*
2C2 ▥▯ *300 rms* ⊂⊃ ⚋ AE CB
⊙ ▨ VISA ⚬ ≋

Governors House Holiday Inn
1615 Rhode Island Ave. NW,
DC 20036 ☎*296–2100. Map*
3E6 ▥▯ *to* ▥▮ *152 rms* ⊂⊃ ⚋ AE
CB ⊙ ▨ VISA *Metro: Farragut*
North.
⚬ ≋

Holiday Inn Thomas Circle
1155 14th St. NW, DC 20005
☎*737–1200. Map 3E7* ▯ *to* ▥▯
208 rms ⊂⊃ ⚋ AE CB ⊙ ▨
VISA *Metro: McPherson Square.*
⚬ ≋

The Washington Holiday Inns
vary slightly in price but are all
broadly similar in character. They
do not pretend to offer great
luxury or superior service, but you
can rely on a good standard of
comfort and efficiency.

Howard Johnson's
Wellington Hotel
2505 Wisconsin Ave. NW,
DC 20007 ☎*337–7400* ▥▯
147 rms ⚋ ⊂⊃ AE CB ⊙ ▨ VISA
Location: Upper Northwest. A
converted building in a pleasant
location near the upper end of
Embassy Row. Much of its
business is connected with the
embassies. It has an attractive
restaurant called **The Gazebo**.
⚬ ≋

Hyatt Regency Bethesda
1 Bethesda Metro Center,
Bethesda, Md. 20814
☎*(301) 657–1234* ▥▮ *383 rms*
⚋ ⊂⊃ ⚋ AE CB ⊙ ▨ VISA *Metro:*
Bethesda.
Location: Directly above Bethesda
Metro station, 5 miles (8km) from
central Washington. Opened in
November 1985, this hotel is
located in the business and
shopping area of downtown
Bethesda.
⚬ ≋ ♟

Hyatt Regency Crystal City
2799 Jefferson Davis Highway,
Arlington, Va. 22202
☎*486–1234* ☏*901943* ▥▮
685 rms ⚋ ⊂⊃ AE CB ⊙ ▨
VISA *Metro: Crystal City.*
Location: Next to National
Airport. A handsome hotel,
recognizably Hyatt in style with its
five-storey atrium full of greenery
and glassed-in elevators. The bulk
of the clientele is corporate.
⚬ ◁€ ≋

Hyatt Regency Washington
on Capitol Hill
400 New Jersey Ave. NW,
DC 20001 ☎*737–1234*
☏*897432. Map 7F9* ▥▯ *to* ▥▮
842 rms ⚋ ⊂⊃ AE CB ⊙ ▨ ⊙
VISA *Metro: Union Station.*
Location: Near Union Station.
The most striking feature of this
hotel is its huge skylit atrium with
a fountain and forest of trees. The
usual Hyatt standard of comfort
and facilities prevails. There is a
good view from the rooftop dining
room.
⚬ ≋

Jefferson
1200 16th St. NW, DC 20036
☎*347–2200* ☏*248879. Map*
3E6 ▥▮ *104 rms* ⚋ ⊂⊃ AE CB
⊙ ▨ VISA *Metro: Farragut North.*
Location: Five blocks N of the White
House. The Jefferson in its present
form is the creation of one of
Washington's most gifted
hoteliers, Mrs Rose Narva, who
also masterminded the renovation
of the Hay-Adams and the
Sheraton Carlton. At the Jefferson
she has created a highly civilized
environment. The prevailing style
is 18thC English. Mrs Narva and
her staff go out of their way to
ensure that their guests feel at
home in this unique hotel.
⚬ ◁€

Loews L'Enfant Plaza
480 L'Enfant Plaza East SW,
DC 20024 ☎*484–1000* ☏*89657.*
Map 6H7 ▥▮ *372 rms* ⚋ ⊂⊃ AE
CB ⊙ ▨ VISA *Metro: L'Enfant*
Plaza.
Location: Between the Mall and the
SW waterfront. In a somewhat stark
and characterless environment but
well placed for the Smithsonian
museums on the S Mall. The
cabaret, Comedy à la Carte, runs
on Fri and Sat evenings (see
Nightlife).
◁€ ≋

Madison
15th and M St. NW, DC 20005
☎*862–1600* ☏*64245. Map 3E6*
▥▮ *368 rms* ⚋ ⊂⊃ AE CB ⊙
▨ VISA *Metro: McPherson*
Square.
Location: Five blocks N of the White
House. One of Washington's top
hotels. Each room has an
individual touch, and the
furnishings and decoration are
comprised of items from the
proprietor's own collection,
including many Oriental *objets*
d'art.

Hotels

J. W. Marriott
*1331 Pennsylvania Ave. NW,
DC 20004* ☎*393–2000*
🕔*7108229638. Map 6F7* ▯▯▯▯
774 rms ⇌ 🍴 AE CB ⓘ ⓒ
VISA *Metro: Metro Center.*
Location: *Old Downtown, near the
White House and next door to the
National Theater*. Opened in 1984
as part of the new National Place
complex. The lobby is a striking
four-storey atrium of pink marble
and mahogany. Below are
restaurants, meeting rooms and
two grand ballrooms. Above are
the guest rooms, some with
magnificent views over the city.
♿ ◁€ ⇌ 🍸

Marriott – Key Bridge
*1401 Lee Highway, Arlington,
Va. 22209* ☎*524–6400. Map
4F2* ▯▯▯▯ *558 rms* ⇌ AE CB
ⓘ ⓒ VISA *Metro: Rosslyn.*
Location: *Directly across the river
from Georgetown*. Built about
20yrs ago, this attractively
furnished hotel is the second oldest
of the Marriott chain. Its rooftop
View restaurant commands a fine
panorama over the Washington
skyline.
♿ ◁€ ⇌

Mayflower
*1127 Connecticut Ave. NW,
DC 20036* ☎*347–3000*
🕔*892324. Map 3E6* ▯▯▯▯ *to* ▯▯▯▯
724 rms ⇌ ⇌ AE CB ⓘ ⓒ
VISA *Metro: Farragut North.*
Location: *New Downtown.* One of
the grandest of *grande dame* hotels.
Opened in 1925, in time for
President Coolidge's inaugural
ball, it has recently undergone
renovation and has re-emerged in
all its finery. In the richly ornate
lobby there is a model of the ship
after which the hotel was named. It
has two restaurants: **Nicholas,** a
high-class, formal dining room,
and the **Café Promenade** for
more casual meals. The latter has
some charming murals of garden
scenes painted by Edward Lanning
under the auspices of the Works
Progress Administration in the
1930s. They were covered in the
1950s and only rediscovered
during the recent restoration.
♿

Morrison House
*116 S Alfred St., Alexandria,
Va. 22314* ☎*838–8000*
🕔*3792672* ▯▯▯ *47 rms* ⇌ ⇌ AE
CB ⓘ ⓒ VISA *Metro: King Street.*
Location: *Near the centre of
Alexandria.* A small European-
style hotel, which is very elegant
and intimate. Afternoon tea is
served in the cosy parlour and
library. There is a high-class
French restaurant, Le Chardon
d'Or, serving *nouvelle cuisine* (see
also *Restaurants*).

Normandy Inn
*2118 Wyoming Ave. NW,
DC 20008* ☎*483–1350. Map
3C5* ▯ ▯ AE CB ⓘ ⓒ VISA
Metro: Dupont Circle.
Location: *NW of Dupont Circle, in
the embassy district.* A small
European-style bed and breakfast
hotel which hosts a free wine and
cheese tasting every Tues
5.30–7.30pm.

Omni Georgetown Hotel
2121 P St. NW, DC 20037
☎*293–3100. Map 3D5* ▯▯▯▯
300 rms ⇌ ⇌ AE CB ⓘ ⓒ
VISA *Metro: Dupont Circle.*
Location: *Just w of Dupont Circle
and near, but not in, Georgetown.*
The building is a former
apartment block with spacious
rooms all of which have recently
been completely refurbished.
♿ ⇌ 🍸

Omni Shoreham
2500 Calvert St. NW, DC 20008
☎*235–0700* 🕔*7108220142.
Map 2B4* ▯▯▯▯ *to* ▯▯▯▯ *884 rms* ⇌
⇌ AE CB ⓘ ⓒ VISA *Metro:
Woodley Park-Zoo.*
Location: *Upper Northwest, near
the Zoo.* A large and imposing
1930s art deco-style building,
which has been recently renovated.
It is in a pleasant residential part of
town with direct access to *Rock
Creek Park*. There is dancing
nightly in the **Marquee Lounge**
and a comedy cabaret Fri–Sun
evenings as well as a Sun matinée.
⇌ 🏊

Phoenix Park
*520 North Capitol St. NW,
DC 20001* ☎*638–6900*
🕔*904104. Map 7F9* ▯▯▯ *84 rms*
⇌ ⇌ AE CB ⓘ ⓒ VISA *Metro:
Union Station.*
Location: *Close to Union Station.*
Named after the famous Dublin
park, this is a small, elegant hotel
with an atmosphere as warm as the
Irish accents that can often be
heard here. Its high-class
restaurant, the **Powerscourt**, is
much frequented by members of
Congress. Next door, under the
same management, is the
Dubliner pub.
♿

Quality Inn Capitol Hill
*415 New Jersey Ave. NW,
DC 20001* ☎638–1616
☎7108220153. *Map 7F9* ▨
341 rms ⇔ ⇌ AE CB ◎ ◎
VISA *Metro: Union Station.*
*Location: Near Union Station and
the Capitol.* A modern ten-storey
hotel, not in the luxury class, but
functional and comfortable.
Ᏸ ⇌

Radisson Henley Park
*926 Massachusetts Ave. NW,
DC 20001* ☎638–5200
☎904059 WSH ▨ *96 rms* ⇔
⇌ AE CB ◎ ◎ VISA *Metro:
Gallery Place, Metro Center.*
*Location: On the N edge of Old
Downtown.* An exceptionally
attractive, quiet, small hotel with a
cosy European atmosphere and
carefully chosen furnishings to
match, a stone's throw from the
Washington Convention Center.

Ramada Renaissance
*1143 New Hampshire Ave. NW,
DC 20037* ☎755–0800
☎7108229209. *Map 3E5* ▨
355 rms ⇔ ⇌ AE CB ◎ ◎
VISA *Metro: Dupont Circle, Foggy
Bottom.*
*Location: W side of New Downtown,
within easy walking distance of
Georgetown, the Kennedy Center
and Dupont Circle.* A hotel of
decidedly contemporary elegance,
characterized by a bright, marble-
floored lobby with a large glass
front and a mass of potted plants.
It has two restaurants,
Summerfield's, for casual meals,
and the slightly more formal **La
Cloche**, which specializes in
seafood.
Ᏸ

Ritz Carlton
*2100 Massachusetts Ave. NW,
DC 20008* ☎293–2100
☎263758. *Map 3D5* ▨ *250 rms*
⇔ ⇌ AE CB ◎ ◎ VISA *Metro:
Dupont Circle.*
*Location: Embassy Row, near
Dupont Circle.* Formerly known as
the Fairfax, this handsome hotel
became the Ritz Carlton in 1982
and has since been extended by 100
rooms. It amply lives up to its
prestigious location in the embassy
district. There is a small exercise
room on each guest floor, where
you can work off any excess weight
acquired in the hotel's Jockey Club
restaurant, one of Washington's
smartest venues (see also
Restaurants).
Ᏸ ⚲

Rock Creek
1925 Belmont Rd. NW, DC 20009
☎462–6007. *Map 2C4* ▨
54 rms ⇔ *Metro: Woodley Park-
Zoo.*
*Location: Upper Northwest, on the
edge of Rock Creek Park.* A low-
priced hotel, where the rooms are
simply furnished and clean, and
avoid being poky. The location is
pleasant and convenient.

Sheraton Carlton
923 16th St. NW, DC 20009
☎638–2626 ☎440650. *Map
3E6* ▨ *250 rms* ⇔ ⇌ AE CB
◎ ◎ *Metro: Farragut North,
McPherson Square.*
*Location: Two blocks N of the White
House.* A gracious hotel built in
1926, which was extensively
renovated under the supervision of
Mrs Rose Narva who runs the
Jefferson. It is now one of the most
elegantly opulent of Washington
hotels.

Sheraton Grand on Capitol Hill
*525 New Jersey Ave. NW,
DC 20001* ☎628–2100
☎4970525 GRAND. *Map 7F9*
▨ to ▨ *272 rms* ⇔ ⇌ AE CB
◎ ◎ *Metro: Union Station.*
*Location: Near Union Station and
the Capitol.* The salient feature of
this hotel is its striking three-
storey atrium. Some $150,000 was
spent on the greenery alone,
brought from all over the world.
The mezzanine café in the atrium
makes a delightful spot for a light
meal, and there is also a more
formal restaurant called the
Signature Room. Decor
combines traditional with modern.
Guests have the use of the Capitol
Hill Squash Club.
Ᏸ

Sheraton Washington
*2660 Woodley Rd. NW,
DC 20008* ☎328–2000
☎892630. *Map 2B4* ▨ to ▨
1,500 rms ⇔ ⇌ AE CB ◎ ◎
VISA *Metro: Woodley Park-Zoo.*
*Location: Upper Northwest, near
the Zoo and Rock Creek Park.* A
huge hotel incorporating two
modern buildings and a historic
former apartment house. It has
three restaurants, two lounges (one
with live music Mon–Sat
evenings) and a variety of shops
including a hairdresser, beauty
salon and post office. On Sun there
is a gargantuan American buffet
with over 175 items.
Ᏸ ⇌

Hotels

Tabard Inn
1739 N St. NW, DC 20036
☎785−1277. Map **3E6** ☐ to ☐
40 rms ⚌ 🅾 VISA *Metro: Dupont
Circle.*

*Location: Two blocks SE of Dupont
Circle.* One of the most intimately
charming of Washington hotels.
Its lounge is a cosy, panelled
sanctum reminiscent of an English
country inn.
❧

Vista International Hotel
1400 M St. NW, DC 20005
☎429−1700 ☏440237 VISTA
WASH DC. Map **3E6** ⏥ to ⏥
396 rms ⚌ ➟ 🖃 AE CB 🅾 🄼
VISA *Metro: McPherson Square.*
*Location: Five blocks N of the White
House.* Glassed-in atriums have
become popular features in
American hotels. This hotel has a
particularly striking one 14 storeys
high – a delightful place in which
to listen to the chamber orchestra
that plays in the evenings.
⚱ ➟ ♨

Hotel Washington
*15th St. and Pennsylvania Ave.
NW, DC 20004* ☎638−5900
☏7108220105. Map **6F6** ⏥
370 rms ⚌ ➟ AE CB 🅾 🄼
VISA *Metro: Metro Center.*
Location: Close to the White House.
A fine old hotel in a prime
position, the Washington has been
in operation since 1918 and
recently was totally renovated.
From the top floor, with its
restaurant and open-air terrace
bar, there is an unparalleled view
of central Washington.
⚱ ◁€

Washington Hilton and Towers
*1919 Connecticut Ave. NW,
DC 20009* ☎483−3000
☏248761 WHDC. Map **3C5** ⏥
to ⏥ 1,154 rms ⚌ ➟ AE CB
🅾 🄼 VISA *Metro: Dupont Circle.*
Location: N of Dupont Circle. This
large, modern hotel commands
fine views out over the city.
Popular with conferences and tour
groups, it has the largest ballroom
in Washington.
⚱ ❧ ◁€ ➟ ⚶ ♨

Washington Marriott
1221 22nd St. NW, DC 20037
☎872−1500 ☏7108221195.
Map **3E5** ⏥ 350 rms ⚌ ➟ AE
🅾 🄼 VISA *Metro: Foggy
Bottom.*
*Location: A 10min walk from
Georgetown, in New Downtown.* A

comfortable, modern hotel
(opened in 1981) with rooms
furnished in contemporary style.
⚱ ➟

Watergate Hotel
*2600 Virginia Ave. NW,
DC 20037* ☎298−4450
☏904994 WAHO. Map **2F4** ⏥
238 rms ⚌ ➟ AE CB 🅾 🄼
VISA *Metro: Foggy Bottom.*
*Location: Foggy Bottom, near the
Kennedy Center.* Part of a large
conglomeration of buildings
overlooking the Potomac (see
Watergate Complex), this
luxurious hotel, set in attractively
landscaped grounds, is run with
tremendous style and polish. It has
two restaurants, one of which is the
well-known Jean-Louis (see
Restaurants).
⚱ ❧ ◁€ ➟ ♨

Westin
2401 M St. NW, DC 20037
☎429−2400 ☏4979800. Map
3E5 ⏥ to ⏥ 416 rms ⚌ ➟ AE
CB 🅾 🄼 VISA *Metro: Foggy
Bottom.*
Location: N of Washington Circle.
Opened at the end of 1985, this is a
luxury hotel of very attractive
design, focusing on a charming
garden courtyard with trees,
shrubs and a stone Italian fountain
in the centre. The accent
throughout is on traditional
elegance coupled with modern
convenience.
⚱ ❧ ➟ ♨

Willard Inter-Continental
*1401 Pennsylvania Ave. NW,
DC 20008* ☎483−7700
☏3725559 WILLARD HOTEL
UB. Map **6F7** ⏥ 395 rms ⚌ ➟
AE CB 🅾 🄼 VISA *Metro: Metro
Center.*
*Location: In the hub of Washington,
close to the White House and the
Mall.* Not just a hotel but one of
Washington's great historic
landmarks. In existence since 1850
and rebuilt in its present palatial
Beaux-Arts form around the turn
of the century, the Willard has
played a key role in Washington
life. Presidents, senators, heads of
state, diplomats, tycoons have all
gathered and conferred in its
sumptuous rooms. Closed during
the 1968 riots, the building was
threatened with demolition but
fortunately saved and entirely
renovated. It has now re-emerged
in all its ornate glory as a jewel of
the resurrected Old Downtown.
⚱ ◁€

Where to eat

In the days when Washington was a federal government "company town", it was as hard to discover an interesting restaurant as it was to find an intelligent person who could converse about anything other than politics. Steak and potatoes and Southern fried chicken were the staple diet, and foreign cuisine meant little more than a handful of Italian, French and Chinese restaurants. Tight government expense accounts exacerbated the situation, and cuisine was generally a low priority. Circumstances have now changed, partly thanks to the large corporations that have recently moved their headquarters into the Washington suburbs, bringing with them a huge influx of expense-account customers who demand quality and variety.

There are now about 150 different nationalities of cuisine represented in the city, the only notable exception being Scandinavian. Successful ethnic restaurants of all types cluster in Adams-Morgan, Georgetown and the suburbs. Take the Metro to Arlington and it's like being in little Saigon; the Chinese stronghold is still in its Old Downtown position around H St. Regional differences have also become important. Exciting northern Italian cooking has largely replaced spaghetti and meatballs, and Chinese no longer means just Cantonese but also Hunan and Szechuan. At the same time Washingtonians still relish their local specialities: the fresh bounty of Chesapeake Bay, the cornucopia of products from Maryland and Virginia farms (ham, game, fruit, vegetables, dairy products) and the beef from America's heartland.

Today the diner seeking interesting experiences will find Indian, Creole, Cuban, Spanish, Ethiopian, Guatemalan, Mexican, Brazilian, German, Hungarian and French restaurants in various parts of Washington. Meanwhile tradition still reigns along "Restaurant Row" – K St. w of Connecticut Ave. – where prices tend to match the elaborately stylized menu designs.

Power lunches are a Washington speciality; and for many people the venue and the customers are more important considerations than the menu. Status comes with a centre table at the **Maison Blanche**, close to the White House, or at **Duke Zeibert's** on Connecticut Ave. Media moguls even gather for power breakfasts at **Joe and Mo's**, also on Connecticut Ave. On Capitol Hill, places where you may catch a glimpse of a member of Congress or two include **The Monocle**, **La Colline**, the **Sheraton Grand** hotel, **La Brasserie** and the **American Café** – or you could sample the famous Senate bean soup in the *Capitol* cafeteria.

Waterfront restaurants seem to blossom as regularly as the cherry trees around the Tidal Basin. New at the time of writing is the huge **Potomac on the River** in the Washington Harbour complex. And recently opened in a new incarnation is **Phillips Flagship** on Maine Ave. SW, one of many excellent seafood restaurants in Washington.

With the renaissance of *Old Downtown* has come a mushrooming of restaurants in that area, and several new hotels with first-class restaurants have upgraded the standard of dining in the West End. Furthermore, at any high-class restaurant you can now count on an excellent selection of wines, usually from America and Europe. So today you need never go far in Washington to find an acceptable place to eat and drink.

When reading a menu bear in mind that prices do not include tax, and a basic tip is about 15 percent.

Restaurants

Restaurants classified by area

Adams-Morgan
Axum ▯ Ethiop
Kalorama Café ▯ whlfd
New Orleans Emporium ▯
   Creole
Capitol Hill
American Café (1) ▯ Am
La Brasserie ▯ Fr
The Chef's Table ▯ Soul
La Colline ▯ Fr
The Monocle ▯ Am
Dupont Circle
El Bodegon ▯ Sp
Galileo ▯ It
The Jockey Club ▯ Fr
Foggy Bottom/West End
Jean-Louis ▯ Fr
Maison Blanche ▯ Fr
Georgetown
American Café (3) ▯ Am
Au Pied de Cochon ▯ Fr
Aux Fruits de Mer ▯ Fr fish
Bamiyan (1) ▯ Afghan
Clyde's ▯ Am
Himalaya ▯ Ind veg
Madurai ▯ Ind veg
Martin's Tavern ▯ Am
Potomac on the River ▯
   Am intnl
Maryland
O'Brien's Pit Barbecue (1) and (2)
   ▯ S Am
New Downtown
Bacchus ▯ Leb
Charley's Crab ▯ fish
Dominique's ▯ Fr
Duke Zeibert's ▯ Am
Hunan Rose ▯ Ch
Joe and Mo's ▯ Am fish
Le Lion d'Or ▯ Fr
Le Pavillon ▯ Fr
Takesushi ▯ Jap
Tiberio ▯ It

Old Downtown
Big Wong ▯ Ch
The Bread Oven ▯ Fr
Café Mozart ▯ Ger
Dutch Mill Deli ▯ Am
Marrakesh ▯ Moroc
Old Ebbitt Grill ▯ Am
Pavilion at the Old Post Office ▯
   to ▯ intnl
Southwest
Hogate's ▯ Am fish
Phillips Flagship ▯ Am fish
Upper Northwest
American Café (2) and (4) ▯ Am
Dancing Crab ▯ fish
Old Europe ▯ Ger
Viet Château ▯ Viet
Virginia
L'Auberge Chez Francois ▯ Fr
Bamiyan (2) ▯ Afghan
Le Chardon d'Or ▯ Fr
O'Brien's Pit Barbecue (3) ▯
   S Am
Potowmack Landing ▯ Am

Key to types of cuisine

Am American
Ch Chinese
Ethiop Ethiopian
Fr French
Ger German
Ind Indian
intnl international
It Italian
Jap Japanese
Leb Lebanese
Moroc Moroccan
S Am South American
Sp Spanish
veg vegetarian
Viet Vietnamese
whlfd wholefood

American Café (1)
227 Massachusetts Ave. NE
☎547–8500. Map **7F9** ▯ AE
CB ▯ ▯ VISA *Closed Christmas,
Thanksgiving. Metro:* Union
Station.
American Café (2)
1300 F St. NW ☎737–5153.
Map **6F7** ▯ AE CB ▯ ▯ VISA
*Closed Christmas, Thanksgiving.
Metro: Metro Center.*
American Café (3)
1211 Wisconsin Ave. NW
☎337–3606. Map **2E3** ▯ AE
CB ▯ ▯ VISA *Closed Christmas,
Thanksgiving.*
American Café (4)
5200 Wisconsin Ave. NW
☎363–7773 ▯ AE CB ▯ ▯
VISA *Closed Christmas,
Thanksgiving. Metro: Friendship
Heights.*
This chain has four restaurants in
the District. Dishes rotate

seasonally, but the food is basically
light, standard American fare. It is
variable in quality, but pasta,
quiches and salads – especially the
chicken and tarragon salad – are
good. The wines are all American.

Au Pied de Cochon
1335 Wisconsin Ave. NW
☎333–5440. Map **2E3** ▯ AE
CB ▯ ▯ VISA *Closed Mon
1.30–10am.*
This establishment hit the
headlines in Nov 1985 when it was
the scene of an embarrassing
incident involving a Russian KGB
defector, Vitaly Yurchenko. He
was dining here with his CIA
keepers when, in the middle of the
meal, he left the restaurant and
walked to the Soviet Embassy
compound farther up Wisconsin
Ave., where he defected back to the
Russians. This is no reflection on

the food at Au Pied de Cochon, which is good, solid bistro-type French fare. The restaurant stays open 24hrs except on Mon.

L'Auberge Chez Francois
322 Springvale Rd., Great Falls, Va. ☎*(703) 759–3800* ⫴ ⇒ AE ⬤ VISA *Closed Mon, Christmas, New Year's Day.*
About 15 miles (22.5km) up the Potomac from central Washington, this French country inn has a long-standing and devoted following. The menu is *prix fixe* only with a choice of such entrées as peppered swordfish steak, salmon soufflé and duck *choucroute*. It is essential to reserve in advance.

Aux Fruits de Mer
1329 Wisconsin Ave. NW ☎*965–2377. Map 2E3* ⫴ AE CB ⬤ ⬤ VISA *Closes Sun – Thurs 1.30am, Fri, Sat 2.30am.*
A suitably nautical decor complements the wide range of seafood on offer at this busy Georgetown restaurant. It shares a kitchen with the adjacent Au Pied de Cochon, but the menu is different.

Axum
2307 18th St. NW ☎*232–8844. Map 3C6* ⫴ ⇒ AE ⬤ VISA
If you have never tried Ethiopian or Sudanese cooking, this friendly, relaxed restaurant will show you what you have been missing. You don't eat with a knife and fork but with pieces of Ethiopian bread that look like freshly laundered napkins. Excellent value for money.

Bacchus
1827 Jefferson Pl. NW ☎*785–0734. Map 3E5* ⫴ ⇒ AE ⬤ VISA *Closed Sun, major hols. Metro: Dupont Circle.*
A small, elegant Lebanese restaurant, serving consistently good food. The menu includes such exotic-sounding dishes as *ouzi* (lamb served on a bed of spiced rice with minced meat, almonds and pine kernels) and *warak inab mahshi* (stuffed vine leaves).

Bamiyan (1)
3320 M St. NW ☎*338–1896. Map 2E3* ⫴ ⇒ AE ⬤ VISA *Closed Sun, Christmas, Thanksgiving and for lunch.*
Bamiyan (2)
300 King St., Alexandria, Va. ☎*548–9006* ⫴ ⇒ AE ⬤ VISA *Closed Sun, Christmas, Thanksgiving and for lunch.*
The two branches of this restaurant have won fervent converts to Afghan food among Washingtonians. As well as wonderfully spicy kebabs and other meat dishes, there is a choice of vegetarian fare.

Big Wong
610 H St. NW ☎*638–0116. Map 7F8* □ AE ⬤ VISA *Metro: Gallery Place.*
Located in Chinatown, this simply decorated restaurant offers a wide range of delicious Cantonese dishes at very reasonable prices. Bear in mind that no wine is served here, only beer and soft drinks. Popular for a *dim sum* Sun brunch.

El Bodegon
1637 R St. NW ☎*667–1710. Map 3D6* ⫴ AE CB ⬤ ⬤ VISA *Closed Sun. Metro: Dupont Circle.*
Authentic Spanish, as opposed to Latin American, food is available here. Specialities include *paella*, Castilian roast suckling pig and *zarzuela* (a seafood casserole cooked in a brandy sauce). There is flamenco music and dancing every evening Mon–Sat.

La Brasserie
239 Massachusetts Ave. NE ☎*546–9154. Map 7F8* ⫴ ⇒ AE ⬤ ⬤ VISA *Metro: Union Station.*
La Brasserie offers *nouvelle cuisine*, exquisitely prepared in tiny portions at vast prices. The decor is intimate and recherché.

The Bread Oven
1201 Pennsylvania Ave. NW ☎*737–7772. Map 7F7* ⫴ ⇒ AE CB ⬤ ⬤ VISA *Closed Sun dinner, major hols. Metro: Metro Center, Federal Triangle.*
A cheerful place serving French country-style food that is reliable if not tremendously exciting. There is live music or other entertainment every evening Mon–Sat; cabaret nights are Thurs, Fri and every other Sat.

Café Mozart
1331 H St. NW ☎*347–5732. Map 6F6* ⫴ ⇒ AE CB ⬤ ⬤ VISA *Closed Christmas, New Year's Day. Metro: Metro Center, McPherson Square.*
The best place in Washington for excellent German food at reasonable prices. The atmosphere

is enriched by music – a different programme every evening, ranging from Viennese chamber music to classical guitar.

Le Chardon d'Or
Morrison House hotel, 116 S Alfred St., Alexandria, Va.
☎*(703) 838–8000* ▥ ▤ ▨
▧ ▨ ▨ *Metro: King Street.*
Nouvelle cuisine with an American accent in an elegant hotel occupying an 18thC building. It is popular for English tea, served daily 3–5pm, and for the fixed price Sun brunch.

Charley's Crab
1101 Connecticut Ave. NW
☎*785–4505. Map 3E6* ▥ ▤
▨ ▨ ▧ ▨ ▨ *Closed Sun, major hols; Sat lunch, saloon only open for light meals. Metro: Farragut North.*
Located in the middle of the busy New Downtown area, within an office and shopping complex linked to Farragut North Metro station, this big restaurant is good for clam chowder, crab meat cakes, broiled fish and other seafood.

The Chef's Table
4414 Benning Rd. NE
☎*6994 ▢ Closed Mon. Metro: Benning Road.*
One of the best places in Washington to go for authentic soul food: spare ribs barbecued on the premises, pigs' feet, chitlings (stuffed innards of pig), baked or fried chicken and turkey rolls. There is a choice of 12 different vegetables and ten desserts.

Clyde's
3236 N St. NW ☎*333–9180. Map 2E3* ▥ ▤ ▨ ▧ *Closed Christmas for lunch.*
Funky, colourful and animated, this is one of the most fashionable of Georgetown haunts. Standard American dishes such as hamburgers and fried chicken are recommended, and there is an omelet room where only egg dishes are served.

La Colline
400 North Capitol St. NW
☎*737–0400. Map 7F9* ▥ ▤
▨ ▧ ▨ ▨ ▨ *Closed major hols. Metro: Union Station.*
A French restaurant, which looks like a cheerful brasserie, and boasts an imaginative menu, including such dishes as shrimp Toulouse-Lautrec (with lobster sauce and a dash of pernod) and suprême of

duckling with blackcurrants. There is a very reasonable *prix fixe* dinner as well as *à la carte*.

Dancing Crab
4611 Wisconsin Ave. NW
☎*244–1882* ▥ ▤ ▨ ▧ ▨
▨ *Closed Christmas.*
A highly informal restaurant where you roll up your sleeves and attack steamed crabs on brown paper tablecloths and can make as much mess as you like. A good place to taste the varied produce of the Chesapeake Bay.

Dominique's
1900 Pennsylvania Ave. NW
☎*452–1126. Map 3F5* ▥ ▤
▨ ▧ ▨ ▨ *Closed Sun, lunch on major hols. Metro: Farragut West.*
A huge, elegant restaurant with a formidably long menu. Owner Dominique d'Erno is a showman and specializes in highly exotic meat dishes. Appetizers include kangaroo *bourgignon*, buffalo sausages, sautéed alligator tail and rattlesnake salad. The bulk of the menu, however, consists of standard French dishes as well as a good range of seafood.

Duke Zeibert's
1050 Connecticut Ave. NW
☎*466–3730. Map 3E6* ▥ ▤
▨ ▧ ▨ ▨ *Closed Sun lunch, major hols. Metro: Farragut North.*
In the glossy new Washington Sq. complex, this large second-floor restaurant is a favourite with politicians and executives of professional associations. Hearty American fare – steaks, roast beef, chicken-in-the-pot – is on offer.

Dutch Mill Deli
639 Indiana Ave. NW
☎*347–3665. Map 7F8* ▢
Closed Sun, most major hols; closes Mon–Fri 7pm, Sat 4pm. Metro: Archives.
Housed in a very old building in the blossoming *Old Downtown* area, this self-service cafeteria is one of the best places in town for breakfast, a sandwich or a wholesome deli meal.

Galileo
2014 P St. NW ☎*293–7191. Map 3D5* ▥ ▤ ▨ ▧ ▨ ▨ *Closed Sun. Metro: Dupont Circle.*
A small, crowded restaurant which has attained a high reputation for authentic Italian cuisine, prepared

by chef and co-owner Roberto Donna from Turin.

Himalaya
1068 31st St. NW ☎*342–0440. Map 2E3* □ AE CB VISA *Closed Mon, some hols. Metro: Foggy Bottom.*

At Himalaya, the Indian vegetarian cooking is delicious enough to win over the most voracious carnivore. This restaurant is unpretentious, friendly and excellent value.

Hogate's
9th St. and Maine Ave. SW ☎*484–6300. Map 6H7* □ ━ AE CB VISA *Closed Christmas. Metro: L'Enfant Plaza.*

A waterfront seafood restaurant with a 550-seat dining room overlooking the Potomac. A popular dish is "mariner's platter", a combination of flounder, oyster, scallops, clam, shrimp and crab cake, which is served with coleslaw and potatoes.

Hunan Rose
2020 K St. NW ☎*833–8818. Map 3E5* □ AE CB VISA *Metro: Farragut West, Farragut North.*

This is the flagship of Shanghai-born Steven Nelson Yung. His middle name is apt as he is owner of a growing fleet of Chinese restaurants including the Hunan in the Pavilion at the Old Post Office. The aim is to mix the best Chinese cuisine with the highest French standards of elegance, presentation and service. The furnishings are quietly luxurious and the food is surprisingly inexpensive for its quality. This is one of the few places where you can dine late in this part of town.

Jean-Louis
Watergate Hotel, 2650 Virginia Ave. NW ☎*337–7750. Map 2F4* □ ━ AE CB VISA *Closed Aug, some major hols. Metro: Foggy Bottom.*

Jean-Louis Palladin was lured from the South of France in 1979 to become chef at this small, hushed sanctum in the basement of the Watergate Hotel (see *Hotels*). Jean-Louis applies his masterly French cuisine to the local produce with great success, and each dish is a delight to both the eye and the taste buds. Prices at dinner are commensurately high, but the lunch menu is a good bargain. All menus are fixed-price.

Jockey Club
Ritz Carlton hotel, 2100 Massachusetts Ave. NW ☎*293–2100. Map 3D5* ━ CB VISA *Metro: Dupont Circle.*

One of Washington's prestige restaurants, this is a place to see and be seen in. Prices are predictably high, but so is the standard of food. The chef is an Italian-trained Japanese, Hede Yamamoto, who practises a sophisticated French cuisine with a touch of *nouvelle*. He is strong on fresh seafoods, including fish imported from France. The decor has the wood-panelled cosiness of an English country inn and the walls are hung with prints of horse-racing scenes. (See also *Hotels*.)

Joe and Mo's
1211 Connecticut Ave. NW ☎*659–1211. Map 3E6* □ AE CB VISA *Closed Sat lunch, Sun, hols. Metro: Dupont Circle, Farragut North.*

A steak and seafood restaurant which has become one of the fashionable places in Washington. Breakfast is popular, not only for the food but also for spotting the media moguls who often start the day here. There is no Joe, but the host, Mo Sussman, runs the place with great panache.

Kalorama Café
2228 18th St. NW ☎*667–1022. Map 3D6* □ *Closed Mon lunch, Sun dinner. Metro: Dupont Circle.*

One of the few wholefood havens in Washington. The food is wholesome and so is the atmosphere, with plenty of natural wood, exposed brick and hanging plants. The menu covers fish as well as vegetarian dishes, and drinks include organically produced wines. Mon evenings are reserved for macrobiotic food.

Le Lion d'Or
1150 Connecticut Ave. NW ☎*296–7972. Map 3E6* □ ━ AE CB VISA *Closed Sat lunch, Sun, most major hols. Metro: Farragut North.*

The inconspicuous location of this restaurant – downstairs in a large office building – does not prepare you for the château-style elegance of its decoration, nor for the superb cuisine, generally rated as among the best of its kind in Washington. This is French *haute cuisine* with some interesting innovations, such as duck sausages, as well as standard dishes, always prepared with great finesse and subtlety of flavouring. Tables must be reserved in advance.

Madurai
3318 M St. NW ☎333-0997. Map 2E3 🖂 AE CB ⊙ ⊙ VISA

A restaurant that proves how delicious and endlessly varied Indian vegetarian food can be. Portions are generous, and the restaurant is very good value, especially the Sun fixed-price buffet lunch, where you help yourself to as much as you want.

Maison Blanche
1725 F St. NW ☎842-0070. Map 6F6 🖂 ⇌ AE CB ⊙ ⊙ VISA *Closed Sun, some major hols. Metro: Farragut West.*

Where you are seated at this restaurant can be more important than what you eat, as it is a haunt of politicians, lobbyists and White House staff. The decor re-creates old-world elegance, with tapestries and crystal chandeliers. The food is best described as "modern" French, that is, classical with some innovative touches, such as duck with blackcurrant sauce.

Marrakesh
617 New York Ave. NW ☎393-9393. Map 7E8 🖂 *Closed Christmas, Thanksgiving. Metro: Gallery Place.*

A colourful corner of Morocco in the Old Downtown area, where the fixed-price dinner menu is excellent value.

Martin's Tavern
1264 Wisconsin Ave. NW ☎333-7370. Map 2E3 🖂 AE CB ⊙ ⊙ VISA *Closed Christmas.*

A bar-restaurant with a welcoming wood-panelled interior decorated with sculptures and English racing prints from President Madison's collection. Opened in 1933 on the very day prohibition was repealed, Martin's is renowned for its hearty meat dishes. It's an excellent place too for a substantial breakfast.

The Monocle
107 D St. NE ☎546-4488. Map 7F9 🖂 ⇌ AE CB ⊙ ⊙ VISA *Closed Sun. Metro: Union Station.*

A Capitol Hill institution which has been in the hands of the same family since 1960. It comprises both a cosy pub and a quietly

elegant restaurant with a good selection of seafood and standard meat dishes.

New Orleans Emporium
2477 18th St. NW ☎328-3421. Map 3C5 🖂 AE CB ⊙ ⊙ VISA *Closed Christmas, Thanksgiving. Metro: Woodley Park-Zoo, Dupont Circle.*

A small, noisy, friendly place where you quickly get to know your neighbours at the next table whether you like it or not. The food is Cajun, a currently fashionable form of Louisiana Creole cuisine, using a variety of strong spices and herbs. Highlights include blackened redfish, barbecued shrimp and lump crab meat Creole.

O'Brien's Pit Barbecue (1)
7305 Waverly St., Bethesda, Md. ☎(301) 654-9004 🖂 ⊙ *Closed major hols. Metro: Bethesda.*
O'Brien's Pit Barbecue (2)
1314 E Gude Dr., Rockville, Md. ☎(301) 340-8596 🖂 ⊙ *Closed major hols. Metro: Rockville.*
O'Brien's Pit Barbecue (3)
6820 Commerce St., Springfield, Va. ☎(703) 569-7801 🖂 ⊙ VISA *Closed major hols.*

At the three suburban locations of this local institution, barbecued meat is prepared in the authentic pit style, served with delicious spicy sauces and accompanied by potato salad and coleslaw. People come here for the food rather than the decor, which is plastic and modern.

Old Ebbitt Grill
675 15th St. NW ☎347-4801. Map 6F6 🖂 ⇌ AE CB ⊙ ⊙ VISA *Metro: Metro Center.*

Housed in a converted cinema and fitted out with great style and opulence, this establishment has basically the same type of American menu as Clyde's in Georgetown, except that there is no omelet room. Located near the National Theater, National Press Club, Willard Inter-Continental (see *Hotels*) and White House, it is much patronized by the young executive class.

Old Europe
2434 Wisconsin Ave. NW ☎333-7600 🖂 ⇌ AE CB ⊙ ⊙ VISA *Closed Christmas.*

A microcosm of Germany, complete with waitresses in dirndl dresses, paintings of Alpine scenery and cosily Teutonic decoration. Every evening a pianist plays folksy German melodies, and on Fri and Sat evenings downstairs in the "Rathskeller" the lively Alpine duo Brian and Alois sing songs. The food is solid German cuisine. Try the succulent venison or the *Kasseler Rippenspeer* with dumplings and *Sauerkraut*.

Pavilion at the Old Post Office

1100 Pennsylvania Ave. NW. Map 6F7. For ☎ and prices see individual restaurants below. Metro: Federal Triangle.

The multiple facilities here are divided into two basic categories. On the lower level, counters serve a variety of foods of different nationalities, including Indian, Greek and Chinese. The idea is to buy a tray and carry it to a table in the atrium in front of a stage where there is often live entertainment. On the floors above there are a number of restaurants, including: **Richard's and Fettucine's** (☎789–0393 ▥), which is divided into two, with one half serving seafood, the other pasta; **Blossoms** (☎371–1838 ▥), a brasserie-style restaurant with an oyster bar as well; **Fitch, Fox and Brown** (☎289–1100 ▥), serving up-market American fare; and **Hunan** (☎371–2828 ▥), where you can eat good Chinese food at reasonable prices in an attractive dining room.

Le Pavillon

1050 Connecticut Ave. NW ☎833–3846. Map 3E6 ▥ ▭ AE CB ◉ ◉ VISA Closed Sat lunch, Sun, major hols. Metro: Farragut North.

One of the contenders for top spot among Washington restaurants. The cuisine is vaguely *nouvelle*, but chef-owner Yannick Cam prefers to call it "*cuisine personalisée*". His combinations are interesting, for example, breast of duck with a wild honey and vinegar sauce.

Phillips Flagship

900 Water St. SW ☎488–8515. Map 6H7 ▥ ▭ AE CB ◉ ◉ VISA Closed Christmas, Thanksgiving. Metro: L'Enfant Plaza.

Formerly just called The Flagship, this enormous waterfront restaurant opened after redecoration at the end of 1985. The menu covers a wide range of seafood dishes.

Potomac on the River

30th and K St. NW ☎944–4200. Map 2E4 ▥ ▭ AE CB ◉ ◉ VISA Metro: Foggy Bottom.

At the time of writing this monumental restaurant is about to open in the new Washington Harbour complex. Its vast seating capacity includes a terraced outdoor dining area facing the river. The menu will present a broad range of American and foreign cuisine.

Potowmack Landing

George Washington Memorial Parkway, Alexandria, Va. ☎548–0001 ▥ ▭ AE ◉ ◉ VISA Metro: National Airport.

A restaurant to visit as much for the setting as for the food. From the glass-walled dining room there is a fine view across the river. The decoration is appropriately nautical and the fare includes steak and fish cooked over a mesquite grill.

Takesushi

1010 20th St. NW ☎466–3798. Map 3E5 ▥ ▭ AE ◉ ◉ VISA Closed Sat lunch, Sun, hols. Metro: Farragut North.

If you are attracted by the Japanese style of eating, with its multitude of small dishes, exquisitely presented, this popular *sushi* bar is unbeatable. At lunchtime there is a special selection of seafood and other attractive morsels served in a box tray.

Tiberio

1915 K St. NW ☎452–1915. Map 3E5 ▥ ▭ AE CB ◉ ◉ VISA Closed Sat lunch, Sun, major hols. Metro: Farragut West.

High-quality Italian cuisine with a northern regional bias in the K St. expense-account belt. Specialities include pasta and hearty meat dishes, such as sliced tenderloin of beef in a thick wine sauce with a touch of garlic. There is a list of more than 1,000 wines.

Viet Château

2637 Connecticut Ave. NW ☎232–6464. Map 2B4 ▥ ▭ AE CB ◉ ◉ VISA Metro: Woodley Park-Zoo.

Vietnam, like other countries, has its regional styles: Hanoi (subtle), Hue (spicy), Saigon (rich). This restaurant approaches them all in a delicate, innovative way. Caramel shrimp, spring rolls and beef soup anise are some of the many specialities.

Nightlife and the arts

Washington's nightlife and performing arts menu, like its gastronomic one, has greatly increased in variety and scope in recent years. There is something here for everyone, whether they want a classical concert, a cabaret with dinner, or an evening of frenzied dancing and laser lights.

In DC nightspots, live entertainment usually begins between 9 and 9.30pm and continues until 1.30 or 2am during the week and until 2.30 or 3am at weekends. Due to stricter licensing laws in the Virginia and Maryland suburbs, the entertainment in clubs there tends to start at about 8pm and finish at midnight or 1am throughout the entire week.

Many of the clubs will charge a "cover", a "minimum" or both, depending on the calibre and celebrity of the featured entertainers. "Cover" is simply an admission fee. "Minimum" is an additional charge that can be offset by ordering an equivalent value in food or drink.

While after-dark entertainment is found in many parts of the city and suburbs, the greatest concentration is in Georgetown along Wisconsin Ave. and M St. NW. Other havens are found on Connecticut Ave. NW, N and S of Dupont Circle in the region of 19th St. in New Downtown and 7th St. NW in Old Downtown. Certain areas are rich in particular styles of music or entertainment. For example, many bluegrass and country-and-western venues are located near the Interstate 495 section of the Capital Beltway in the Maryland and Virginia suburbs. The red-light district will soon no longer be found along DC's 14th St., which is undergoing extensive redevelopment, and where it re-emerges remains to be seen.

Celebrity-spotting is rather haphazard, except on gala opening nights at the opera, symphony or ballet. Washington's mighty meet publicly at business lunches in exclusive restaurants, then retreat to private dinner parties.

The following is only a selective list, divided into very broad categories. For a full weekly briefing on the current nightlife agenda, read the *Weekend* section of the Fri *Washington Post*, or the free *City Paper*, which appears every Thurs.

Two ticket-buying services are useful and convenient. **Ticketplace** (*12th and F St. NW* ☎*842–5357*) sells cut-price tickets on the day of the performance. **Ticketron** (*1101 17th St. NW* ☎*659–2601*), a computerized agency with several branches, is open Mon–Fri. Both accept major credit cards.

Ballet, contemporary dance and opera

Although for ballet Washington hardly matches London, New York or Moscow, it nevertheless mounts a significant share of high-level performances. The two main venues for ballet are supplemented by smaller stages which offer more modern dance.

The Dance Place
2424 18th St. NW ☎*462–1321. Map 3C6.*
Troupes such as Liz Larman and the Dance Exchange and Toe Jam and Jelly alternate performances with daily technique classes.

John F. Kennedy Center for the Performing Arts
New Hampshire Ave. and Rock Creek Parkway NW ☎*254–3600. Map 5F4. Metro: Foggy Bottom.*
Many distinguished visiting ballet companies such as the New York City Ballet, the American Ballet Theater and the Joffrey Ballet come here to perform anything from *Swan Lake* to works by Balanchine, in the 2,300-seat Opera House. The Kennedy Center is also home to the Washington

Performing Arts Society.

Lisner Auditorium
21st and H St. NW
☎676–6800. Map 3F5. Metro:
Foggy Bottom.
This auditorium in the George
Washington University complex
is, among other things, the home of
the Washington Ballet, a company
with a wide repertoire whose
brilliant Singapore-born
choreographer Choo-San Goh has
won international acclaim.

The New Dance Place
3225 8th St. NE ☎269–1600.
New troupes come here to perform

a variety of dance idioms, many
ethnically rooted.

The Washington Opera
Kennedy Center ☎223–4757.
Map 5F4 AE CD VISA Metro:
Foggy Bottom.
A small but well-regarded
company, The Washington Opera
struggles yearly to raise enough
funds to see itself through a short
four-opera season. It performs
Nov–Feb and productions are
usually sold out. Now that the
Metropolitan Opera of New York
has suspended touring, this is the
only opportunity in town to see
opera.

Cabarets, comedy theatres and supper clubs
Cabaret flourishes in Washington in many restaurants, cafés
and cabaret theatres that also serve food and drink. Here are
some of the places where you can test the proposition that
laughter is good for the digestion.

Artists' Room
Bread Oven Restaurant, 1201
Pennsylvania Ave. NW
☎737–7772. Map 6F7 ≊ AE
CD VISA Open Thurs–Sat
8.30pm–after midnight. Cover for
Capitol Steps performances.
Metro: Federal Triangle, Metro
Center.
Carol Lehan is artistic director for
a polished cabaret show of
highlights from Broadway and old-
time radio, which alternates
weekly with a riotous troupe called
The Capitol Steps.

Café Lafayette
105 N Alfred St., Alexandria, Va.
☎548–0076 ≊ CD Shows
Fri, Sat 9.30pm, 11.30pm.
The long-running character "Mrs
Foggy Bottom", created and
performed by Joan Cushing,
delivers her jaundiced and satiric
view of Washington's influential
elite.

Comedy à la Carte
Loews L'Enfant Plaza Hotel, 480
L'Enfant Plaza E SW ☎646–4400
(weekdays), 667–2701 (eves,
weekends). Map 6H7 ≊ AE CD
VISA Shows Fri and Sat only; Fri
dinner 6.30pm, shows 7.30pm,
8.30pm; Sat dinner 7.30pm,
shows 8.30pm, 10.30pm. Cover.
Metro: L'Enfant Plaza.
A sparkling 90mins of skits on
timely topics, performed by the
Park Place Players under their
producer Zina Greene whose Park
Place Café was the original venue.

Food and drink are served during
the second show only.

Comedy Café
1520 K St. NW ☎638–JOKE.
Map 3E6 ≊ CD VISA Shows Thurs
8.30pm; Fri 8.30pm, 10.30pm; Sat
7.30pm, 9.30pm, 11.30pm.
Cover. Metro: McPherson Square.
National and local comedy acts
give their all on weekends; would-
be comics are Walter Mitty types
who take their turns at "Open
Mike" every Thurs, when all you
can be sure of is bravery.

Garvin's Laugh Inn
Holiday Inn Georgetown, 2101
Wisconsin Ave. NW
☎342–2026. Map 2C2 AE CD
VISA Two shows Fri, Sat 8.30pm,
10.30pm. Cover and minimum.
More local and national comedy
performers.

Marquee Lounge
Omni Shoreham Hotel, 2500
Calvert St. NW ☎232–1122.
Map 2B4 ≊ AE CD VISA Open
8pm–2am. Metro: Woodley Park-
Zoo.
The satirical "Forbidden
Broadway" revue runs at
weekends, with star turns by Ethel
Merman and Carol Channing
lookalikes. On weekdays, dance to
the nostalgic sound of big band
music, enjoy the art deco decor and
step back in time. Clark Gable and
Marilyn Monroe were fond of
staying at this luxurious and
historic old Washington hotel.

Nightlife and the arts

Old Vat Room
Arena Stage, 6th and M St. SW
☎*488–3300. Map 7/8* ≒ ⬤
[VISA] *Shows Thurs, Fri, 8pm; Sat 7pm, 10pm. Metro: L'Enfant Plaza.*
This 180-seat auditorium at Arena Stage is the home of one of the longest-running and most popular shows in Washington: Stephen Wade's one-man *Banjo Dancing*. Wade plays five different types of banjo, performs clog-dancing and tells stories full of folksy humour. Two bars sell drinks and light snacks.

Cafés and bars
A convivial atmosphere and, occasionally, live entertainment can be found in a number of Washington's cafés and bars. The Dubliner also appears under *Nightclubs*.

Brickskeller
1523 22nd St. NW ☎*293–1885. Map 3D5* ⬤ [VISA] *Open 5pm–2am. Metro: Dupont Circle.*
A mecca for drinkers of beer, with over 500 varieties on sale. Similar to a neighbourhood pub in atmosphere and locale.

Clyde's
3236 N Capitol St. NW, Georgetown
☎*333–9180. Map 2E3* ≒ [AE]
[CB] *Closes Mon–Thurs 2am, Fri–Sat 3am, Sun 6pm.*
A stylish Georgetown bar-restaurant. See also *Restaurants*.

The Dubliner
520 N Capitol St. NE
☎*737–3773. Map 7F9* ≒ [AE]
[CB] ⊕ ⬤ [VISA] *Open Sun–Thurs 11.30am–2am, Fri, Sat noon–3am. Metro: Union Station.*
An attractive evocation of a Dublin pub, with two bars, and a restaurant serving hearty pub food. Irish folk groups or other live entertainers perform every eve.

F. Scott's
1232 36th St. NW, Georgetown
☎*965–1789. Map 2E2* ≒ [AE]
⊕ ⬤ [VISA] *Closes Mon–Thurs 2am, Fri, Sat 3am, Sun 10.30pm.*
Named after the famous American novelist, author of the *Lost Generation*, this cosy, mirrored bar, poised on the edge of Georgetown University's campus, is filled with art deco chic. The 18thC townhouse is also home of the 1789 restaurant and the Tombs Bar, all owned and managed by the same organization as Clyde's.

Kramerbooks and Afterwords Café
1517 Connecticut Ave. NW
☎*387–1462. Map 2D5* ≒ [AE]
⬤ *Open Sun–Thurs 8am–1am, Fri, Sat for 24hrs. Metro: Dupont Circle.*
This bookshop-cum-café is one of the most civilized features of the Dupont Circle area. After browsing in the well-stocked front section you can repair to the back for a drink or a meal. Occasionally there is live entertainment.

Pavilion at the Old Post Office
1100 Pennsylvania Ave. Map 6F7. Metro: Federal Triangle.
A complex of cafés and restaurants in one of the most striking buildings in Washington, featuring regular live entertainment. See also *Restaurants*.

Cinema
In spite of the meteoric rise of home video movie rentals, Washington is still very much a cinema city. Its *aficionados* can find anything from first-run Hollywood hits to foreign-language releases, martial-arts flicks to evergreen movie classics.

Many of the theatres have several showings daily, beginning in the afternoon (often at a reduced matinée price), and several theatres have multiple cinemas under one roof. There are one or two of the grand old movie palaces left, but generally the interior decor is disappointingly utilitarian rather than awe-inspiring.

Attractions generally change on Fri; the *Weekend* section of the *Washington Post* carries synopses of those films currently playing, as well as their location. Cash only is accepted by the box office and refreshment counter of cinemas, and smoking is forbidden by District law.

American Film Institute Theater
John F. Kennedy Center, New Hampshire Ave. and Rock Creek Parkway NW ☎785–4600 (recorded). Map **5**F4 ⎓ Metro: Foggy Bottom.
This national non-profit-making organization, formed to preserve the best in American film, regularly presents classic movies in a well-designed auditorium. Nightly showings offer several films sequentially.

American Theater
10th and D St. SW ☎554–2111. Map **6**H7. Metro: L'Enfant Plaza.
Occasionally a venue for experimental theatre, but more usually a showcase of martial arts films.

Bethesda Cinema 'N' Drafthouse
7719 Wisconsin Ave. NW, Bethesda, Md. ☎656–3337. Metro: Bethesda.
Current films at half-price, with the civilizing touch of sitting at café tables, sipping beer or wine and smoking cigarettes. (Also in Arlington.)

Biograph
2819 M St. NW, Georgetown ☎333–2969. Map **2**E4. Metro: Foggy Bottom.
Frequently runs mini film festivals.

Circle Theater
2105 Pennsylvania Ave. NW ☎331–7480. Map **3**E5. Metro: Foggy Bottom.
First-run releases; first showing each day is at reduced prices. There are two screens.

Dupont Circle
1329 Connecticut Ave. NW ☎785–2300. Map **3**D5. Metro: Dupont Circle.
Frequent exclusive releases; reduced prices for first showing on weekdays only.

Georgetown
1351 Wisconsin Ave. NW, Georgetown ☎333–5555. Map **2**E3.
Second-run releases; X-rated midnight movie at weekends.

Inner Circle
2105 Pennsylvania Ave. NW ☎331–7480. Map **3**E5. Metro: Foggy Bottom.
The remaining two screens of the Circle Theater; mainly re-runs.

K-B Cerberus
3040 M St. NW, Georgetown ☎337–1311. Map **2**E4. Metro: Foggy Bottom.
First-run offerings on three screens; Dolby music system.

K-B Fine Arts
1919 M St. NW ☎223–4438. Map **3**E5. Metro: Farragut North.
New releases at reduced prices.

K-B Janus
1660 Connecticut Ave. NW ☎232–8900. Map **3**D5. Metro: Dupont Circle.
Three screens showing first-run releases and classics.

Key
1222 Wisconsin Ave. NW, Georgetown ☎333–5100. Map **2**E3.
Four screens showing major films. Reduced prices for first showings.

Library of Congress
1st St. and Independence Ave. SE ☎287–5677. Map **8**G10. Open Tues, Thurs, Fri at 7.30pm. Metro: Capitol South, Union Station.
The library has an extensive film archive which it draws on for regular showings in the Mary Pickford Theater.

West End Circle
23rd and L St. NW ☎293–3152. Map **3**E5. Metro: Foggy Bottom.
Seven screens showing first-run releases. Reduced prices for first showings.

Classical music
Although the Kennedy Center, with its programme of large orchestral performances, dominates the musical scene in Washington, music can also be heard in many other places in the city and its environs, such as concert halls, churches, museums, galleries, libraries and historic houses. Many of

these concerts are free. Indeed, few cities in the world offer so much free music every day of the week. A selection of venues where a range of music can be heard is listed here. For a full list, consult the sources given on p.112. Another source of information for major performances is the **Washington Performing Arts Society** (*425 13th St. NW, DC 20004* ☎*393–3600*), which will send a schedule on request.

Anderson House (Society of the Cincinnati)
2118 Massachusetts Ave. NW ☎*785–0540. Map 3D5. Metro: Dupont Circle.*
Occasional free concerts in this historic Palladian townhouse full of treasured art and furnishings.

Church of the Epiphany
1317 G St. NW ☎*347–2635. Map 6F7. Metro: Metro Center.*
Free organ recitals every Fri at noon, except during Lent.

Corcoran Gallery
17th St. and New York Ave. NW ☎*638–3211. Map 6F6. Metro: Farragut West.*
Free classical concerts are frequently held here; the weekly programme is available by telephone. The gallery also holds a Contemporary Music Forum at 8pm on the third Mon of every month Sept–May.

DAR Constitution Hall
18th and D St. NW ☎*767–5658. Map 6F6. Metro: Farragut West.*
The hall where for racial reasons the great soprano Marian Anderson was once forbidden to perform is now occasionally the venue for rock bands, as well as other musical groups. The 4,000-seat auditorium has been somewhat eclipsed by the Kennedy Center, but its handsome Beaux-Arts appearance is unique.

John F. Kennedy Center
New Hampshire Ave. and Rock Creek Parkway NW ☎*254–3600. Map 5F4* ≡ *Metro: Foggy Bottom.*
The Concert Hall at the Kennedy Center is the scene of many concerts by distinguished orchestras. The National Symphony Orchestra's concert series runs Oct–Apr.

Library of Congress
1st St. and Independence Ave. SE ☎*287–5000. Map 8G10. Metro: Capitol South.*
The library has a fine collection of musical instruments, including

several Stradivarius violins, which require constant exercise to keep them fit – one reason for the regular concerts held in the library's **Coolidge Auditorium**. Tickets are available on the Mon morning preceding the concert. Performances are Oct–Apr Fri at 8pm, Sat at 5.30pm.

Lisner Auditorium
21st and H St. NW ☎*676–6800. Map 3F5. Metro: Foggy Bottom.*
The 1,500-seat auditorium, part of the George Washington University, is the site of occasional free concerts, as well as the home of the Washington Ballet. Phone for programme information.

National Gallery of Art
6th St. and Constitution Ave. NW ☎*842–6076. Map 7G8. Metro: Gallery Place.*
Free Sun concerts at 7pm.

New York Ave. Presbyterian Church
1313 New York Ave. NW ☎*588–1895. Map 3F7. Metro: Metro Center.*
Free Fri morning concerts are held at this church in Old Downtown.

Phillips Collection
1600 21st St. NW ☎*387–2151. Map 3D5. Metro: Dupont Circle.*
Sun eve concerts at 5pm in this once-private collection of exceptional Impressionist art, now a public museum.

Smithsonian Museums
☎*287–3350.*
The Smithsonian's Division of Performing Arts is responsible for concerts held frequently in various museums. For details consult the Smithsonian bulletin of events in the *Washington Post* on the last Sun of every month (see *Sights* for individual museum addresses).

Washington Cathedral
Wisconsin Ave. and Massachusetts Ave. NW ☎*537–6247. Map 2A2.*
After nearly 80yrs, this magnificent example of Gothic

ecclesiastical architecture is still under construction using the medieval craft of stone carving. The cathedral has regularly scheduled recitals after Sun evensong, and carillon performances on Sat afternoons; other music is frequently scheduled.

Wolf Trap Farm Park
1551 Trap Rd., Vienna, Va.
☎*938–2404.*
This national performing arts

centre is set amid almost 120 acres (49ha) of gently rolling Virginia farmland. The permanent stage and wooden three-sided auditorium of the **Filene Center** are surrounded by grassy terraces where you can picnic while listening to the New York City Opera or Charley Pride. Many Sun afternoon concerts are free. The principal season is May–Sept, though there are occasional performances at the Barns during the winter months.

Lectures and literary events

You can usually find an interesting lecture in Washington on any day of the week, whether the subject is astronomy at the *National Air and Space Museum*, Japanese embroidery at the *Textile Museum* or Renaissance painting at the *National Gallery of Art*. There are also guided walks in parts of the city. For information, consult the *City Paper* or *Smithsonian Calendar* in the *Washington Post*, or phone Smithsonian Resident Associates (☎*357–3030*) for a bulletin of lectures.

For anyone with a literary bent, Washington offers many lectures and readings, by visiting authors and members of the city's own growing band of poets and creative writers. A strong focus of activity is the **Writer's Center** (*7815 Old Georgetown Rd., Bethesda, Md.* ☎*654–8664*), which will give details of their own programme and other events. The *Washington Post* publishes a *Literary Calendar* on the last Sun of each month.

Nightclubs and music venues

The following list is subdivided by type of music, although of course many venues present a variety of styles.

Country-and-western/bluegrass

Birchmere
3901 Mount Vernon Ave., Alexandria, Va. ☎*549–5919*
This rustic outpost in a converted supermarket between Arlington and Alexandria is a real mecca for bluegrass fans (the Seldom Scene play on Thurs eve). Also a venue for folk, Celtic and cowboy artists.

Bronco Billy's
1823 L St. NW ☎*887–5141.*
Map 3E6 AE CB ⓒ ⓓ VISA
Metro: Farragut North.
This is the Wild West with a vengeance – all kinds of cowboy antics accompany the music and dancing. An extensive happy hour buffet and reduced-priced drinks 4.30–8.30pm on weekdays.

Discos

Annie's
3204 M St. NW ☎*333–6767.*
Map 2E3 AE ⓒ VISA
A Georgetown venue with more

than a touch of Texas. Let yourself go on the large dance floor to some of the best country disco music in town. Much more a singles bar than a neighbourhood pub.

The Bank
915 9th St. NW ☎*393–3632.*
Map 7E8 AE ⓒ VISA *Open Wed–Sun. Metro: Gallery Place.*
Three levels of dancing to top-40/ Eurodisco DJ, music videos or jazz. Emerald laser show and a way-out clientele in a refurbished 100yr-old bank.

East Side
1824 Half St. SW ☎*488–1206.*
Map 7I9 ⓒ VISA
Once a gay disco called The Pier which also welcomed straights, this nightspot in the warehouse district has become a determinedly heterosexual dance club with a slick lightshow, sophisticated sound system and refurbished decor.

117

Nightlife and the arts

Numbers
1330 19th St. NW ☎463–8888.
Map 3E5 AE CB VISA *Metro:*
Dupont Circle.

A video DJ and lots of single folk
who don't want to end their day
downtown by spending the night
alone in front of the television.

Folk and ethnic

The Dubliner
520 N Capitol St. NE
☎737–3773. Map 7F9 CB
VISA *Metro: Union Station.*
See Cafés and bars.

Gallagher's Pub
3391 Connecticut Ave. NW
☎686–9189 ☰ AE ◈ CB VISA

The original Gallagher's, where
Irish stew is mixed with Irish folk
ballads and plenty of Irish spirits.
Young musicians, reminiscent of
the folksingers of the 1960s, play
acoustic guitars, small harps and
flutes.

Ireland's Four Provinces
3412 Connecticut Ave. NW
☎244–0860 ☰ CB VISA

Folk balladeers perform every
weekend in this neighbourhood
pub.

Mr Henry's Washington Circle
2134 Pennsylvania Ave NW
☎337–0222. Map 3E5 ☰ AE
◈ CB VISA *Metro: Foggy Bottom.*

A friendly neighbourhood bar/
restaurant that draws its share of
tourists, moviegoers from the
Circle across the street, and
George Washington University
students. Weekday happy hour
4–7pm features reduced-priced
drinks. Live folk music nightly.

Jazz

Blues Alley
Blues Alley off Wisconsin Ave.
NW (⅓ block s of M St.)
☎337–4141, 337–2338 for
group rates. Map 2E3 ☰ AE CB
VISA *Dinner at 6.30pm. Shows*
Sun–Thurs 8.10pm, Fri, Sat
midnight. Cover and minimum.

One of the last regular venues for
top jazz performers – Sarah
Vaughan, Buddy Rich, Mel
Torme, Charlie Byrd and the like.
Restaurant seating with dinner
available; sandwich menu for
midnight shows. Well worth the
substantial cover and minimum
charge.

One Step Down
2517 Pennsylvania Ave. NW
☎331–8863. Map 2E4 AE CB
VISA *Closes Sun–Thurs 2am, Fri,*
Sat 3am. Cover. Metro: Foggy
Bottom.

An authentic jazz bar featuring
some of the East Coast's most
talented musicians. Jam sessions
Sat and Sun afternoons.

Park Place Café
2651 Connecticut Ave. NW
☎667–2701. Map 2B4 ☰ AE
CB VISA *Cover. Metro: Woodley*
Park-Zoo.

Weekends are devoted to jazz in
this chic, cosy restaurant.

Potter's House
1658 Columbia Rd. NW
☎232–5483. Map 3B6 CB VISA

In the Adams-Morgan
neighbourhood, which has a strong
Latin influence and is dotted with
emerging art galleries. You can
enjoy anything here from open
auditions to ethnic performances.

Tucson Cantina
2605 Connecticut Ave. NW
☎462–6410. Map 2B4 ☰ AE
CB VISA *Metro: Woodley Park-Zoo.*

Live entertainment with a country
jazz swing, aimed at a clientele in
their 30s. Frequented by many
regulars as well as tourists from
nearby hotels. Tex-Mex cuisine.

The Wintergarden
Embassy Row Hotel, 2015
Massachusetts Ave. NW
☎265–1600. Map 3D5 AE CB
◈ CB VISA *Metro: Dupont Circle.*

John Eaton, Washington's premier
jazz pianist, performs current hits
plus his own evergreen
arrangements of oldies, in this
small, pricey hotel. Reservations
are strongly advised Thurs–Sat.

Pop/Rock/New Wave

The Bayou
3135 K St. NW, Georgetown
☎333–2897 (recorded concert
listings). Map 2E3 AE CB VISA
Admission by ticket only. Metro:
Foggy Bottom.

Down by the Potomac at the foot
of Georgetown, this is one of the
few showcases for live rock by
well-known performers in the city.

DC Space
443 7th St. NW ☎347–4960.
Map 7F8 CB *Metro:*
Gallery Place, Judiciary Square.
The feel is Greenwich Village in

DC, surrounded by art boutiques and mammoth office construction. Young poets, artists and musicians wait on tables by day and perform at night in front of an audience seated at a bizarre collection of old diner tables and movie theatre seats.

9.30 Club
930 F St. NW ☎*393–0930. Map 6F7* [CC] [VISA] *Metro: Gallery Place.*
Every garage band in the metropolitan area dreams of getting its big break at this showcase for new music.

Incredibly smoky, crowded and loud. Not for the faint-hearted nor the claustrophobic.

The Roxy
1214 18th St. NW ☎*296–9292. Map 3E6* [CC] [VISA] *Cover. Metro: Dupont Circle, Farragut North.*
The management has spent far more on the acoustic system than on the seating arrangements, which are benches at tables and unpadded accountants' stools. Expect anything from reincarnations of folk groups to would-be acid rock stars.

Theatre

Washington has several theatres of national stature, presenting performances by either resident or touring professional companies. Performances are listed in the *Washington Post*.

Arena Stage
6th St. and Maine Ave. SW ☎*488–3300. Map 7I8* [AE] [CC] [VISA] *Metro: L'Enfant Plaza.*
Washington's original theatre-in-the-round and first professional repertory company is nationally regarded for its acting, directing and producing talents. The founders, Zelda and Tom Fichandler, oversee the 800-seat Arena Stage, the 500-seat **Kreeger Theater** and the 180-seat **Old Vat Room**, stocking them with a full range of exciting drama and entertainment each season.

The Folger Shakespeare Theater
201 E Capitol St. SE ☎*546–4000. Map 8G10* [AE] [CC] [VISA] *Metro: Capitol South.*
Not only the Bard, but other classic dramatists such as Molière are presented in an authentic 16thC theatre. The library also has an excellent collection of manuscripts and memorabilia from Shakespeare's time.

Ford's Theatre
511 10th St. NW ☎*426–6924. Map 6F7* [AE] [CC] [VISA] *Metro: Gallery Place, Metro Center.*
Our American Cousin, the play during which President Lincoln was shot, may have been their most notorious production, but these days Ford's Theatre offerings range from current musicals to political satire. Local theatre-goers applaud the new reproduction theatre seats that replaced the uncomfortable "authentic" period pieces.

Kennedy Center Eisenhower Theater
New Hampshire Ave. and Rock Creek Parkway ☎*254–3670. Map 5F4* ⇌ [AE] [CC] [VISA] *Metro: Foggy Bottom.*
Director Peter Sellars has mounted some startling productions of Chekhov classics and modern-day angst in this 1,200-seat jewel box of a theatre. Not the type of drama the local supporters of the arts had in mind for a national arts centre, but the adventurous can't wait for another controversial season.

The National Theater
1321 E St. NW ☎*628–6161. Map 6F7* [CC] [VISA] *Metro: Federal Triangle, Metro Center.*
The *grande dame* of Washington theatres, established in 1835, has recently emerged from a multi-million dollar renovation by renowned theatre designer Oliver Smith. Now owned by the Schubert Organization, the 1,672-seat house shows Broadway musicals and other lavish productions.

The Source Theater
1809 14th St. NW ☎*462–1073. Map 3D7* [CC] [VISA]
Three stages present a range of drama from American classics to experimental plays.

Warner Theater
513 13th St. NW ☎*626–1050. Map 6F7* [AE] [CC] [VISA] *Metro: Federal Triangle, Metro Center.*
Once a vaudeville palace, this 2,000-seat auditorium has been splendidly renovated and now serves as a concert hall.

119

Shopping

Washington provides a myriad of opportunities to buy anything from souvenir T-shirts sold by grizzled street vendors to *haute couture* reluctantly offered by disdainful shop assistants. What Washington does not provide, however, is a major geographic concentration of elegance such as that found in downtown New York, for example.

In this sprawling metropolitan area convenient public transport did not arrive until the late 1970s with the opening of the Metro; the car is, therefore, historically the vehicle of choice for many local residents. The downtown department stores and speciality shops dwindled to a paltry few as more and more local and regional merchants relocated in vast shopping malls in the Maryland and Virginia suburbs, conveniently near an interstate highway off-ramp, inconveniently 10–25 miles (15–37km) from downtown.

However, there are still old pockets of urban retail sophistication, and indications of a revived interest in serving all the shopping needs of Washington's inhabitants as well as the city's frequent visitors. **Hecht's**, a local department store chain, relocated its flagship store in 1985 to Metro Center (the square encompassed by 11th and 12th, F and G St.), an area that is well served by the Metro and is currently undergoing renovation. Other local landmarks include the department stores, **Garfinkel's** and **Woodward and Lothrop**. **Georgetown Park**, a "vertical" mall with Victorian overtones and a recent addition to Georgetown, has begun a major expansion which will include a market garden among its furniture, fashion, confectioners and craftsmen.

Comfortably shod window shoppers will be rewarded in browsing along Connecticut Ave. between K St. and R St. (Metro: Dupont Circle and Farragut North), crowded with boutiques, book stores, galleries, jewellers, shoe shops, record stores, street musicians and restaurants. The avenue provides a delightful day's shopping, and you are sure to find something here you never knew you needed.

Another part of Georgetown that is attractive to shoppers lies about 2½ miles (4km) w of Metro Center. To preserve the community's narrow streets, its citizens decided that they did not want their roads destroyed during the years of Metro construction, so there is no underground stop, but buses run frequently to and from this district; the cab ride is only one zone from downtown, so the fare is modest. Wisconsin Ave. and M St. and its offshoots offer contemporary and antique furnishings, rare books and prints, fine fabrics, jewellery, and clothes for all the family from running gear to evening wear. Restaurants are varied both in character and price.

Fortunately the citizens of upper Wisconsin Ave. in Chevy Chase did not veto a Metro stop at Friendship Heights (5400 Wisconsin Ave. NW). Exit here and you will find yourself in a shopper's paradise that includes **Mazza Gallerie** to the E and **Saks-Jandel** and **Saks Fifth Avenue** to the w. Here decidedly up-market local retailers have a long-established, luxury-conscious clientele that has attracted like-minded retailers from New York, Texas and California. Browsers are welcome, and there are always surprisingly inexpensive, yet elegant, small items at the most exclusive boutiques.

Tyson's Corner Mall, near McLean, Va., and **White Flint Mall**, near Bethesda, Md., are the nearest large shopping

centres, each with close to 200 shops, as well as cinemas, cafés and amusement arcades, under one roof. The malls are served by Metrobus routes and White Flint has an underground stop.

At the other end of the scale are the cut-price stores which sell manufacturers' seconds. Beware the "suggested retail price" which is listed above "our sales price". It may bear no relation to the real economic world. You usually get what you pay for; the question is, how much is it worth? If you loathe paying retail for anything, visit **Potomac Mills Mall**, a collection of shops that sells well-priced merchandise ranging from family clothing to European furniture. The mall is 30 miles (45km) s of Washington on I-95, and can only be reached by car.

Each of the many museums in Washington has a gift shop, where reasonably priced mementoes and some astonishing bargains may be found, and where shoppers gain the satisfaction of knowing they have contributed something to the upkeep and expansion of the museum.

Antiques
While there are no bargains in Washington's antique shops, you can find a host of beautiful and rare examples of decorative furniture, silver, jewellery, art and fabrics from Amish quilts to Chinese silks.

The Black Cocker
911 N Quincy St, Arlington, Va. ☎527-9673 ⬤ 🆅🆂🅰
Conveniently near a Metro stop, this shop specializes in cut glass, Staffordshire china and silver.

Peter Mack Brown
1525 Wisconsin Ave. NW, Georgetown ☎338-8484. Map **2D3** 🅰🅴
Elegant displays of 18thC French, English and American furniture.

GKS Bush Company
2828 Pennsylvania Ave. NW ☎965-0653. Map **2E4**.
The place for original American antiques.

Marston Luce
1314 21st St. NW ☎775-0460. Map **3D5** 🅰🅴
A selection of 19thC painted furniture, folk art and quilts, which are enjoying increasing popularity and are priced accordingly.

Nelson-French Antiques Inc.
1629 Wisconsin Ave. NW, Georgetown ☎342-1643. Map **2D3** 🅰🅴 ⬤ 🆅🆂🅰
18thC antiques well-loved by interior designers and Washington hostesses.

Tiny Jewel Box
1143 Connecticut Ave. NW ☎393-2747. Map **3E6** 🅰🅴 ⬤ 🆅🆂🅰
This shop specializes in diamonds, other precious gems and antique jewellery.

Beauty salons and hairdressers
The leisurely day at the hairdresser is all but forgotten in large American cities. The customers, both male and female, are hard at work in downtown offices, dashing in after work or in their lunch hour for a quick cut and blow dry at a convenient "no appointment necessary" unisex salon. But bastions of luxury still exist, where, for a price, women and men can enjoy a "day of beauty", including a skin treatment and massage. Some hotels and major department stores also have hairdressers on the premises.

Shopping

Walk-in shops

Daniel's   1831 M St. NW ☎296–4856. Map **3E5** 🏧 🆅🆂🅰 Open Sun.

The Hair Loft   1715 I St. NW ☎298–7228. Map **3E6**.

Raphael of Montreal Coiffures   1821½ L St. NW ☎785–0474. Map **3E5**.

Shears   822 15th St. NW (at I St.) ☎842–4070. Map **3E6**.

Luxury salons

Elizabeth Arden Salon   5225 Wisconsin Ave. NW ☎362–9890 🄰🄴 🏧 🆅🆂🅰

Robin Weir and Co.   2134 P St. NW ☎861–0444. Map **3D5** 🄰🄴 🏧 🆅🆂🅰 Hairdressers to the First Lady, Nancy Reagan.

Suissa Hair & Skin Salon   3068 M St. NW, Georgetown ☎833–1066. Map **2E4** 🄰🄴 🏧 🆅🆂🅰

Watergate Salon   2532 Virginia Ave. NW ☎333–3488. Map **2F4**.

Books and records

Washington is blessed with a huge selection of book and record shops catering to any taste from the classical to the avant-garde.

Booked Up
1209 31st St. NW, Georgetown
☎965–3244. Map **2E3**.

A store devoted to first editions, fine, rare and unusual books.

Crown Books
2020 K St. NW (and other branches) ☎659–2030. Map **3E5** 🄰🄴 🏧

This local chain sells every book at a discount. Hardcover and paperback bestsellers, popular consumer and specialized magazines sell for 15–40 percent off the retail price.

B. Dalton
Mazza Gallerie, Wisconsin Ave. and Military Rd. ☎362–7055 🄰🄴 🏧 🆅🆂🅰

This nationwide chain carries national and local bestsellers.

Globe Book Shop
1700 Pennsylvania Ave. NW
☎393–1490. Map **3F6** 🄰🄴 🏧 🆅🆂🅰

Foreign language publications and recordings are available here.

Kramer Books and Afterwords
1347 Connecticut Ave. NW
☎387–1400. Map **3D5** 🄰🄴 🏧 🆅🆂🅰

A Dupont Circle institution, this cosy bookshop-café welcomes browsers and bibliophiles alike. The café serves excellent soups, salads and desserts, plus beer and wine, and keeps late hours.

Olsson's
1239 Wisconsin Ave. NW, Georgetown (and other branches) ☎338–6712. Map **2E3** 🄰🄴 🏧 🆅🆂🅰

An extensive inventory of books, from bestsellers to scholarly tomes, as well as a treasure-trove of classic and jazz recordings and tapes.

Penguin Feather Records and Tapes
3225 M St. NW, Georgetown (and other branches)
☎965–7172. Map **2E3** 🄰🄴 🏧 🆅🆂🅰

Funk, punk, reggae or retro-rock in a trendy setting.

Second Story Books
2000 P St. NW ☎659–8884. Map **3D5** 🄰🄴 🏧 🆅🆂🅰

If it's old, out of print, custom-bound or a small press publication, this is where to find it.

Tower Records
21st and I St. ☎331–2400. Map **3E5** 🄰🄴 🏧 🆅🆂🅰

A gigantic store with a wide choice of records, cassettes and compact discs in every category.

Waldenbooks
Georgetown Park, 33rd and M St. NW ☎333–8033. Map **2E3** 🄰🄴 🏧 🆅🆂🅰

Another bestseller chain.

Cameras and photographic equipment

A wide range of services and supplies, from inexpensive point-and-shoot cameras to de luxe German and Japanese equipment, is available at competitive prices. Some shops offer repair services and have staff who speak other languages.

Baker's Photo Supply
4433 Wisconsin Ave. NW ☎362–9100 AE ⬤ VISA

Hasselblad, Nikon, Graflex, Beseler and other less expensive equipment are on sale. There is also a repair service.

Congressional Photo
209 Pennsylvania Ave. SE (2nd floor) ☎543–3206. Map *8G10* AE ⬤ VISA

The professionals' choice for custom finishing. A full camera repair service and budget processing are available.

Embassy Camera Center
1709 Connecticut Ave. NW ☎483–7448. Map *3C5* ⬤ VISA

Assistants are fluent in Spanish, French and German and the range includes American and Japanese cameras, accessories and film.

Potomac Photo
1819 H St. NW ☎822–9001. Map *3F5* AE ⬤ VISA

Provides same-day slide service, and sells national brand cameras and accessories.

Chemists

The sensible traveller always carries a signed prescription form for any necessary medication. Luggage can be lost, medicines can be spilled or spoiled, and a trip to a private physician or clinic can cost precious time and money just for a replacement prescription. Chemist shops carry a wide variety of over-the-counter remedies, but some of those customarily available overseas may only be obtained by prescription. American chemists also stock perfume, cosmetics, greetings cards, film, paperback novels and detergents.

Dart Drugs
1275 K St. NW ☎682–2155. Map *6E7*.

A major local chain, open daily.

Drug Fair
1815 Connecticut Ave. NW ☎332–1718. Map *3D5* ⬤ VISA

One of several Drug Fair stores in the downtown area, open daily.

Foggy Bottom Apothecary
2421 Pennsylvania Ave. NW ☎296–9314. Map *2E4* AE ⬤ VISA

Located in a hospital area, this chemist is good for unusual prescriptions.

Morgan Pharmacy
3001 P St. NW, Georgetown ☎337–4100. Map *2D4* AE ⬤ VISA

Free delivery, open every Sun till noon.

People's Drug Store
14th St. and Thomas Circle NW ☎628–0720. Map *3E7* ⬤ VISA

The only 24-hr pharmacy downtown.

Clothes and shoes for men

Like much else in Washington, men's clothes have become more cosmopolitan and adventurous in recent years, and the shops have kept pace. The following list covers a wide range of clothing from traditional three-piece suits to jeans and safari jackets.

Arthur A. Adler Inc.
1101 Connecticut Ave. NW ☎628–0131. Map *3E6* AE ⬤ VISA

Tailored menswear geared to the tastes of Washington executives.

Athlete's Foot
3222 M St. NW, Georgetown ☎965–7262. Map *2E3* AE ⬤ VISA

Exercise gear and footwear for almost every sport.

Shopping

Banana Republic
14th and F St. NW ☎*783–1400.
Map 6F7* AE ⊙ ⊙ VISA

Safari styling in casual shirts,
jackets, sweaters, trousers and
accessories. (There is another
branch in Georgetown.)

Britches of Georgetown
1219 Connecticut Ave. NW
☎*347–8994. Map 3E6* AE CB
⊙ ⊙ VISA

The downtown branch offers trim
tailoring in tuxedos, tweed jackets,
traditional suits and casual wear, as
well as shoes and accessories.
(There is another branch in
Georgetown.)

The Gap
1217 Connecticut Ave. NW
☎*638–4603. Map 3E6* AE CB
⊙ ⊙ VISA

Blue, white, grey and striped jeans,
sweaters and sports shirts can be
bought here.

Georgetown University Shop
1248 36th St. NW, Georgetown
☎*337–8100. Map 2E2* AE ⊙
⊙ VISA

On the edge of campus, this shop
features Ivy League styles
designed for the student or the
still-slim graduate.

Raleigh's
*Mazza Galleries, Wisconsin Ave.
and Military Rd.* ☎*785–7011* AE
⊙ VISA

A long-standing local source for
correct menswear, now featuring
European designers as well. Shoes
and accessories are also available
here.

Watergate Men's Wear
2520 Virginia Ave. NW
☎*333–0299. Map 2F4* AE ⊙
VISA

A good range of expensive
imported menswear, knitwear and
executive gifts.

Clothes and shoes for women

Geoffrey Beene, Bill Blass, Liz Claiborne, Perry Ellis,
Alexander Julian, Donna Karan, Ann Klein, Calvin Klein and
Ralph Lauren are the top names in American design. Their
clothes, from leisure to luxurious evening wear, are
characterized by simple, unfussy lines and natural fabrics.
They are stylish, yet at the same time practical and
comfortable. At the shops listed below will be found a wide
selection of daywear, evening wear, sportswear, shoes and
accessories by these and other American designers, as well as
by European and Oriental designers. Many of the men's stores
also feature a large selection of women's clothing.

Alcott and Andres
2000 Pennsylvania Ave. NW
☎*822–9476. Map 3E5* AE ⊙
VISA

Office and leisure wear for the
contemporary executive woman.

Jos. A. Bank Clothier
1118 19th St. NW ☎*466–2282.
Map 3E5* AE ⊙ VISA

Traditional suits and accessories
for successful women executives.

Commander Salamander
*1420 Wisconsin Ave. NW,
Georgetown* ☎*333–9599. Map
2D3* AE ⊙ VISA

Funky clothes and accessories in a
way-out setting

Claire Dratch
1224 Connecticut Ave. NW
☎*466–6500. Map 3E6* AE ⊙
VISA

A well-established local designer
boutique, selling sophisticated

clothing. (There are also branches
downtown and in Bethesda, Md.)

Guy Laroche Boutique/Saint
Laurent Rive Gauche
600 New Hampshire Ave. NW
☎*333–3702. Map 2F4* AE ⊙
VISA

Ready-to-wear clothes by the
famous Parisian designers.

Saks-Jandel
*5514 Wisconsin Ave. NW, Chevy
Chase* ☎*652–2250* AE ⊙ ⊙
VISA

Elegant afternoon and evening
wear.

Ann Taylor
*Mazza Galleries, Wisconsin Ave.
and Military Rd.* ☎*244–1940* AE
⊙ VISA

Chic clothing and footwear with
the American look. (There is
another branch in Georgetown
Park.)

Department stores

Recently many new department stores have opened in the burgeoning shopping centres of Washington's suburbs. But if you prefer to shop in the city, the three stalwarts of Old Downtown – Garfinkel's, Hecht's and Woodward and Lothrop – are enjoying a new lease of life as the area revives.

Bloomingdale's
Tyson's Corner Mall, McLean, Va.
☎*556–4600* AE CB
Outpost of the famous New York-based chain featuring trendsetting fashions for men, women and children, shoes and accessories, household goods and soft furnishings.

Garfinkel's
14th and F St. NW ☎*628–7730.*
Map 6F7 AE ◉ ⬡ VISA
Long-standing local retailer with a carefully selected stock of fine clothing, jewellery, tableware and linen.

Hecht's
Metro Center, 12th and G St. NW
☎*628–6661. Map* 6F7 AE ◉ VISA
Anything from mattresses to video cameras, children's socks to bridal gowns can be bought in this store, which has become a local institution. Well located in the centre of Washington.

Lord and Taylor's
5255 Western Ave. NW
☎*362–9600* AE
Another New York shopping giant transplanted to Washington. (There is another branch at Seven Corners.)

Neiman-Marcus
Mazza Gallerie, 5300 Wisconsin Ave. NW ☎*966–9700.*
The great Texas institution whose his-and-hers Christmas gifts are exercises in conspicuous consumption. Remarkably good bargains at their "Last Call" half-yearly sales.

J. C. Penney's
Springfield Mall, Springfield, Va.
☎*971–8850* AE ◉ VISA
The century-old king of mail order companies now transformed into a store selling well-designed and keenly priced family clothing and the Rolls Royce-on-tea-cups that drew Princess Diana to this shop on her first American visit.

Saks Fifth Avenue
5555 Wisconsin Ave. NW, Chevy Chase ☎*657–9000* AE CB ◉
The Washington branch of one of the loftiest names in New York retailing.

Woodward and Lothrop
11th and F St. NW ☎*347–5300.*
Map 6F7 AE ◉ VISA
Much of the same merchandise as that found at Hecht's, though there are some slightly more expensive lines as well.

Food

Only in the last ten years has Washington developed a cosmopolitan restaurant presence, so it is no surprise that there are very few suppliers to the gastronome at home. But those that do exist can hold their own with other cities for variety, quality and price.

Cannon's Seafood
1065 31st St. NW, Georgetown
☎*337–8366. Map* 2E3.
The finest fresh seafood at prices to match. It is often crowded at lunchtime with Georgetown shoppers.

Eastern Market
400 E Capitol St. SE
☎*543–2444. Map* 8G10.
This farmers' market is so famous that there is a Metro stop named after it. Fresh turkeys, dewy vegetables, home-cured sausages, local colour, bustle and bargains are all to be found here.

Neam's Market
3217 P St. NW, Georgetown
☎*338–4694. Map* 2D3.
Splash out here on such luxuries as white asparagus, caviar, Columbian coffee and French wines. A boy will carry your bags to your car for you.

Sutton Place Gourmet
3201 New Mexico Ave. NW
☎*363–5800* AE ◉ VISA
Stargaze on noted politicians and TV personalities as you shop for mouthwatering delicacies, including a fine choice of wines and cheeses.

Shopping

Jewellery

Luxurious, close-carpeted boutiques, brightly lit middle-price shops and bustling department stores feature a variety of precious and semi-precious jewellery from heirloom to souvenir quality, and prices range accordingly.

Bailey, Banks and Biddle   Tyson's Corner Mall, McLean, Va. ☎883–1400 AE CD VISA

W. Bell   1901 L St. NW ☎881–2000. Map 3E5 CD VISA

J. E. Caldwell Co.   1140 Connecticut Ave. NW ☎466–6780. Map 3E6 AE CD VISA

Melart Jewelers   National Pl. NW ☎737–8772. Map 6F7 AE CB CD CD VISA

Les Must de Cartier   1127 Connecticut Ave. NW ☎887–5888. Map 3E6 AE CD CD VISA

Pampillonia Jewelers   Mazza Gallerie, Wisconsin Ave. and Military Rd. ☎363–6305 AE CD VISA

Sports and camping

Name the sport and there will be a Washington merchant who can supply the equipment or clothing. Favourite weekend activities for Washingtonians are hiking, canoeing and camping, so sports shops carry everything from tent stakes to freeze-dried meals, trail boots and bed rolls.

Eddie Bauer   1800 M St. NW ☎331–8009. Map 3E6 AE CB CD CD VISA

Herman's World of Sporting Goods   800 E St. NW ☎638–6434. Map 7F8 AE CB CD CD VISA

Hudson Trail Outfitters   National Pl. ☎393–1244. Map 6F7 CD VISA

Irving's Sports Shops   1203 Connecticut Ave. NW ☎466–8830. Map 3E6 AE CD VISA

Moss Brown and Co.   1522 Wisconsin Ave. NW, Georgetown ☎965–4350. Map 2D3 AE CD VISA

Toys

Beatrix Potter books, snakes and ladder games and toys remembered from the nursery vie with the latest movable plastic cartoon monsters and video games on the shelves of the modern metropolitan toy shop. Some shops specialize in handcrafted or educational toys.

Georgetown Zoo   3222 M St. NW, Georgetown Park ☎338–4182. Map 2E3 AE CD VISA

Red Balloon   1073 Wisconsin Ave. NW, Georgetown ☎965–1200. Map 2E3 CD VISA

FAO Schwarz   Mazza Gallerie, Wisconsin Ave. and Military Rd. ☎363–8455 AE CB CD VISA

Toys "Я" Us   8449 Leesburg Pike, Tyson's Corner, Va. ☎893–2223 AE CD VISA

Wine and spirits

The following list of off-licences are among the best in the city in terms of choice and value.

Calvert Woodley Liquors   4339 Connecticut Ave. NW ☎966–4400. Map 2B4 CD VISA

Colonial Liquor Shoppe   1800 I St. NW ☎338–4500. Map 3E6 CD VISA

Mayflower Wines and Spirits   2115 M St. NW ☎463–7950. Map 3E5 CD VISA

Wagner's Liquor Shop   1717 Wisconsin Ave. NW, Georgetown ☎232–1900. Map 2D3.

Biographies

It would be an impossible task to list here all the famous people, politicians included, associated with Washington. The following is a selection of those who, either by birthright, noteworthy deed or influence, have contributed to the history of the city.

Adams, Henry (1838–1918)
Historian and philosopher. Grandson of President John Quincy Adams and son of the diplomat Charles Francis Adams. Although his best-known book is his autobiographical work *The Education of Henry Adams*, he also wrote a monumental *History of the United States*. He settled in Washington in 1877 in a house on the site of the present Hay-Adams Hotel.

Barry, Marion S., Jr (born 1936)
Mayor of Washington since 1979, the second holder of the office. Barry is an ebullient character who was formerly an activist for black civil rights.

Bradlee, Benjamin (born 1921)
Executive Editor of the *Washington Post*. He steered the *Post* through the period of the Watergate investigation (1972–4), conducted by the journalists Carl Bernstein and Bob Woodward.

Buchwald, Art (born 1925)
Syndicated newspaper columnist living in Washington who writes with mischievous wit and humour about life and politics in the capital. His column appears in about 500 newspapers in many countries, and several collections of his articles have been published as books.

Douglass, Frederick (c.1817–95)
Leading pioneer of black liberation. His real name was Frederick Augustus Washington Bailey, but he assumed the alias Douglass after escaping from the slavery into which he was born. He dedicated his life to writing, lecturing and campaigning for the cause of black freedom and equality. See *Frederick Douglass House*.

Ellicott, Andrew (1754–1820)
Surveyor who helped L'Enfant lay out the area that is now DC. He took over after L'Enfant's dismissal, and the map of the territory published in 1793 was in his name, although it was mostly L'Enfant's work.

Ellington, Duke (1899–1974)
Seminal jazz composer, band leader and pianist, born in Washington. His real name was Edward Kennedy Ellington.

L'Enfant, Pierre Charles (1754–1825)
The brilliant, temperamental French engineer and architect who, more than anyone else, is responsible for the shape of Washington today. Having come to America to fight in George Washington's army against the British, he was commissioned in 1791 to prepare a plan for the federal capital. The following year he was dismissed after quarrelling with the Commissioners of the District of Columbia. He spent the latter part of his life fighting for greater compensation and died in poverty. Posthumous recognition came in 1909 when his remains were moved to *Arlington National Cemetery* and a monument to him was erected there.

Graham, Katharine ((born 1917)
Chairman and Chief Executive Officer of the Washington Post Company. Her son, Donald E. Graham, is publisher of the

Biographies

Washington Post newspaper. See also Benjamin Bradlee above.

Hayes, Helen *(born 1900)*
Actress, born in Washington. Helen Hayes became a star after appearing in James Barrie's play *Dear Brutus* in 1918. Probably her most famous role was as Queen Victoria in the play *Victoria Regina* (1935).

Hoban, James *(1762–1831)*
Irish-born architect who designed and supervised the construction of the *White House*.

Hooker, General Joseph *(1814–79)*
A name that has achieved a dubious immortality. Hooker was a Union general during the Civil War who tried to restrict prostitution in the capital by confining camp followers (nearly 4,000) to one part of the city. Hence the term "hooker".

Hoover, J. Edgar *(1895–1972)*
Director of the Federal Bureau of Investigation for 48yrs from 1924 until his death. Born in Washington and a graduate of George Washington University Law School, Hoover built the FBI into the powerful organization that it is today. A tough, combative figure, he was both widely respected and much disliked. For 20yrs he lunched regularly at the Mayflower Hotel, and after his death his customary table was draped in red, white and blue for a week, in mourning.

Jolson, Al *(1886–1950)*
Popular singer and actor. Originally named Asa Yoelson, he was born in Russia and raised in SW Washington where his father was a rabbi.

Latrobe, Benjamin Henry *(1764–1820)*
English-born architect. He came to America in 1796 and designed a number of buildings in Washington including *Decatur House* and parts of the *Capitol* and *White House*.

Pope, John Russell *(1874–1937)*
Architect whose serene neoclassical buildings are a major feature of Washington. They include the *National Archives*, the West Building of the *National Gallery of Art*, the *Jefferson Memorial* and *House of the Temple*.

Shepherd, Alexander Robey *("Boss") (1835–1902)*
Shepherd was to Washington what Baron Haussmann was to Paris. He became Head of the Board of Public Works in 1871 and Governor of the District of Columbia in 1873. Under his regime a vast programme of public works was undertaken which bankrupted Washington but for the first time gave it adequate pavements, water mains, sewerage, lighting and other amenities.

Smith, Captain John *(1580–1631)*
English adventurer who, in 1608, accompanied by "7 souldiers and 7 gentlemen" sailed up the Potomac. Where Washington now stands he discovered a settlement of Algonquin Indians. Charmed with the place, he encouraged colonists to settle here.

Smithson, James *(1765–1829)*
Although Smithson never came to Washington the city would have been a very different place without him. He was a British scientist whose bequest of $500,000 to the USA, resulted in the creation of the Smithsonian Institution.

Sousa, John Philip *(1854–1932)*
Bandmaster and composer. Born in a house on Capitol Hill, Sousa was for many years leader of the US Marine Band before forming his own. Composer of many styles of music, he is most famous for his rousing marches which include *Liberty Bell*, *Semper Fidelis*, *The Stars and Stripes Forever* and the

Washington Post march which is played every time a band passes the newspaper's offices. He also wrote five novels and an autobiography, *Marching Along*. Of Polish parentage, his real name was So, to which he later added the letters USA.

Thornton, William *(1759–1828)*

Scottish-born doctor, architect and inventor. He emigrated to the USA in 1787, and won the competition for the design of the Capitol in 1792 and supervised the construction of the building until he was replaced by Latrobe.

Washington, George *(1732–99)*

First President of the United States, he chose the location of the city named in his honour. With great practicality he selected a site far enough inland to be safe from surprise naval attack yet at the same time accessible to ocean-going vessels. His own home was nearby at Mount Vernon (see *Excursions*).

Washington, Walter E. *(born 1915)*

What more appropriate name for the man who became the first mayor of Washington in 1975? A black and a lawyer by profession, he held the office for four years.

Chronology of US presidents

Name	Party	Years in office
George Washington	None	1789–97
John Adams	Federalist	1797–1801
Thomas Jefferson	Democratic-Republican	1801–9
James Madison	Democratic-Republican	1809–17
James Monroe	Democratic-Republican	1817–25
John Quincy Adams	Democratic-Republican	1825–9
Andrew Jackson	Democrat	1829–37
Martin Van Buren	Democrat	1837–41
William H. Harrison	Whig	1841
John Tyler	Whig	1841–5
James K. Polk	Democrat	1845–9
Zachary Taylor	Whig	1849–50
Millard Fillmore	Whig	1850–3
Franklin Pierce	Democrat	1853–7
James Buchanan	Democrat	1857–61
Abraham Lincoln	Republican	1861–5
Andrew Johnson	National Union	1865–9
Ulysses S. Grant	Republican	1869–77
Rutherford B. Hayes	Republican	1877–81
James A. Garfield	Republican	1881
Chester A. Arthur	Republican	1881–5
Grover Cleveland	Democrat	1885–9
Benjamin Harrison	Republican	1889–93
Grover Cleveland	Democrat	1893–7
William McKinley	Republican	1897–1901
Theodore Roosevelt	Republican	1901–9
William H. Taft	Republican	1909–13
Woodrow Wilson	Democrat	1913–21
Warren G. Harding	Republican	1921–3
Calvin Coolidge	Republican	1923–9
Herbert C. Hoover	Republican	1929–33
Franklin D. Roosevelt	Democrat	1933–45
Harry S. Truman	Democrat	1945–53
Dwight D. Eisenhower	Republican	1953–61
John F. Kennedy	Democrat	1961–3
Lyndon B. Johnson	Democrat	1963–9
Richard M. Nixon	Republican	1969–74
Gerald R. Ford	Republican	1974–7
James E. Carter, Jr	Democrat	1977–81
Ronald W. Reagan	Republican	1981–

Washington for children

A city whose *raison d'être* is government might be expected to provide little opportunity for children's pleasures. On the contrary, Washington offers a positive *embarras de richesses*, especially for children with curiosity and stamina; in addition to the many museums, monuments and sights that are of interest to both children and parents alike, there are also numerous museums designed specifically for children, and a host of parks with playgrounds. And, if you want a change from urban activities, the nearest beach is only an hour's drive away (see *Swimming* in *Sports and activities*).

An invaluable book for parents visiting or living in Washington is *Going Places with Children in Washington*, edited by Salley Shannon and Ruth Ann Phang, available from selected book shops or from the publisher, Green Acres School (*11701 Danville Dr., Rockville, Md. 20852* ☎*881–4100*). Another useful source of information is *Kiosk*, a free monthly bulletin of events; to be added to their mailing list, write to the Public Affairs Office (*National Capital Parks, 1100 Ohio Dr. SW, Washington DC 20242* ☎*426–6700*). Coming events for children are listed in the "Where and when" section of the *Washingtonian* monthly magazine and in the "Carousel" section of the *Washington Post*'s *Weekend* supplement, published Fri. The *Post* publishes a *Calendar of the Smithsonian* towards the end of each month. Recorded telephone messages also provide information on a range of services (see *Telephone services* in *Basic information*) such as the **DC Recreation Department** (☎*673–7660*) and "**dial-a-park**" (☎*426–6975*).

Parks

Whether your kids want to play on a swing, picnic, watch birds or go roller-skating, there is bound to be a park in Washington or its environs to satisfy these needs. The following organizations will direct you to a suitable park in their area.

Alexandria Department of Recreation and Parks ☎*838–4343*

Arlington County Recreation Division ☎*558–2700*

Fairfax County Park Authority ☎*941–5000*

Maryland-National Capital Park and Planning Commission ☎*565–7417*

National Park Service ☎*426–6700*

Prince Georges County Parks and Recreation ☎*699–2407*

Most parks allow picnicking but no alcoholic beverages, and many have special picnic areas. Normally there are no restrictions about walking on the grass. Individual parks are too numerous to be listed, but the following are a few of the most attractive for children. *Rock Creek Park* (☎*426–6833*), which runs in a long strip through NW DC, has miles of leafy paths to explore, picnic places, playgrounds, a Nature Center and a Planetarium. Battery Kemble and Fort Stevens Parks fall under its jurisdiction. **Battery Kemble Park** (*Chain Bridge Rd. NW, near American University* ☎*426–6833*) is ideal for kite-flying and for tobogganing in snowy weather. **Fort Stevens Park** (*Piney Branch Rd. and Quakerbos St. NW* ☎*426–6833*) has restored earthworks and gun emplacements from a Civil War fort. The Tidal Basin in West *Potomac Park* has pedal boats to rent (see *Boating* in *Sports and activities*).

Outside DC the attractions are richer. **Cabin John Regional Park** (*Rockville, Md.* ☎299–4555) has train rides, a seasonal ice rink, a miniature zoo and a special playground for children under six. **Glen Echo Park** (*Bethesda, Md.* ☎492–6282) has theatre classes for children aged five and older, and free art workshops on Sun afternoons in spring and summer. **Wheaton Regional Park** (*Wheaton, Md.* ☎622–0056) has train rides, a collection of animals called "Old MacDonald's Farm" and miles of wild country to explore.

Zoos, nature places and farms

In addition to the *National Zoological Park* with its 165 acres (66ha) and superb cross-section of the animal kingdom, there are many other places where children can delight in animals, nature and wildlife. At **Columbia Children's Zoo** (*Columbia, Md.* ☎ *(301) 997–7535*) the kids are allowed to stroke and feed all the animals. **The Audubon Naturalist Society** (*Chevy Chase, Md.* ☎652–5964) has a nature trail and special programmes for children aged four and older. **Roaches Run Waterfowl Sanctuary**, on the NW side of Washington Airport, has a lake with a variety of ducks and other waterfowl. **Turkey Run Farm** (*McLean, Va.* ☎557–1356) is a re-creation of a Colonial farm, which includes a family in period costume carrying out the farm chores. Other working farms that can be visited are **Frying Pan Farm Park** (*Herndon, Va.* ☎437–9101), **National Colonial Farm** (*Accokeek, Md.* ☎283–2113), and **Oxon Hill Farm** (*Oxon Hill, Md.* ☎839–1177). Youngsters also enjoy **Carroll County Farm Museum** (*Westminster, Md.* ☎ *(301) 848–7775*) and **Pet Farm Park** (*Vienna, Va.* ☎759–3636); the latter allow petting and feeding of their animals.

Nature centres and trails are always popular with children; the following are located in the Washington area.

Brookside Nature Center   *Wheaton Regional Park, Md.* ☎946–9071

Clearwater Nature Center   *Cosca Regional Park, Thrift Rd., Clinton, Md.* ☎297–4575

Gulf Branch Nature Center   *3608 N Military Rd., Arlington, Va.* ☎558–2340

Hidden Oaks Nature Center   *4030 Hummer Rd., Annandale, Va.* ☎941–1065

Hidden Pond Nature Center   *8511 Greeley Blvd., W Springfield, Va.* ☎451–9588

Lathrop E. Smith Meadowside Nature Center   *5100 Meadowside Lane, Rockville, Md.* ☎924–4141

Long Branch Nature Center   *625 S Carlin Springs Rd., Arlington, Va.* ☎845–7640

Riverbend Nature Center   *8814 Jeffrey Rd., Great Falls, Va.* ☎759–3211

Rock Creek Nature Center   *Rock Creek Park, Military and Glover Rd. NW* ☎426–6829

Don't forget the underwater world: there is a small but interesting *National Aquarium* in the basement of the Department of Commerce building.

Amusement parks

This form of attraction, which America has developed to an advanced degree, is a great hit with children. An old favourite is **Glen Echo Park Carousel** (*MacArthur Blvd. and Goldsboro Rd., Glen Echo, Md.* ☎ *492–6282*). **Kings Dominion** (☎ *(804) 876–5000; closed winter*), located 75 miles (120km) S of DC just N of Richmond, Va., on route 1-95, is a spectacular amusement park, complete with rollercoaster, 33-storey Eiffel Tower, steam train, safari park, fantasy rides, shops, restaurants and all kinds of live entertainment. It is possible to include nearby Colonial Williamsburg on the same trip (see *Excursions*). Closer to DC and just outside Baltimore is **Enchanted Forest** (☎ *(301) 465–0707; closed winter*), which includes re-creations of fairy tales and children's fiction, as well as delightful grounds in which to wander, play or picnic.

Museums and workshops

The only museum in Washington specifically for the young is the *Capital Children's Museum*, an exciting "hands-on" museum where kids can learn about the world around them through a variety of workshops and exhibits. They can try their hand at writing with a quill pen, operating a printing press, making a radio programme or working with a computer. Many of Washington's other museums are equally interesting for both adults and children. An example is the *National Geographic Society Explorers Hall*, with its striking displays which convey the romance of discovery and exploration. Another example is the *National Air and Space Museum* where all ages appreciate the fascination of aeroplanes, rockets, satellites and other paraphernalia of modern air and space travel. Other places for space buffs are the **Goddard Visitor Center and Museum** (*Greenbelt, Md.* ☎ *334–8101*), run by NASA and with exhibits on all aspects of the Space Programme; the **Rock Creek Nature Center Planetarium** (☎ *426–6829*); and the *United States Naval Observatory* (☎ *653–1543*). Technologically minded children will also love the participatory exhibits at the *National Museum of American History*. The *National Museum of Natural History* is always a favourite, with its vast range of stuffed animals and a superb section on Native American life.

Many museums have special sections for children. The Natural History Museum, for example, has a "hands-on" **Discovery Room**, while the National Museum of American Art has an **Explore Gallery**, a multi-media experience through which children can explore different sensory effects. Children interested in military matters will enjoy the **US Marine Corps Museum** and **US Navy Memorial Museum** at *Navy Yard*, and the **Fort Ward Museum** (☎ *838–4848 for details*), which has Civil War memorabilia and occasionally stages re-enactments of events of the period. More peacefully minded youngsters will enjoy the *Dolls' House and Toy Museum*, and transport buffs will like the **National Capital Trolley Museum** (*Colesville Branch, Silver Spring, Md.* ☎ *(301) 384–9797* ✆ *open noon–5pm, Wed in July, Aug noon–4pm; closed mid-Dec to early Jan*). The **Wax Museum**, with tableaux from the Bible and from American history, is usually a great success with kids.

Film, theatre and music

Watch the periodicals listed in the introduction to this section for children's performances of all kinds. For film enthusiasts there are many possibilities. The *Hirshhorn Museum* and the

National Air and Space Museum both have lively film shows. In theatre the choice is even wider. Listed below are some of the children's theatre ventures in the DC area.

Adventure Theater (*Glen Echo Park, Glen Echo, Md.* ☎320–5331). Plays, music and puppetry; at weekends.

Theater of Arlington (*Arlington County Visual and Performing Arts, 300 North Park Dr., Arlington, Va.* ☎558–2161).

Maryland Children's Theater (*4930 Cordell Ave., Bethesda, Md.* ☎ 652–7999).

Programs for Children and Youth (*Education Office, John F. Kennedy Center for the Performing Arts, New Hampshire Ave. and Rock Creek Parkway* ☎254–7190).

The Round House Theater (*Montgomery County Recreation Dept, 12210 Bushey Dr., Wheaton, Md.* ☎468–4172 *office, 468–4234 box office*). An adult theatre which also has classes and performances for children.

Smithsonian Discovery Theater (*Arts and Industries Building, 900 Jefferson Dr., SW* ☎357–1500).

Sylvan Theater (*Washington Monument grounds* ☎426–6975). Outdoor plays, ballets, musicals and puppet shows in spring and summer.

The Vagabond Puppet People (*47 South Aberdeen St., Arlington, Va.* ☎892–6252). Performances once a month Oct–Mar.

For children who like to listen to music, numerous open-air concerts are given in Washington during the summer, such as the military concerts at the Jefferson Memorial or the Marine Corps Sunset Parade (see also p.35). The National Symphony also performs a series of young people's concerts at the Kennedy Center (☎785–8100) in the spring and autumn.

Other ideas
A climb up the *Washington Monument*, a cruise on the Potomac or a barge up the *Chesapeake and Ohio Canal* all make ideal family outings, as does a visit to the *Federal Bureau of Investigation*, with its fascinating museum of crime and detection and its displays of firearm shooting. Rather more peaceful is the *National Aquarium* in the Department of Commerce building. Budding racing drivers can try the **Skelterama Go-cart Track** (*4300 Kenilworth Ave., Bladensburg, Md.* ☎864–0110), while kids with a taste for digging in the garden might enjoy one of the practice sessions organized for children at **Washington Youth Gardens** in the *National Arboretum*.

Check the *Calendar of events* in *Planning* for any that your children might particularly enjoy. The following may be of special appeal: **The Kite Carnival**, held on a Sat in Mar or Apr near the Washington Monument (☎357–3244 *for info*); the Easter Monday **Easter Egg Roll** on the White House lawn; free Sun afternoon concerts and the **International Children's Festival** of dance, theatre and music, held on Labor Day weekend at **Wolf Trap Farm Park** (*Vienna, Va.* ☎255–1800).

Toy shops and book shops
Capital Children's Museum has a shop selling an interesting selection of books and toys. The only children's book store in Washington is **Cheshire Cat Book Store** (*5512 Connecticut Ave. NW* ☎244–3956), which has a good selection for all ages.

Toy shops include the following:

Granny's Place *303 Cameron St., Alexandria, Va.*
☎*549–0119*
John Davy Toys *301 Cameron St., Alexandria, Va.*
☎*683–0079*
Little Caledonia *1419 Wisconsin Ave. NW* ☎*333–4700*
The Red Balloon *1073 Wisconsin Ave. NW* ☎*965–1200*
F. A. O. Schwarz *Mazza Gallerie, 5300 Wisconsin Ave.
NW* ☎*363–8455, and Georgetown Park, 3222 M St. NW*
☎*342–2285*
Sullivan's Toy Stores *3412 Wisconsin Ave. NW*
☎*362–1343, and other branches*
Treetop Toys *3301 New Mexico Ave. NW* ☎*244–3500*
Why Not Shop *200 King St., Alexandria, Va.* ☎*548–4420*

For discount toy shops, try **Juvenile Sales** (*2321 University
Blvd., Wheaton, Md.* ☎*949–5157; 6612 Richmond Highway,
Alexandria, Va.* ☎*768–7500; and other branches*) or **Toys
"Я" Us** (*Tyson's Corner, Va.* ☎*893–2223; Springfield, Va.*
☎*922–7876; and other branches*), a chain of discount toy and
children's furniture shops.

Babysitters

Assistants, Inc. *2909 Wilson Blvd., Arlington, Va. 22201*
☎*(703) 524–1131/0666;* **Child Care Agency** *Woodward
Building, 733 15th St. NW, DC 20005* ☎*783–8573;* **Sitters
Unlimited** *DC and Va.* ☎*823–0888.*

Sports and activities

Active sports enthusiasts who come to Washington will be
either disappointed or delighted, depending on their particular
sport and how far they are willing to travel outside the city. In
DC itself there is a marked lack of sporting opportunities for the
visitor. The only large-scale general sports complex is run by
the **YMCA** (*1711 Rhode Island Ave. NW* ☎*862–9622*) and is
open only to members or those who belong to other YMCA
branches. If you are lucky enough to be one of these, you will
have the use of, among other things, a swimming pool, squash
courts, gymnasium and sauna. The only remotely comparable
facility open to the public is the excellent **Watergate Health
Club** (*2650 Virginia Ave. NW* ☎*298–4460*), with swimming
pool, gymnasium, sauna, massage and exercise classes.

Otherwise, for the ordinary tourist there are limited facilities
in the city for swimming (in a few hotels), golf and tennis, but
very little else. The free *Recreation Guide Book* from the **DC
Recreation Department** (*3149 16th St. NW, Room 22, DC
20010* ☎*673–7660*) gives a list of municipal facilities.

Outside the city the choice becomes wider, especially in
outdoor sports, but it can still be frustrating if you are not a
member of a club. One organization with a superb range of
activities is **Outdoor University** (*508 N Washington St.,
Alexandria, Va. 22314* ☎*548–3838*).

In spectator sports, the prospect in DC is better. There are
stadiums for professional games such as American football,
soccer and ice-hockey. Interesting amateur events can be
watched free in parks, including jousting, polo, rugby and
hockey; for information phone **National Capital Parks**
(☎*426–6700*) or **"dial-a-park"** (☎*426–6975 daily bulletin*).

The following A-Z includes not only sports but also activities and facilities that come under the general heading of recreation.

Ballooning
Fly high on an introductory flight, with a glass of champagne to help you on your way up. There are several ballooning clubs in the vicinity of Washington. Contact the **Chesapeake Balloon Association** (☎987–5914) or the *Weekend* section of the *Washington Post*.

Baseball
Washington no longer has its own major-league baseball team. The nearest is the Baltimore Orioles, who play out of **Memorial Stadium** (*1,000 block of E 33rd St., Baltimore, Md.* ☎(301) 338–1300). There is also a minor-league team, the Alexandria Dukes, who play at **Four-Mile Run Park** (*3600 Commonwealth Ave., Alexandria, Va.*). The season is Apr–Oct.

Basketball
The Washington Bullets play out of the **Capital Centre Stadium** (*1 Harry S. Truman Dr., Landover, Md., off the Beltway from exit 15A or 17A* ☎350–3400). The season is Oct–Apr.

Bicycling
In a land where the automobile is worshipped, cycling still holds its own, and there are many delightful cycle routes in and around Washington. For information contact the **Potomac Pedalers Touring Club** (*Box 23610, DC 20026* ☎363–8687), which provides maps and advice. See also *Basic information* for a list of bicycle rental firms in Washington.

Boating
You can rent pedal boats on the Tidal Basin, from the **Tidal Basin Boating Center** (*15th St. and Maine Ave. SW* ☎484–3475). For the Potomac and/or C&O Canal, try the following: **Fletcher's Boat House** (*4940 Canal Rd. NW* ☎244–0461) – canoes and rowboats on the canal and Potomac; **Jack's Boats** (*3500 K St. NW, Georgetown* ☎337–9642) – canoes and rowboats on the Potomac; **Thompson Boat Center** (*Rock Creek Parkway and Virginia Ave. NW* ☎333–4861) – canoes on the Potomac.

Bowling
A classic American indoor sport and a good way to get a cheap evening's entertainment. Most of the bowling alleys are outside DC. The most pleasant and accessible is probably **Brunswick River Bowl** (*5225 River Rd., Bethesda, Md. 20816* ☎656–5531).

Bridge
There are many bridge clubs in Washington and its suburbs. Contact Charlotte Miller of the **Washington Bridge League** (*1111 University Blvd. W, Silver Spring, Md. 20902* ☎649–1812).

Chess
There are a number of open-air chess tables in Dupont Circle and on the w side of *Lafayette Park*, and on a fine day there are

usually several games in progress either of chess or chequers (draughts). For information on chess clubs in DC, Virginia and Maryland, contact the **United States Chess Federation** (*186 Route 9W, New Windsor, NY 12550* ☎562–8350).

Dance
In Washington you can cavort to music in any number of ways from classical ballet to clogging. There are too many dance places to list even a fraction of them, but the following addresses might be useful.

Schools
Dance for Washington (*2801 Connecticut Ave. NW* ☎797–1746)
Joy of Motion (*1643 Connecticut Ave. NW* ☎362–1320)
Washington School of the Ballet (*3515 Wisconsin Ave. NW* ☎362–1683)

Associations
Square Dance Information Center (*1014 22nd St. S, Arlington, Va. 22202* ☎979–1647)

Fishing
Whether you want to charter a boat and go deep-sea fishing off the Maryland coast or try your luck upriver on the Potomac or the Shenandoah, there are endless opportunities for the angler. Read the regular feature called "Fish Lines" in the *Weekend* section of the *Washington Post* to find out where the best catches are currently to be found. Fishing maps of both fresh and saltwater fishing grounds are published by the **Alexandria Drafting Company** (*6440 General Green Way, Alexandria, Va. 22310* ☎750–0510), obtainable from them or from book stores.

Football (American)
Washington's professional team, the Redskins, plays out of **Robert F. Kennedy Stadium** (*E Capitol and 22nd St. SE* ☎543–6465). The season runs approximately from Sept to Dec.

Gardens
"A garden is a lovesome thing", especially on a hot day in Washington when you want to escape from the streets and enjoy the solace of trees and plants. See also *A–Z* entries for *Dumbarton Oaks, Franciscan Monastery, Hillwood, Lady Bird Johnson Park, Meridian Hill Park, National Arboretum, United States Botanic Gardens, Washington Cathedral* and *Mormon Temple*.

The following places offer a green respite:
Brookside Gardens (*1500 Glenallan Ave., Wheaton, Md.* ☎949–8230). 50 beautifully planted acres (20ha), including a herb, aquatic and Japanese garden.
Constitution Gardens (*in the Mall, just N of the Lincoln Memorial reflecting pool*). A relaxed place for walkers, joggers and picnickers, with a lake, 5,000 trees and some 10,000 other plants.
Dumbarton Oaks Gardens (*3101 R St. NW* ☎342–3200). An oasis in Georgetown, with a delightful mixture of formal and informal planting.
Floral Library (*between the Tidal Basin and the Washington Monument*). A small but colourful array of many different flowers.

Franciscan Monastery (*1400 Quincy St. NE* ☎*526–6800*). Glorious grounds, beautifully tended.
Gunston Hall (*Route 242, Lorton, Va.* ☎*550–9220*). A Colonial garden, complete with a 200-year-old boxwood hedge.
Hillwood (*4155 Linnean Ave. NW* ☎*636–5807*). 25 acres (10ha) of superb grounds, with Japanese and French formal gardens and a greenhouse with 5,000 orchids.
Japanese Embassy Gardens (*2500 Massachusetts Ave. NW* ☎*234–2266*). An authentic Japanese garden, open May–Oct by appt only.
Kenilworth Aquatic Gardens (*Anacostia Ave. and Douglas St. NE* ☎*426–6905*). A delightful maze of ponds full of irises, lotuses and water-lilies – not to mention frogs, turtles, waterfowl, muskrats and other fauna.
Lady Bird Johnson Park and **LBJ Memorial Grove** (*George Washington Memorial Parkway between Memorial and 14th St. Bridges* ☎*426–6700*). 15 acres (6ha) of white pine, dogwood, azalea, rhododendron and much else.
Meridian Hill Park (*16th and Euclid St. NW*). A Franco-Italian formal garden, once belonging to a now-demolished private house.
Mormon Temple (*9900 Stoneybrook Dr., Kensington, Md.* ☎*587–0144*). An award-winning garden, attractive at any time of year.
National Arboretum (*3501 New York Ave. NE* ☎*475–4815*). A veritable tree museum, covering over 400 acres (162ha).
United States Botanic Gardens (*1st St. and Maryland Ave.* ☎*225–7099/226–8333*). A jungle at the foot of Capitol Hill.
Washington Cathedral grounds (*Massachusetts and Wisconsin Ave. NW* ☎*537–6200*). A tranquil place with shaded walkways, medieval herbs and flowers, and a greenhouse where plants are sold.

Gliding (soaring)

The **Outdoor University** (see introduction to this section) and **Bay Soaring** (*P.O. Box 257, Woodbine, Md. 21797* ☎*(301) 731–6095*) both organize gliding.

Golf

Difficult in the Washington area unless you are a member of a club or the guest of a member. The **Washingtonian Motel and Country Club** (*Shady Grove Rd., off Interstate 70 at Gaithersburg, Md.* ☎*248–2200*), with two very fine courses, occasionally allows non-members to play unaccompanied by members; confirm in advance by telephone. Less interesting to play on, but much cheaper and more convenient for the city, are the three public courses and driving range at **East Potomac Park** (☎*554–7660*); **Langston Park** (*Benmangs Rd.* ☎*397–8638*); and **Rock Creek Park** (☎*727–9332*).

Health clubs and fitness centres

Washingtonians sweat themselves into shape in a variety of ways. One of the most popular is the muscle-conditioning equipment developed by the **Nautilus Fitness Centers** (*1901 Pennsylvania Ave., Md.* ☎*867–0760* and *1101 Vermont Ave. NW* ☎*289–0081*) Other centrally located health clubs are the excellent **Watergate Health Club** (*2650 Virginia Ave. NW* ☎*298–4460*) with swimming pool, gymnasium, massage and exercise classes; **Holiday Spa** (*1750 K St.* ☎*296–0711*) and the **Office Health Center** (*1990 M St. NW* ☎872–0222); all of these have saunas. The **Washington Hilton**, (*1919 Connecticut Ave. NW* ☎483–3000) has sauna, exercise room and outdoor swimming pool, all open to the public. The **Washington Marriott** (*22nd and M St. NW* ☎872–1500) has indoor swimming pool, sauna and whirlpool, but non-residents must join the hotel's club for at least one month.

Hiking, walking and rambling

Rock Creek Park and *Chesapeake and Ohio Canal* provide enjoyable walking. There are also good trails along the Potomac around Great Falls, 15 miles (24km) upriver from Washington. In addition to the **National Park Service** (☎426–6700), the following park authorities can provide further information about trails under their jurisdiction:

Alexandria Department of Recreation and Parks ☎838–4343
Arlington County Park Division ☎558–2426
Fairfax County Park Authority ☎941–5000
Maryland State Parks ☎(301) 269–3761
Prince Georges Park and Planning Commission ☎699–2407

Other sources of information are the **Appalachian Trail Club** (*1718 N St. NW* ☎638–5306) and the **Sierra Club** (☎547–2326 *for recorded info.*). For organized hikes try also the **Outdoor University** (see introduction to this section).

Horse-racing

In America, harness racing (where the horse is driven from a cart or buggy) is popular. Races are run at: **Rosecroft Raceway** (*Oxon Hill, Md.* ☎567–4000), **Ocean Downs** (*Berlin, Md.* ☎541–0680) and **Freestate Raceway** (*Laurel, Md.* ☎(301) 725–2600). Flat-racing, or steeplechasing, can be watched at: **Bowie Race Course** (*Bowie, Md.* ☎(301) 262–8111), **Laurel Race Course** (*Laurel, Md.* ☎(301) 539–6242), **Pimlico Race Course** (*Baltimore, Md.* ☎(301) 542–9400) and **Shenandoah Downs** (*Charles Town, W Va.* ☎737–2323).

Hunting and shooting

Whether you prefer shooting at targets or live game, the *National Rifle Association* (*1600 Rhode Island Ave. NW* ☎828–6000) will be able to provide information.

Ice hockey

The local professional team, the Washington Capitals, plays out of the **Capital Centre** (*1 Harry S. Truman Dr., Landover, Md.* ☎350–3400); tickets obtainable from **Capital Ticket Centre** (*1801 K St. NW* ☎296–6970). Season is Oct–Apr.

Ice-skating

When the ice is thick enough (☎426–6841 *US Park Police for an ice report*), skating is permitted on the C&O Canal or the reflecting pools in front of the Lincoln Memorial and the w steps of the Capitol. There are also numerous ice rinks in the Washington area. Outdoor rinks: **Liberty Plaza** (*17th and G St. NW* ☎377–6599); **National Sculpture Garden Ice Rink** (*Constitution Ave. between 7th and 9th St. NW* ☎347–9041/2); **Pershing Park Ice Rink** (*Pennsylvania Ave. between 14th and 15th St.* ☎737–6938). Indoor rinks open all

year: **Fairfax Ice Arena** *(3779 Pickett Rd. Fairfax, Va.*
☎*323–1131)*; **Fort Dupont** *(3779 Ely Pl. SE* ☎*584–3040)*;
Mount Vernon District Park *(2017 Bell Vue Blvd.,
Alexandria, Va.* ☎*768–3223)*. Skate rental is available at all of
these rinks.

Polo
Polo matches are held on Sun afternoons in spring, summer
and autumn on **Lincoln Memorial Polo Field**, between the
Memorial and the Tidal Basin: a good spectator sport which is
free. Call the **National Park Service** (☎*426–6700*) for
information. There are also two polo clubs within easy driving
distance of DC: **Middleburg Polo Club** *(on Route 50, 3 miles
(5km) past Middleburg, Va.)* and **Potomac Polo Club**
(Hughes and River Rd., 12 miles (19km) past Potomac, Md.).

Riding and equestrian events
Riding stables in the area:
Meadowbrook Stables *Meadowbrook Lane, Chevy Chase,
Md.* ☎*588–6935*
Potomac Equitation Farm *5320 Pleasant Valley Rd.,
Centreville, Va.* ☎*631–9720*
Rock Creek Park Horse Center *Military and Glover Rd.
NW* ☎*362–0117*

The main equestrian event in the city is the Washington
International Horse Show, which takes place annually at the
end of Oct at the **Capital Centre** *(1 Harry S. Truman Dr.,
Landover, Md.)*. For general information contact the
American Horse Council *(1700 K St. NW* ☎*296–4031)*.

Roller-skating and skate-boarding
Skate-boarding has waned considerably in the Washington
area. There are no skate-board pistes as such, but die-hard
aficionados can probably find a large enough paved area to use
as an *ad hoc* piste. Roller-skating, on the other hand, continues
to gain popularity and seems to be here to stay. Although one
often sees roller-skaters on the city pavements, there is only
one roller-skating rink near DC: **Alexandria Roller-
Skating Rink** *(807 N and Asaph St., Alexandria, Va.*
☎*836–6167)*.

Rugby
Rugby has a relatively small but enthusiastic following in the
USA. It is occasionally played at **West Potomac Park**, near
the Lincoln Memorial. Contact the **National Park Service**
(☎*426–6700*) for information about matches.

Running and jogging
Another national craze. For information and advice contact the
American Running and Fitness Association *(2420 K St.
NW* ☎*667–4150)*. The main running event of the year is the
Marine Corps Marathon in Oct.

Sailing
Whether you plan to rent a dinghy for an afternoon or charter a
large boat for several days, there are abundant opportunities
for sailing near Washington. For a short sail on the Potomac,
try renting a boat from **Buzzard Point Marina** *(at the foot of
1st St. SW* ☎*488–8400)*. Farther afield, Annapolis on the
splendid Chesapeake Bay has several boat rental services, such

as the **Annapolis Sailing School** (*601 6th St.*
☎ *(301) 267–7205*). At nearby Edgwater, **Pier Seven** (*48
South River* ☎ *(301) 956–2288*) rents a wide variety of boats,
from 16ft (5m) upwards. Charter firms at Annapolis include
Bay Yacht Agency (*2nd St. and Spa Creek*
☎ *(301) 269–6772*) and **Dockside Yacht Charters** (*326 1st
St.* ☎ *(301) 437–7190*). Chesapeake Bay Yacht Racing Week
takes place at Annapolis in early July, and the President's Cup
Regatta (hydroplanes, rowing and canoe races) in early June.

Soccer
Washington's professional soccer team, the Diplomats, plays
Apr–Aug at the **Robert F. Kennedy Stadium** (*E Capitol and
22nd St. SE* ☎ *543–6465*).

Squash and racquetball
These two games, which are close relatives, can be played at
many places in the Washington area where entry is not
restricted to members. Court time tends to be expensive,
however. Clubs include: **Capitol Hill Squash Club** (*214 D
St. SE* ☎ *547–2255*) – squash; **Courts Royal Merrifield**
(*2733 Merrilee Dr., Fairfax, Va.* ☎ *560–1215*) – squash and
racquetball; **Courts Royal White Oak** (*11313 Lockwood Dr.,
Silver Spring, Md.* ☎ *593–7626*) – racquetball.

Swimming
Facilities in the city are not very extensive. The DC
government runs a number of pools (☎ *673–7660 for info.*), as
do the various suburban and county authorities. Among the
few hotels with a pool are the **Washington Hilton** (*1919
Connecticut Ave. NW* ☎ *483–3000*) and the **Washington
Marriott** (*22nd and M St. NW* ☎ *872–1500*), but at the latter
you must join the club for a month. The **Watergate Health
Club** (see introduction to this section) has an indoor pool
which non-members can use.

For other outdoor swimming avoid the local rivers, which
are polluted. The nearest good beach is about an hour's drive
away at **Sandy Point State Park**, by the w end of the
Chesapeake Bay Bridge. The best beaches, however, are on the
Delaware coast and a small part of the Virginia coast facing the
Atlantic, for example at **Dewey Beach**, **Ocean City** and on
Assateague Island. The disadvantage of these is their
distance – at least a three-hour drive – from DC.

Tennis
There are many public tennis courts run by DC and by the
surrounding county and suburban authorities (☎ *673–7660 for
info.*). Some private tennis clubs allow non-members to play.
Examples are **Cabin John Indoor Tennis Court** (*7801
Democracy Blvd., Bethesda, Md.* ☎ *469–7300*) and **Courts
Royal Annandale** (*4317 Ravensworth Rd., Annandale, Va.*
☎ *256–6600*); the latter are also indoors.

Spectator tennis events include the Women's Championship
in Jan and the DC National Bank Tennis Classic in July. For
further details contact the **Washington Area Tennis
Patrons** (*800 18th St. NW* ☎ *429–0661*).

Zoos
The *National Zoological Park* is the only zoo in DC. For
farms and nature centres, see *Washington for children*.

Excursions

It would be a pity to visit Washington and see only the metropolitan area, for the city lies in a fascinating part of America, full of natural beauty and historic interest. This section describes five selected places within a day's excursion from the capital, but first take a look at a map of the region and note some of the other possibilities.

A couple of hours' drive to the E via the Chesapeake Bay Bridge takes you to the eastern shore of Maryland, an area of quiet, rich countryside, wooded inlets, charming old-world towns and an abundance of excellent seafood. More accessible from Washington is the peninsula that juts down into the Chesapeake to the SE of the city, another deeply rural part of Maryland where occasionally you will catch sight of the black-clad Amish in their horse-drawn buggies.

To the SW lies Virginia, a state that is very conscious of its importance in America's history and the many US presidents that it has produced. One of them, Thomas Jefferson, lived at **Monticello**, just over 100 miles (150km) from Washington, a beautiful hilltop house which he designed for himself and which is now a museum. Nearby is the town of **Charlottesville** where the splendid university, also designed by Jefferson, can be toured. Tobacco planting was one of the industries that made Virginia rich, and there are many old plantation houses that can be visited, including a number that lie along the James River between Richmond, the state capital, and Williamsburg.

Scenically, Virginia has much to be proud of in the **Shenandoah National Park**, which extends for 85 miles (127.5km) along the crest of the Blue Ridge Mountains. The Skyline Drive through the park affords wonderful panoramas.

For those interested in military history there are many Civil War battlefields within reach of Washington. Four of them lie in the vicinity of **Fredericksburg**, 50 miles (75km) from Washington, where there is a **Battlefield Park Museum**. Two more battles took place at **Manassas**, some 25 miles (37.5km) W of Washington, where there is also a battlefield park and museum. Another Civil War site is **Harpers Ferry** in W Virginia, about 50 miles (75km) NW of the capital, a charming town which was the scene of much action including John Brown's raid in 1859. The fort in which he was captured is now a museum. Not far away is the **Antietam** battlefield, also known as Sharpsburg. But the most famous of all Civil War battlefields is probably **Gettysburg** in Pennsylvania, about 80 miles (120km) N of Washington. The vast battle site, with its many relics and markers, is best toured with a guide.

Note that many of these destinations can be visited on organized bus tours.

Alexandria

*6 miles (10km) s of Washington. Population: 111,000.
Getting there: By car, Route 1; by Metro to King Street or
Braddock Road; by Metrobus, or tour with Gray Line (333 E
St. SW ☎479–5900), which also includes Mount Vernon.*
Although now part of the Washington metropolitan area and a fashionable residential enclave for the city's professional people, Alexandria is still very much a town in its own right, with an old-world Virginian atmosphere which is entirely different from DC. The spirit of the Confederacy lives on in

the old houses, the mellow, tree-lined streets and the twang of the local accent. But Alexandria also has its chic, modern side. In and around its main artery, **King St.**, there are many smart shops and a proportionally richer selection of good restaurants than in the capital.

Allow an entire day if you want to appreciate Alexandria to the full. A good place to start your visit is the **Ramsay House Visitors' Center** (*221 King St.* ☎*549–0205*), a small 18thC clapboard house, the oldest surviving Alexandria property, which was the home of William Ramsay, a Scottish merchant who was one of the founders of Alexandria and the town's first postmaster. Here you can obtain brochures, tourist advice and a free parking pass if you are from outside the town. From here walk along to Alexandria's heritage museum housed in the **Lyceum** (*201 S Washington St.* ☎*838–4994* ⊠ *open 10am–5pm; closed major hols*), an imposing Greek revival building of 1839. In the Lyceum, Alexandria is reviving its first cultural centre, with a museum of decorative arts and artifacts, plus free concerts and performances.

By now you will have become aware of Alexandria's strong sense of history. The town is named not after Alexander the Great but after a Scotsman named John Alexander who settled here in 1669. As Alexandria developed into an important port for tobacco and other goods, the Scottish connection continued. It was a Scotsman, John Carlyle, who built the grand stone building called **Carlyle House** (*121 N Fairfax St.* ☎*549–2997* ⊠ *open Tues–Sat 10am–5pm, Sun noon–5pm; closed Mon, some hols*). There is a guided tour of the interior, which has been restored as near to its original state as possible. Another reminder of the city's Scottish founders is the **Old Presbyterian Meeting House** (*321 S Fairfax St.* ☎*549–6670* ⊠), a dignified, red-brick building.

There is a link with the town's Egyptian namesake in the form of the **George Washington National Masonic Memorial** on Old Shuter's Hill (*King St. and Callahan Dr.* ☎*683–2007* ⊠ *open 9am–5pm; closed some major hols*). This 333 ft-high (101.5m) edifice, built in the 1920s, is based on the Pharos Lighthouse at Alexandria in Egypt, one of the Seven Wonders of the World. Masons and non-masons alike can visit the interior. It contains a replica of the lodge room of Alexandria Lodge No. 22, of which Washington was Worshipful Master. There are various memorabilia of Washington the man and the mason, both here and in the **George Washington Museum**, on a higher floor. The observation floor at the top of the tower affords a fine view of the town, and children are always intrigued by the mechanical parade perpetually filing past a model of the Taj Mahal in one of the Shrine Rooms on the first floor.

Although he had his main home at nearby Mount Vernon, Washington kept a house in Alexandria and was one of the town's leading citizens. A pew was reserved for him at **Christ Church ★** (*Cameron and N Washington St.* ⊠)

Other prominent Alexandrians included General "Light Horse" Harry Lee, a hero of the Revolutionary War, and his son Robert E. Lee, the famous Confederate general in the Civil War. The Lee family is associated especially with two houses in Alexandria. The **Lee-Fendall House** (*614 Oronoco St., on the corner of N Washington St.* ☎*548–1789* ⊠ *open Tues–Fri 10am–4pm, Sat, Sun by appt*) was built by Harry Lee's relative, Philip Richard Fendall. It was there that Harry Lee wrote the funeral oration for George Washington containing the famous words "First in war, first in peace, and first in the hearts of his countrymen". Besides Lee heirlooms and furnishings, the house possesses a fine collection of antique doll's houses. The other house linked with the Lees, which is across the road, was Harry Lee's last residence and is now known as the **Boyhood Home of Robert E. Lee** (*607 Oronoco St.* ☎*548–8454* 📷 *open Mon–Sat 10am–4pm, Sun noon–4pm; closed mid-Dec to Jan*). Beautifully furnished, the house contains many Lee portraits and memorabilia.

If historical sightseeing leaves you cold, just stroll through the streets between the town centre and the Potomac River, enjoying the charm of the architecture for its own sake, and browsing in the shops and galleries. On the s side of Prince St. near its eastern end stand two charming groups of houses, **Gentry Row** and **Captain's Row**. On the opposite side of Prince St. at No. 201 is the **Athenaeum** (☎*548–0035* 📷), a Greek revival building of about 1850, once a bank but now an art gallery showing temporary exhibitions. Around the corner at 101 N Union St. is the **Torpedo Factory**, a grim building from the outside, but imaginatively converted to a complex of artists' studios and craft shops where you can buy handicrafts or simply watch the artists at work.

The **Book Annex**, at 106 S Union St. in the next block, has a bright, welcoming tearoom at the back overlooking the river – a delightful spot for a tea, coffee or light meal. If you want something more substantial in more traditional surroundings, go to ⟺ **Gadsby's Tavern** (*138 N Royal St.* ☎*548–1288*), a famous hostelry which was once a haunt of many of the Founding Fathers. The older part of the tavern, next door to the restaurant at No. 134, is a museum (☎*834–4242* 📷).

Many traditional events take place in Alexandria every year. In Aug, for example, a Civil War battle is re-enacted in costume at **Fort Ward** (*4301 W Braddock Rd.* ☎*838–4848* 📷 *open Tues–Sat 9am–5pm, Sun noon–5pm; closed Mon, some major hols*), a partially restored Civil War Fort, now a park and museum. On the first Sat in Dec, the town's Scottish heritage is celebrated by the **Annual Scottish Christmas Walk**, when the pipes are played, the kilts twirl and Gaelic greetings are exchanged. Whenever you visit Alexandria, indeed, there is sure to be something going on. A calendar of events is available from the Visitors' Center.

Alexandria lies on the route to Mount Vernon, and the two can easily be combined in one excursion.

Annapolis

33 miles (53km) E of Washington. Population: 37,000. Getting there: By car, Route 50.

Annapolis, capital of Maryland, is one of the places where you can still catch a glimpse of the gracious, old-world face of America. On the Severn River close to where it meets Chesapeake Bay, the town thrives on two things: the sea and history. It was the sea that brought Annapolis its early prosperity as a trading port; and today it retains its maritime image through its great Naval Academy and its fame as a sailing and fishing centre. Many Washingtonians keep their weekend yachts in the large marina here. If you want to go out into the bay sailing boats can be rented or chartered (see *Sailing* in *Sports and activities*); or take a 40-min narrated tour on the steamer *The Harbor Queen*.

Excursions

There are few towns in the USA with so proud and so well-presented a heritage. Originally settled in 1649 by Puritans from Virginia, Annapolis was first laid out as a planned unit in 1694 when Washington was still a swamp. In the same year it became the capital of Maryland, and for a short period (Nov 1783–Aug 1784) it was actually the capital of the USA.

Today it is a charming town with quiet, brick-paved, tree-lined streets and an abundance of fine architecture. As the historic centre is small, the best way to see it is on foot, and you may wish to follow one of the guided walks organized by **Historic Annapolis Tours** (*Old Treasury Building, State Circle, Annapolis* ☎ *(301) 267–8149*) or by **Three Centuries Tours** (*48 Maryland Ave., Annapolis* ☎ *(301) 263–5357*), whose guides dress in 18thC costume. The most significant old buildings are marked with plaques, colour-coded according to period: terra cotta for pre-Revolutionary; blue for Federal (from the Revolution to about 1820); green for Greek revival (1820–40); mauve for Victorian (after 1840). Annapolis brick is a beautiful soft red, and in the older buildings the mortar is made out of burned and crushed oyster shells.

Chase-Lloyd House
Maryland Ave. ☎ *(301) 263–2723* ◌ *Open Tues–Sat 2–4pm. Closed Sun, Mon.*
In this fine 18thC building, across the road from the Hammond Harwood House and possessing a similar doorway, Mary Lloyd married Francis Scott Key, author of *The Star Spangled Banner*. It is now a ladies' retirement home.

City Dock
This is an attractive harbour, busy with pleasure craft and fishing boats and lined with historic buildings. **Middletown Tavern** (☎ *(301) 263–3323*) was established at No. 2 Market Pl. in 1750 and is still going strong. Washington, Jefferson and Franklin were among its patrons. You can dine or lunch here on such traditional fare as oysters or Maryland crab. Note also the 19thC **Market House**, once condemned to demolition but reprieved and now containing retail food shops.

Hammond Harwood House
Maryland Ave. and King George St. ☎ *(301) 269–1714* ▨ *Open summer Tues–Sat 10am–5pm, Sun 2–5pm; winter Tues–Sat 10am–4pm, Sun 2–4pm. Closed Mon.*
This graceful Georgian house, now a museum, was designed by William Buckland, architect of Gunston Hall in Virginia and many other fine houses. It has a particularly elegant doorway with egg-and-dart mouldings, Ionic columns and a fan window. The house is filled with 18thC furniture and *objets d'art*.

Maryland State House
State Circle ☎ *(301) 269–3400 Open 9am–5pm. Closed Christmas.*
This beautiful building is the oldest state capitol in the country that has remained in continuous use. Its dome, which dominates the town centre, was built entirely without nails, using only wooden pegs. The building contains many portraits of men prominent in the history of Maryland, from the first Lord Baltimore onwards. You can view the present **House of Delegates** and **Senate chambers** and also the **Old Senate chamber**, now a museum and preserved exactly as it was in 1783 when George Washington stood here to resign his commission as Commander-in-Chief of the Continental Army. The scene is depicted in a painting that hangs in the room.

Old Treasury Building
This small brick building in the grounds of the State House is
believed to be the oldest public building in Maryland. It was
here that the country's first paper money, in the form of Bills
of Credit, was kept. Restored in 1950, it now houses the tour
offices of Historic Annapolis Inc. Exhibits relevant to the
town's history are on display.

St John's College
60 College Ave. ☎(301) 263-2371 ▣
This was one of the first public schools in America, opened in
1696 as King William's School, and the campus contains many
historic buildings. It is now part of the University of
Maryland. In the grounds is the so-called **Liberty Tree**,
under which many ceremonies have been held. In the mid-
19thC some rowdy youths tried to blow the tree up with
gunpowder, but in doing so, they unwittingly saved the tree by
killing all the vermin in it.

United States Naval Academy
Ricketts Hall USNA ☎(301) 267-3363 ▣ ⚑ *Open Mon–Sat
9am–4pm, Sun 11am–4pm. Tours: early spring and late
autumn every hr on the hr 10am–2pm; June–Aug and Sat,
Sun until Dec every half hr 9.30am–4pm.*
Founded in 1845, the US Naval Academy was designated a
National Historic Site in 1963. It has beautifully laid-out
grounds and some fine buildings, notably **Bancroft Hall**, a
dormitory for the 4,400 midshipmen, and the **Chapel** with its
crypt containing the remains of the naval hero John Paul
Jones. Model ships, paintings, nautical relics and other items
relating to naval history are on display in the museum, housed
in **Preble Hall**.

The guided tours start from the **Visitors' Information
Center** in Ricketts Hall (☎ *(301) 263–6933; open 9am–4pm;
closed some major hols*), reached via Gate 1 at the foot of King
George St.

William Paca House
186 Prince George St. ☎263–5553 ▣*includes garden.
Open Tues–Sat 10am–4pm, Sun noon–4pm. Closed Mon.*
Built in 1765 by William Paca, a signer of the Declaration of
Independence and three times Governor of Maryland, this
mansion is now beautifully restored. The delightful garden
(*open Mon–Sat 10am–4pm, Sun noon–4pm*), entered from 1
Martin St., is also well worth a visit.

🛏 Annapolis has hotels to suit most tastes, from the large and modern
Holiday Inn (*Route US 50 going w* ☎ *(301) 224–3150* ▮▮) to
Gibson's Lodgings (*110 Prince George St.* ☎ *(301) 268–5555* ▮▮), a
charming old-world guest house.

🍴 The town also boasts numerous good restaurants, especially around
the harbour area, where the specialities are seafood and other traditional
Maryland fare. For something a little more European, try **Café
Normandy** (*195 Main St.* ☎ *(301) 263–3382* ▮▯), which is excellent
for a coffee and croissant or a full meal.

Baltimore
*35 miles (56km) NE of Washington. Getting there: By car,
Interstate 95; by train, frequent departures from Union
Station.*
Edgar Allan Poe, H. L. Mencken, Babe Ruth, Bromo-Seltzer,
General Motors, Bethlehem Steel are all names associated with

Baltimore, Md., second largest port on the E coast and a proud city whose history dates back to 1729. Although a working city, it possesses a strong sense of culture and a fine architectural heritage. Baltimore has had its ups and downs, but at present is very much enjoying an "up" phase, thanks in large measure to William Donald Schaefer, who became mayor in 1970 and initiated a programme of development that has turned Baltimore into one of America's liveliest and best-run cities.

Epitomizing this transformation is the **Inner Harbor**, until the early 1970s a sad area of rotting buildings, ramshackle piers and rubbish tips, but now the site of one of the most stylish and imaginative urban developments in the world, an object lesson in combining modernity with grace, beauty and the human touch. One of its features is a smart shopping and restaurant complex called **Harbor Place**, comprising two separate pavilions. Sit here on a fine day under the awning of one of the open-air cafés, sipping a cool drink and looking out over the sparkling water as sailing boats come and go, and you will feel that the Riviera has nothing over Baltimore.

The Inner Harbor is dominated by the tall, pentagonal **World Trade Center** (*401 E Pratt St.* ☎(*301*) *837–4515* 🖾), designed by I. M. Pei. Travel up to the 27th-floor **Top of the World** (*open Apr–Labor Day Mon–Thurs 10am–5pm, Fri, Sat 10am–8pm, Sun noon–7pm; rest of yr Mon–Sat 10am–5pm, Sun noon–5pm*), where there is a superb panorama over the city, as well as a boutique, coffee shop and exhibits on Baltimore's history. There is another dramatic view from the 173ft (54m) **Washington Monument** (*N Charles St.* ☎(*301*) *752–9103* 🖾 *open Fri–Tues 10am–4pm; closed Wed, Thurs*).

The **National Aquarium in Baltimore** (*Inner Harbor, open mid-May to mid-Sept Mon–Thurs 10am–5pm, Fri–Sun 10am–8pm; rest of yr Sat–Thurs 10am–5pm, Fri 10am–8pm*) is one of the most imaginative aquariums in the world. Youngsters will love the **Children's Cove**, where they can pick up fearsome-looking but harmless horseshoe crabs. At the top of the building, you walk through a re-creation of a tropical Amazon rain forest, with no glass between you and the iguanas and brightly coloured birds. Another remarkable new museum on the Inner Harbor is the **Maryland Science Center and Planetarium** (☎(*301*) *685–5225* 🖾 *open Mon–Thurs 10am–5pm, Fri, Sat 10am–10pm, Sun noon–6pm*), a kind of huge scientific adventure playground, where you can watch a show in the Planetarium, work on a computer, experiment with illusion-creating devices that tease your perception of reality, and learn about the ecology of the Chesapeake Bay.

The harbour also has three ships that can be visited. Moored on the N side is the graceful sailing ship, the US Frigate *Constellation*, launched in 1797 and the oldest American warship afloat (*open mid-May to mid-Oct 10am–6pm; rest of yr Mon–Sat 10am–4pm, Sun 10am–5pm*). Not far away in the **Baltimore Maritime Museum** (☎(*301*) *396–3854* 🖾 *open Mon, Thurs–Sun 10am–4.30pm; closed Tues, Wed*), two more ships are open to the public, the US Submarine *Torsk* and the Lightship *Chesapeake*. Another feature of the harbour is the warehouse of the **McCormick Spice Company** (*401 Light St.* ☎(*301*) *547–6166*), from which delicious aromas waft over the harbour. Visit their Colonial-style **Tea Room** (*by appt* 🖾), sample tea and coffee and learn about exotic spices.

As a change from sightseeing you can rent a paddleboat, and on certain days watch an open-air show at the NW corner of the harbour. You can also shop in the stylish new **Pratt St. Pavilion**, where there is a wide variety of merchandise and a café or two. The complementary building, the **Light St. Pavilion**, is devoted to a mouth-watering variety of food shops and restaurants. You can eat anything here from a sandwich to a high-class meal. Try the **American Café** or the upper floor of the **City Lights Restaurant**. Both have good food and open-air terraces commanding a fine view of the harbour. After lunch you could take a boat out to **Fort McHenry** on the end of a peninsula in the bay (*boats leave every half hour 10.30am–5pm*). This fort successfully warded off a British attack during the War of 1812 and inspired Francis Scott Key to write *The Star Spangled Banner*, now the US national anthem. The fort is also accessible by land.

From the harbour a pedestrian walkway passes a fountain where it is possible to walk behind the falling water, and on to the award-winning **Convention Center** and the new Hyatt Regency Hotel. The city centre to the N has been revitalized with new plazas, walkways and shopping areas. But the city also has some fine townscapes of an earlier period, notably the magnificent **Mount Vernon Pl.**, with its parks, statues and fountains, dominated by the Washington Monument and surrounded by such fine buildings as the **Peabody Institute of Music**. Unlike Washington, Baltimore has many skyscrapers, some of charmingly whimsical design, such as the **Bromo-Seltzer Tower**, based on the Palazzo Vecchio in Florence.

Sights of historical interest include the 246ft-high (75m) **Shot Tower** (*301 E Fayette St.* ☎ *(301) 396–8256* ⊠ *open 10am–4pm*); **Star Spangled Banner Flag House** (*844 E Pratt St.* ☎ *(301) 837–1793* ⊠ *open Tues–Sat 10am–4pm, Sun 1–4pm; closed Mon*), where the famous flag was sewn by Mary Pickersgill; **Babe Ruth House** (*216 Emory St.* ☎ *(301) 727–1539* ⊠ *open Wed–Sun 10.30am–3.15pm; closed Mon, Tues*), birthplace of the great baseball player; and **Edgar Allan Poe House** (*203 Amity St.* ☎ *(301) 396–7932 for opening hrs* ⊠).

In the art field, Baltimore has two very fine galleries: **Baltimore Museum of Art** (*Art Museum Dr. and 32nd St.* ☎ *(301) 396–7101* ⊠ *open Tues, Wed, Fri 10am–4pm, Thurs 10am–10pm, Sat, Sun 11am–6pm; closed Mon*), which includes a particularly good Impressionist collection, and **Walters Art Gallery** (*Charles and Centre St.* ☎ *(301) 547–9000 for opening times* ⊠), with works from ancient Egyptian times to the early 20thC. A nice feature of the Walters is that relevant books are placed in certain galleries so that you can read up the background to the objects on display.

For children, Baltimore has many attractions, including the **Zoo** (*Druid Hill Park* ☎ *(301) 396–7102* ⊠ *open 10am–4.20pm; closed Christmas*), which has more than 1,000 species of animals and includes a children's zoo with farm animals and playground equipment. Youngsters also love the **B&O Railroad Museum** (*Pratt and Poppleton St.* ☎ *(301) 237–2387* ⊠ *open Wed–Sun 10am–4pm; closed Mon, Tues*), with its superb collection of old locomotives and rolling stock.

One of the most attractive aspects to Baltimore is the presence of many ethnic people from different parts of the world, who retain a pride in their origins and traditions – Black, Hispanic, Polish, German, Greek, Irish and many more. A number of these groups have a festival each year, so there is a continual round of celebrations, which helps to create the colourful and human city that is Baltimore. (*To find out what will be happening during your visit* ☎ *(301) 837–INFO*.)

Mount Vernon and environs

15 miles (24km) s of Washington. Getting there: By car, the George Washington Memorial Parkway or Route 1; by bus, tour with Gray Line (333 E St. SW ☎*479–5900) which also includes Alexandria; by boat, Mar–late autumn with Washington Boat Lines (Pier 4, 6th and Water St. SW* ☎*554–8000); by bicycle, on the Mount Vernon Bike Trail along the Potomac.*

"No estate in United America is more pleasantly situated than this", wrote George Washington to an English friend in 1793, describing his house and farm at Mount Vernon. Now owned and maintained by the Mount Vernon Ladies' Association, it is a popular place of pilgrimage, not only because of its link with America's great hero but because of its singular charm and beauty.

Washington acquired the property in 1754, following the death of his half-brother, and had the house enlarged and redecorated. After an eventful career in the Virginia militia, he settled down there in 1759 with his new wife Martha. Washington adored Mount Vernon and hoped to spend the rest of his life there as a hard-working farmer. But his plans were interrupted first by the War of Independence, in which he commanded the American forces, then by his two terms as President of the United States. Throughout the momentous events of his life he longed for the peace and solace of Mount Vernon. After his final retirement from politics, he enjoyed only a brief period of less than three years on his farm before his death in 1799.

When you visit Mount Vernon today, it is clear to see why Washington loved it so much. The house (☎*780–2000* ▣ *open Mar–Oct 9am–5pm, Nov–Feb 9am–4pm; smoking is forbidden throughout house and grounds*) is a gracefully proportioned building in a Neo-Georgian style with a facade that looks like stone but is in fact painted wood. Washington himself master-minded the alterations to the house, which has many unusual features, such as the twin open colonnades connecting with the dependencies on either side, and the spacious porch at the back known as the "piazza", two storeys high and running the full length of the house. Picture Washington sitting there with his friends on a summer evening looking out over lawn and woodland to the broad sweep of the Potomac.

The restrained, unpretentious dignity of the architecture is in keeping with Washington's character. The interior has been restored as closely as possible to the way it looked in his time. The grandest room in the house is the **Large Dining Room**, with its Hepplewhite and Sheraton furniture, its delicate plaster mouldings and marble mantlepiece carved with agricultural motifs. Most evocative of Washington's spirit, however, is the **Study**, from which he administered his estate. Among the original items are his dressing-table, chair and secretary-desk.

The many outbuildings surrounding the house are worth a visit. The kitchen, smokehouse, coach-house, stable and greenhouse have all been restored to their original state. There is also a small **museum** containing portraits and memorabilia of George and Martha Washington. Their bodies lie in a brick tomb, ordered by Washington in his will, which stands in a secluded part of the grounds to the w of the house. About 50yds (46m) to the sw of this is an area where the slaves of Mount Vernon were buried. Washington came to oppose slavery and in his will provided for the freedom of his slaves.

The formally laid-out **Flower Garden** and **Kitchen Garden** are both delightful. By the Flower Garden is a shop selling souvenirs and a variety of plants and seeds, many of them taken from the garden itself. Along the driveway leading up to the house can be seen elms, tulip poplars and other trees planted by Washington himself – he was no armchair gardener. Just by the main entrance to the estate is a gift shop and a pleasant restaurant ⇌ **Mount Vernon Inn** (☎780–0011 ▮▮▯).

There are a number of other places near Mount Vernon worth visiting. **Woodlawn Plantation** (*3 miles (5km) to the w via Route 235* ☎557–7881 ▨ *✗ compulsory, open 9.30am–4.30pm; closed major hols*) was built in the early 1800s on land given by George Washington to his nephew, Lawrence Lewis, and foster daughter, Eleanor Parke Custis, when they married in 1799. The house, designed by the versatile Dr William Thornton, first architect of the *Capitol*, breathes the atmosphere of gracious Southern living. Set in beautiful grounds, it is a centre for courses in horticulture and landscape architecture. In the grounds of Woodlawn is the crisply modern **Pope-Leighey House** (☎557–7881 ▨ *at Woodlawn; open Mar–Oct Sat, Sun 9.30am–4.30pm and by appt*), built by Frank Lloyd Wright in 1940 and considered a pioneering design in small-scale domestic architecture. It was moved in its entirety from Falls Church, Va., when it stood in the way of highway construction.

Pohick Church (*3 miles (5km) to the w via Route 1* ☎550–9449; *open 8.30am–4pm*) is a chaste, red-brick structure dating from 1774. Washington attended here regularly, sitting in pew No. 28. From Pohick Church continue for about 1½ miles (2.5km) sw on Route 1, then double back 4 miles (6.5km) se down SR 242. This will bring you to **Gunston Hall** (☎550–9220 ▨ *open 9.30am–5pm; closed Christmas*), one of the most elegant Colonial homes in Virginia, built by the Revolutionary statesman George Mason (1725–92). Inside, note particularly the **Chinese Chippendale** and **Palladian Rooms** with their fine wood carvings. The house is set in beautiful grounds, with a grand view over the Potomac.

Williamsburg

150 miles (240km) s of Washington. Population: 10,000. Getting there: By car, Interstate highways 95, 295 and 64; by bus, Greyhound or day tour with Gray Line (333 E St. SW ☎479–5900).

Williamsburg offers the visitor a uniquely vivid illusion of stepping back into an 18thC American town. Capital of Virginia in Colonial and Revolutionary times, Williamsburg was superseded by Richmond as the capital, and for a century and a half remained in obscurity until the 1920s when John D. Rockefeller provided money for its restoration and preservation. Run today by the non-profit-making Colonial Williamsburg Foundation, it is both a working town and a living museum.

Before going into the centre of Williamsburg, it is advisable to report at the **Information Center** (*Colonial Williamsburg*

Index

General index 151
Gazetteer of streets 158

With the exception of a few of the most notable, such as the Willard Hotel and Hecht's department store, individual hotels, restaurants and shops have not been indexed, because they appear in alphabetical order within their appropriate sections. The sections themselves, however, have been indexed. Similarly, although most streets are listed in the gazetteer and not in the index, a few exceptions, such as the Mall, are indexed as well.

Page numbers in bold type indicate the main entry.

151

Index

Index

Index

Gazetteer of streets

Numbers after the street refer to pages on which it is mentioned in the book. Map references refer to the maps that follow this gazetteer.

Numbered streets (1st St., 2nd St., etc) are listed in numerical sequence. Named streets are listed alphabetically.

It has not been possible to label every street drawn on the maps, although all major streets and most smaller ones have been named. Some streets that it has not been possible to label on the maps have been given map references in this gazetteer, however, because this serves as an approximate location, which will nearly always be sufficient for you to find your way.

Gazetteer

L

L St. NW, 117, 122, 126;
Map 3E5–6
Lafayette Sq. NW, 65,
100; Map 3F6
Lee Highway, Arlington,
102; Map 4F2
L'Enfant Plaza East SW,
101, 113;
Map 6H7
Louisiana Ave. NE, 43;
Map 7F9

M

M St. NW, 16, 27, 60, 82,
99, 100, 104, 107, 110,
112, 115, 117, 120, 122,
123, 126, 134, 138;
Maps 2&3E
Rhode Island Ave., 40;
Map 3E6
Maine Ave. SW, 105;
Map 6H7
Mall, The, SW, 20, 21,
26, 34, 35, 36, 40, 68;
Maps 6&7G
Martin Luther King Ave.
SE, 45; Map 8K11
Massachusetts Ave. NE,
9, 107;
Map 8F–G10–11
Delaware Ave., 90; Map
7F9
Massachusetts Ave. NW,
15, 16, 41, 42, 45, 62,
100, 103, 110, 116, 118,
137; Maps 2B–D3–4,
3D–E5–6, 7E–F8–9
Mount Saint Alban NW,
92; Map 2A2

N

N St. NW, 37, 40, 59, 99,
104, 108, 114, 138;
Maps 2–3E
National Pl. NW, 126;
Map 6F7
New Hampshire Ave.
NW, 15, 37, 41, 52, 100,
103, 124;
Maps 3D–E5–6,
5F4
Rock Creek Parkway,
64, 112, 115, 116, 119,
133; Map 5F4
New Jersey Ave. NW, 83,
101, 103; Map 7E–H9
New York Ave. NW, 8,
16, 81, 82, 110, 116;
Maps 6E–F7, 7E8
13th St., 82;
Map 6F7
North Capitol St. NE, 9,
43, 102, 108, 114, 118;
Map 7E–F9
Massachusetts Ave., 12,
14; Map 7F9

N Carolina Ave. SE, 43;
Map 8G–H10
North Fort Myer Dr.,
Arlington, 99; Map 4F2

O

O St. NW, 14; Map 2D3
Observatory Circle NW,
15; Map 2C3
Ohio Dr. SW, 15; Map 5H5

P

P St. NW, 41, 102, 108,
122, 123, 125;
Maps 2&3D
Pennsylvania Ave. NW,
14, 22, 23, 29, 31, 37,
39, 82, 83, 95, 99, 100,
102, 104, 107, 108, 111,
113, 114, 115, 118, 120,
122, 123, 124, 138;
Maps 2E4, 3E5, 6F6–7,
7G8
Pennsylvania Ave. SE, 43,
123; Map 8G–H10–11
Pershing Sq. NW, 40, 83;
Map 6F7

Q

Q St. NW, 59; Map 2D4

R

R St. NW, 60, 107, 120,
136; Map 2&3D
Reservoir Rd. NW, 15,
17; Map 2D2–3
Rhode Island Ave. NW,
16, 40, 48, 79, 87, 100,
101, 134, 138;
Map 3D–E6–7
Rock Creek Parkway NW,
11; Map 2E4
Virginia Ave., 135;
Map 2E4

S

S St. NW, 89, 97;
Maps 2&3D
Scott Circle NW, 40;
Map 3E6
Sheridan Circle NW, 25,
42; Map 3D5
Sunderland Pl. NW, 41;
Map 3D5

V

Vermont Ave. NW, 11,
137; Map 3E6–7
Virginia Ave. NW, 104,
109, 122, 124, 134, 137;
Map 5F4–5
New Hampshire Ave.,
94; Map 5F4

W

W St. SE, 58; Map 8J11
Water St. SW, 99, 111;
Maps 6H7, 7I8
Western Plaza, 40, 83;
Map 6F7
W Potomac Park, 63;
Map 5H5
Whitehaven St. NW, 15;
Map 2C3
Wisconsin Ave. NW, 60,
100, 101, 107, 110, 112,
113, 115, 118, 120, 121,
122, 124, 126, 134, 136;
Map 2C–E3
Woodley Rd. NW, 103;
Map 2B4
Wyoming Ave. NW, 102;
Map 3C5

WASHINGTON

1

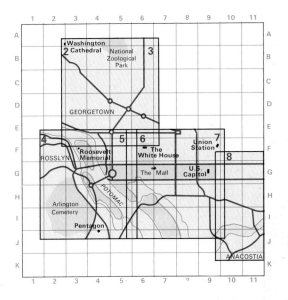

LEGEND

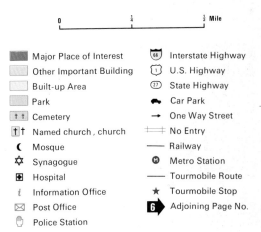

0	¼	½ Mile	

Major Place of Interest	🛡 Interstate Highway
Other Important Building	🛡 U.S. Highway
Built-up Area	㉗ State Highway
Park	🖘 Car Park
†† Cemetery	→ One Way Street
†† Named church , church	⊦⊦ No Entry
☾ Mosque	— Railway
✡ Synagogue	Ⓜ Metro Station
✚ Hospital	— Tourmobile Route
i Information Office	★ Tourmobile Stop
⊠ Post Office	6 Adjoining Page No.
⍩ Police Station	

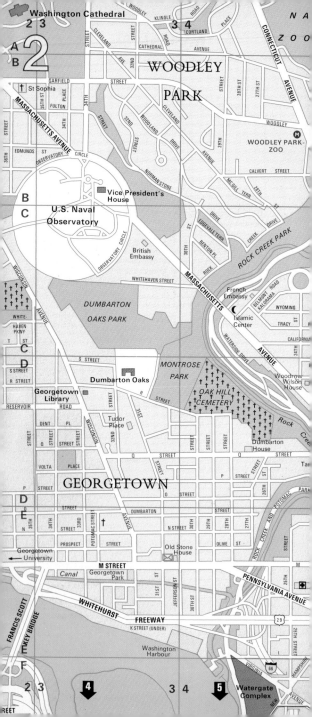

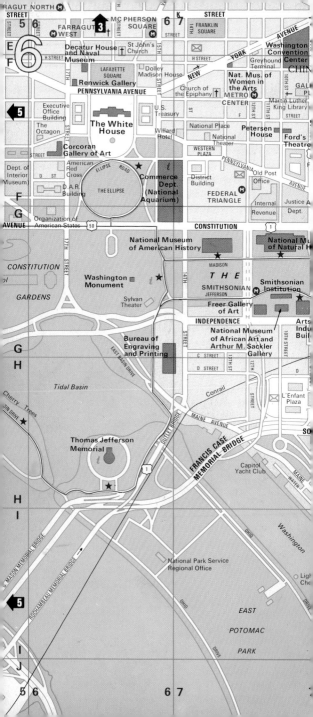

↑Capital Children's Museum

9 10 MASSACHUSETTS 10 11 11

8

F
G

STANTON
SQUARE

CONSTITUTION   AVENUE

LINCOLN
PARK

Supreme
Court
EAST
Library
of
Congress

Folger Shakespeare
Library

INDEPENDENCE   AVENUE

G
G

SEWARD
SQUARE

CAROLINA

Capitol
South

EASTERN
MARKET

PENNSYLVANIA

M

NORTH

MARION
PARK

SOUTH

Christ
Church

AVENUE

GARFIELD PARK

Marine
Corps
Barracks

SOUTHEAST   FREEWAY

H
I

CANAL

K STREET

L   STREET

M   STREET

Washington Navy Yard

Navy Memorial
Museum

J

ANACOSTIA   RIVER

ANACOSTIA BRIDGE

FREDERICK DOUGLASS
BRIDGE

7

NURSERY
GARDENS

ANACOSTIA

FREEWAY

Cedar
Hill

HOWARD   ROAD

J
K

U.S. Naval
Station
Washington

ANACOSTIA

Anacostia
Neighborhood
Museum

SHANNON   PLACE

9 10 10 11 1